The Vietnam War on Trial

LANDMARK LAW CASES

&

AMERICAN SOCIETY

Peter Charles Hoffer
N. E. H. Hull
Series Editors

Titles in the series:

MICHAL R. BELKNAP

The Vietnam War on Trial

The My Lai Massacre and the

Court-Martial of Lieutenant Calley

UNIVERSITY PRESS OF KANSAS

Published by the University Press of Kansas (Lawrence, Kansas 66049),
which was organized by the Kansas Board of Regents and is operated
and funded by Emporia State University, Fort Hays State University,
Kansas State University, Pittsburg State University, the University of Kansas,
and Wichita State University

Library of Congress Cataloging-in-Publication Data

Belknap, Michal R.

The Vietnam War on trial : the My Lai Massacre and the court-martial
of Lieutenant Calley / Michal R. Belknap.

p. cm. — (Landmark law cases & American society)

Includes bibliographical references and index.

ISBN 0-7006-1211-4 (cloth : alk. paper) — ISBN 0-7006-1212-2
(paper : alk. paper)

1. Calley, William Laws, 1943- —Trials, litigation, etc. 2.
Courts-martial and courts of inquiry—United States. 3. Trials
(Murder)—United States. 4. Vietnamese Conflict, 1961–1975—Atrocities.
5. My Lai Massacre, Vietnam, 1968. I. Title. II. Series.

KF7642.C3 B45 2002

343.73'0143—dc21

2002007076

British Library Cataloguing in Publication Data is available.

Printed in the United States of America

10 9 8 7 6 5 4 3 2 1

The paper used in this publication meets the minimum requirements of the
American National Standard for Permanence of Paper for Printed Library
Materials Z39.48-1984.

THIS BOOK IS DEDICATED TO ALL THE GRADUATES

OF THE ARMY ROTC PROGRAM AT UCLA

WHO SERVED IN THE VIETNAM WAR,

AND ESPECIALLY TO THE ONLY ONE WE LOST,

MY CLASSMATE FIRST LIEUTENANT THOMAS BLAKE DAILY,

WHO WAS KILLED IN ACTION AT

BIEN HOA ON 21 MAY 1967.

CONTENTS

For those of us of a certain age, the words "My Lai" conjure up an indelible image, or rather a panorama, of destruction and mayhem. We close our eyes and see ditches filled with mutilated lumps of humanity, women with children in their arms, toddlers disfigured by gunshot wounds, old men in postures of supplication, horribly murdered. A massacre, or, in the words of one of the examiners of the events, a tragedy of war. The killing of civilians in wartime is certainly not new, and the more mechanized and impersonal that war becomes, the more widespread and perhaps even unavoidable will be civilian casualties, or, as they were called in the Vietnam War, collateral damage. In the Vietnam War in particular, ground troops often found it impossible to tell the difference between noncombatants and Vietcong guerrillas; indeed, sometimes apparently friendly and peaceful villagers were Vietcong. And by the spring of 1968, after the casualties they had taken during the preceding Tet Offensive, American combat troops in the country were ill disposed to make such distinctions, despite the army's requirement of fair treatment for civilians.

But My Lai was more. On 16 March 1968, in the course of a search-and-destroy mission in a village suspected of harboring crack Vietcong troops, an American infantry officer ordered others to round up, and joined some of them in butchering, unarmed civilians. Perhaps he himself was ordered to do so, as he later alleged. Perhaps the army itself was to blame for insufficient training or inept control of its ground troops. Whatever the mistakes the upper-echelon commanders made, the outcome was the same. Hundreds dead when not a shot was fired against the American troops.

What followed was a cover-up almost as shocking as the carnage itself. Unit commanders refused to pursue inquiries into reports of misconduct from helicopter pilots accompanying the troops and later by the conscience-striken infantrymen themselves. The cover-up, or at least a minimization of the events, reached to the highest levels of the army and was in a way approved by the president of the United States and members of Congress as well. Fortunately for history, lawyers in uniform on the Judge Advocate General's staff and in other branches of the service, along with courageous army investigators, brought the full scope of the massacre to light and prosecuted the participants.

It would not do in this preface to reveal the outcome of those trials, save to say that they open a window into military justice that is both reassuring (for the trials were eminently fair) and disturbing, for what they reveal of the conduct of the military in war. What is equally important, the way in which the prosecution proceeded tells us something both reassuring and disturbing about how our country goes to war. A democratic nation that holds itself and its principles of self-determination and freedom as a light unto the nations of the world was complicit in the slaughter. Many Americans rushed to support or excuse the actions of the troops at My Lai, arguing that the villagers had brought their fates upon themselves by opposing us, or that any means necessary to defeat communism were acceptable.

Michal Belknap's superbly researched and dramatically retold account of these events sets them in their multiple contexts. My Lai not only was emblematic of the difficulties American troops faced by intervening in a civil war abroad but also became a focal point for protesters at home. But the antiwar forces were not the only ones who found My Lai distressing. Many who had supported the war concluded that even if such atrocities were understandable in the Vietnam conflict (for My Lai was not the only place where American troops disregarded the difference between civilians and combatants), My Lai did not help the United States wage its larger conflict against world communism. In the end, My Lai contributed to the American pullout and the eventual North Vietnamese victory.

As legal history, Belknap's book introduces readers to what has hitherto been a mysterious subject for American civilians—the system of military justice. He reveals how that system works and, with great sympathy and balance, takes us through the preparations for the trials and the actual courtroom give-and-take. We feel that we are there, alongside the legal counsel, or with the officers who sat on the bench watching the witnesses and defendants. This is the highest compliment anyone can pay to legal history—that it makes the law live. In addition, we learn what motivated the various protagonists, for example, the time constraints that forced the prosecutors to hurry their case, lest crimes committed in war go unpunished when the perpetrators left the service.

The story of My Lai as here retold becomes the story of all the atrocities of war. The lessons learned are as applicable to our war in Korea, and our military actions in Libya, Panama, Kosovo, and against the Taliban regime in Afghanistan. Who is to blame when the innocent are slaughtered? What is the law when the legality of the combat itself is in question? Should the "grunt" who takes orders to kill, indeed, who is liable to punishment if he does not obey such orders, bear the burden of punishment if it turns out that the victims are not the enemy at all? What laws should apply, and who is to apply them, when combat becomes carnage? These are the questions that My Lai raised. This book will go a long way toward answering them.

ACKNOWLEDGMENTS

Although my name is on the title page, there are many people without whose contributions this book would not exist. I am especially indebted to my research assistant, Jason Saccuzzo, a lawyer-historian whose tireless efforts unearthed sources I did not realize existed. By now he probably knows more about My Lai and Lieutenant Calley than about any of the subjects on the California bar exam, for which he was beginning to prepare as we were wrapping up this project. I also owe large debts of gratitude to William G. Eckhardt (who shared with me his recollections of his own work on the My Lai cases), Jonathan Lurie (the leading historian of American military justice), and my California Western colleague William C. Lynch (a retired Navy Judge Advocate General's Corps captain), all of whom contributed expert counsel on military law. By carefully reading the entire manuscript, Jon Lurie and Bill Lynch saved me from factual mistakes, while my colleague Thomas D. Barton rescued me from equally embarrassing stylistic blunders. Tom also offered helpful insights into the way Americans reacted to the conviction of Lieutenant Calley, as did Paul J. Gudel, Matthew Ritter, and other participants in the California Western Faculty Development Seminar at which I presented an early version of chapter 10. The typing skill of Cheree Smith and Mary Ellen Norvell turned very rough drafts into a finished manuscript.

That there even was a manuscript is due largely to the staff of the California Western Law Library, which went well beyond the call of duty when presented with the challenge of a project that required heavy use of nonlegal sources. Linda Weathers located and obtained for me (sometimes through interlibrary loan and sometimes by going personally to other libraries in the area) books and articles that I needed. Acquisitions Librarian Carmen Brigandi and Law Library Director Phyllis Marion kept a sharp eye out for new books on Vietnam and purchased far more of those than most law librarians would. Bill Bookheim's ability to track down quickly even the most obscure bits of information was truly amazing.

The staff of the Nixon Materials Project at the National Archives Annex in College Park, Maryland, also assisted me with my research. So did Agnes Kiang, the Librarian of the United States Court of Appeals for the Armed Forces. While working as the historian for that court, Jon Lurie discovered, and set aside for my use, some valuable files on the Calley case. I was able to spend several weeks in the Washington, D.C., area going through those and the collections at the National Archives Annex because of the hospitality of Dick and Joan Sweeney. Marvelous dinners and great conversation with these two old friends brought a pleasant end to many a tedious day of research.

I would also like to thank two other old friends, Peter Hoffer and Natalie Hull, for asking me to write this book and for putting up with the numerous delays in its completion caused by my father's terminal illness and my own bout with cancer. My editor at the University Press of Kansas, Mike Briggs, has also been extremely patient. The positive way he responded to each new excuse for failing to meet a deadline encouraged me to keep working on this book until (perhaps to Mike's surprise) I actually finished it.

While a number of people contributed to the writing of this book, one who ought to have done so did not. Although I contacted William L. Calley Jr., asking to interview him about My Lai and his court-martial, he never responded. I wish that he had agreed to talk with me, for while this book is about much more than just Lieutenant Calley himself, he is at the center of the story that it tells. Unable to question him directly, I have had to rely for his side of the story on the testimony he gave at his court-martial; on what he revealed to a psychiatrist, Dr. Wilbur Hamman, who also testified as a defense witness in that proceeding; and on an as-told-to autobiographical book, *Lieutenant Calley: His Own Story*, by John Sack. To the extent that these sources fail adequately to explain Calley's perceptions, motivations, and feelings and to convey fully his views on the events it discusses, this book is incomplete. If its incompleteness has resulted in any unfairness, the responsibility for that rests with Calley himself. For all this book's other deficiencies, I alone am entirely to blame.

Introduction

"Lieutenant Calley, it is my duty . . . to inform you that the court
. . . finds you . . . guilty of premeditated murder." As Colonel
Clifford H. Ford read the verdict, the small and rather red-faced
soldier standing in front of him trembled. His jaw went slack and
his eyes fluttered as Ford informed First Lieutenant William L.
Calley Jr. that six of his fellow officers had convicted him of murdering twenty-two civilians in the Republic of Vietnam. It was
March 1971, and slightly more than three years had passed since
Calley and other members of his company had rampaged
through a hamlet known as My Lai (4), perpetrating one of the
worst massacres in the annals of American warfare.

Theirs was a crime that "stung the national conscience," as
Telford Taylor observed in a 1970 book. Taylor had prosecuted
Nazi war criminals at Nuremberg, and to him it seemed that
"now the wheel has spun full circle, and the fingers of accusation
are pointed not at others for whom we have felt scorn and contempt, but at ourselves." Forced to confront the awful reality that
young men they had sent off to fight in Vietnam had slaughtered
civilians there, Americans reacted with outrage. They directed
their anger not at Calley and the crimes he had committed, however, but at the verdict against him and the life sentence that the
court-martial had imposed. The reason was that this "outlaw soldier" had become a symbol. As *Time* magazine observed in its report on the verdict, his "case embodied everything that was
wrong with the war [in Vietnam]." It also fed mounting pressures
to end that increasingly unpopular conflict.

Because the Calley case reflects so much about the Vietnam
War, studying his court-martial is an excellent way of gaining a

fuller appreciation and deeper understanding of that national tragedy. Those are things that young Americans at the beginning of the twenty-first century need, for America is again at war. After the United States withdrew from Vietnam, it experienced nearly three decades of peace, interrupted only by the quick and rather painless little Gulf War. The events of 11 September 2001 plunged the nation into what President George W. Bush warned immediately would be a long and difficult military struggle. Suddenly, a generation entirely unfamiliar with life in a country at war found National Guardsmen being summoned to active duty, soldiers and sailors heading overseas to perform missions shrouded in secrecy, and the Justice Department rounding up aliens from certain countries, while politicians and civil libertarians debated unfamiliar issues, such as the use of military tribunals and the need for surveillance of suspect groups. The young men and women of a generation asked to bear the burdens of this new war can learn a great deal from the experiences of their predecessors who fought the one in Vietnam that ended three decades ago. Among those lessons are how and why good people do bad things, and who is responsible for crimes committed on the battlefield.

These issues have fascinated me for decades. Like William Calley, I was a lieutenant in the army during the Vietnam War. Although we never met, the two of us went through infantry officer's training at Fort Benning, Georgia, at the same time, and we even graduated from our respective programs on the same day. For years, I wondered whether, if put in the same situation in which Calley found himself, I would have done what he did. I don't think so, but it is something I ask my students to ponder. I also prod them to think about how they would have reacted had they found themselves in Calley's combat boots.

Besides urging them to consider whether they would have committed the sort of war crimes for which he was prosecuted, I ask my students to look upon Calley's court-martial as a political trial. When they hear the phrase "political trial," what most often leaps to mind is a proceeding in which an oppressive government prosecutes an opposition leader for treason, sedition, or some other crime against the state. If prodded, students will generally acknowledge that the nature of the trial is essentially the same if the charge is murder, the possession of narcotics, or some other ordinary crime, but the government has initiated the prosecution because of the accused's political activities or affiliations. They are somewhat slower to accept the notion that sometimes the defendants politicize criminal cases by seeking to turn the courtroom into a political forum.

Most difficult of all for students to understand is how the context can convert a basically nonpolitical legal proceeding into a political trial. This happens when the crime of which the defendant is accused is the product of political controversy (as were those of the British soldiers prosecuted for perpetrating the Boston Massacre) or when it was committed for political reasons (as was the Watergate burglary). It also happens when the outcome of the trial is determined by political considerations (as, apparently, was that of Washington, D.C., mayor Marion Barry for possession of cocaine). Finally, an otherwise nonpolitical legal proceeding can become a political trial because it has a major impact on the politics of its time. The 1992 prosecution of the Los Angeles police officers accused of beating African-American motorist Rodney King is one example of that kind of political trial.

The court-martial of Lieutenant Calley is another. His case became one of the major political issues of 1971 because those on both sides of a heated debate over Vietnam viewed the verdict as exemplifying what they thought was wrong with the war. To hawks, who supported America's military effort in Southeast Asia, Calley was a patriot. In their eyes he had been prosecuted simply for doing his duty. To them the verdict was proof that their own government would never allow this country's fighting men to do what had to be done to win.

Although convinced the United States should not be involved in the military struggle against Vietnamese Communists that hawks endorsed, doves shared their opponents' outrage over the conviction of Lieutenant Calley. To them he was simply a scapegoat. Responsibility for the My Lai massacre rested not with a lowly lieutenant but with the civilian and military leaders who had sent him to fight in Vietnam and authorized the tactics employed by American forces there. As far as doves were concerned, the slaughter of innocents in which Calley had participated was an inevitable consequence of a war that should never have been fought in the first place. They joined hawks in condemning the court-martial that convicted him.

Grasping the breadth and depth of public hostility to the verdict, President Richard Nixon shamelessly exploited public reaction against it to advance his own political agenda. The White House sought to capitalize on the Calley case, even though doing so required intervening in the military legal process in a way that seriously undermined the rule of law. Although he championed Lieutenant Calley when his case was a hot political issue, Nixon abandoned him once the war was over and the public no longer cared passionately about his fate.

That fate was not a harsh one. Lieutenant Calley served only a few months in a military prison and a few years confined to his apartment in the bachelor officers quarters (BOQ) at Fort Benning, not much punishment for a man convicted of twenty-two murders, who probably committed several times that many. But the Calley case raises for a later generation, as it did for Americans in 1971, the issue of who, if anyone, should have been punished for those killings.

As the United States undertakes a war against the terrorists who slaughtered thousands of innocent civilians on 11 September 2001, it must address again the issue of who is responsible for such atrocities. Is it the individuals who look the victims in the eye and brutally take their lives? Is it the leaders who order their actions? Or is it the nation-states, or political or religious movements, for whom the killers fight? Answers to those questions tend to come easily when it is the enemy who committed the war crimes. They are harder to answer when it is American soldiers who did so.

As the famous Union general William T. Sherman once observed, "War is hell." But does that mean that all of the deaths that result from a war are simply inevitable consequences of the political decision to resort to military force in the first place? Or

{ *The Vietnam War on Trial* }

are some of them crimes for which individuals can and should be held accountable? Should those who go "too far" in battle and violate the international law of war be placed on trial for their actions? Or should they be excused because they were simply doing their duty? These are questions to which the court-martial of Lieutenant William L. Calley Jr. offers ambiguous answers. They are ones that students should consider as they read this account of his trial and the public and political reactions it evoked.

CHAPTER I

Going to Hell

Fort Benning was the front porch of hell. At least that is the way it seemed in the summer of 1967. The blistering Georgia sun beat down relentlessly on the young soldiers, whose neatly starched fatigue uniforms trapped the sweat against their bodies as they sweltered hour after hour on shadeless firing ranges (where they blazed away with outmoded rifles at lifeless targets that resembled not at all the enemies who would soon be trying to kill them); on dusty red clay roads (over which they tramped for miles in heavy combat gear to toughen soft civilian bodies into "lean, mean fighting machines"); and in insect- and snake-infested pine woods (through which they stumbled with map and compass in hand, supposedly mastering the art of land navigation, but all too often "temporarily disoriented"). During the few breaks in their gruelling training, the soldiers swallowed gallons of water and scores of salt tablets in a futile effort to replace what the sun had boiled away.

It was not just the heat that made Fort Benning seem very close to hell. It was also what awaited the soldiers when they finished Officer Candidate School (OCS). Most of them were headed for Vietnam. Soon they would be commanding rifle platoons in combat. Sometimes the recent graduates of military academies and college Reserve Officers' Training Corps (ROTC) programs with whom they shared training facilities at the Infantry School referred to them contemptuously as "cannon fodder." Many would not return from their tours of duty in Southeast Asia. William L. Calley Jr. would come home to stand trial for murder.

Like thousands of other young men of his generation, "Rusty"

Calley had been sucked into what would prove to be the longest war in American history. He was going to Vietnam to fight communism. In 1945, when Calley was two years old, a Communist, Ho Chi Minh, had launched a nationalist revolution there, seeking to prevent France from reasserting colonial control over an area the Japanese had dominated during World War II. Ho sought the support of the United States, but the administration of President Harry Truman cared more about preventing the Soviet Union, a Communist power that it viewed as a threat to U.S. interests, from expanding its sphere of influence into Western Europe than it did about Vietnamese independence. In 1946 France launched a war against Ho's Vietminh movement, and after Mao Tse-tung's Communist forces won a civil war in neighboring China, the United States, convinced it had to prop up France in order to contain communism, began providing assistance both to the French and to the puppet regime they set up under Emperor Boa Dai. By 1952 the United States was paying about one-third of the cost of France's war against the Vietminh. Although American assistance increased after Dwight Eisenhower became president in 1953, in May 1954 the French suffered a disastrous defeat at Dienbienphu. The chairman of the Joint Chiefs of Staff wanted to launch air strikes to save that besieged fortress, but other military leaders opposed the idea, and neither America's allies nor congressional leaders would support military intervention.

Although unwilling to intervene militarily to save Dienbienphu, the Eisenhower administration remained committed to containing communism in Vietnam. On 21 July 1954 the participants in a peace conference held in Geneva, Switzerland, signed a series of agreements providing for a cease-fire, the temporary division of the country between French and Vietminh forces at the seventeenth parallel, and elections within twenty-four months to determine the future of a unified Vietnam. The United States did not sign the Geneva Accords, but it pledged to respect them. Despite this commitment, the Central Intelligence Agency (CIA) immediately began developing plans to harass the Vietminh regime in Hanoi by covert means. Secretary of State John Foster

Dulles organized the Southeast Asia Treaty Organization (SEATO) to provide security for Laos, Cambodia, and the southern part of Vietnam, and the United States threw its support behind Ngo Dinh Diem, who on 18 June 1954 became prime minister under Boa Dai and a year later deposed the emperor. Like Ho, Diem was a Vietnamese nationalist. Unlike him, he was a Catholic and an anti-Communist. Diem made himself the president of a separate country south of the seventeenth parallel with its capital in Saigon, called the Republic of Vietnam, and refused to participate in the nationwide elections the Geneva negotiators had scheduled for 1956, realizing that if these were held, Ho would surely win. With military and economic assistance from the United States, Diem built up a national police force and an army, which he used to kill and arrest the operatives the Vietminh had left behind in the South. The desperate Communists fought back, kidnapping, torturing, and killing local officials. In 1959 a somewhat reluctant Hanoi regime, whose top priority was the development of the North, authorized the resumption of armed struggle below the seventeenth parallel. To promote it, 90,000 Vietminh cadre infiltrated the South. In December 1960, at Hanoi's direction, the southern revolutionaries, called "Vietcong" (VC) by the Saigon government, created the National Liberation Front (NLF), a Communist-led but broadly based organization designed to unite all of those disaffected with Diem's narrowly based and rather oppressive government. In battling the Vietcong, Diem had the firm support of the United States, which in early 1956 had taken over from the French responsibility for training the Vietnamese armed forces. During the Eisenhower years the U.S. Military Assistance Advisory Group (MAAG) grew to 692. America supplied South Vietnam with $85 million per year worth of military equipment, financed the construction of military installations, underwrote the cost of military training programs, and even paid the salaries of South Vietnamese soldiers.

The United States was heavily involved in preventing a Communist takeover of South Vietnam when John F. Kennedy became president in 1961. "Inheriting from Eisenhower an increasingly dangerous if still limited commitment," historian George Herring writes, "he plunged deeper into the morass." Like most Americans, Kennedy believed the Cold War between the United States and the Soviet Union was a global struggle and consequently that Communist revolutionaries in Third World countries were direct threats to American interests. In his first year in office, he sent 100 more MAAG advisers to South Vietnam, along with 400 Special Forces troops to provide training in counterinsurgency techniques. Kennedy also approved an additional $42 million to support expansion of Diem's army. The CIA initiated a program designed to help villagers defend themselves against the Communists and sent clandestine teams of South Vietnamese into the North to engage in sabotage and disruption. Despite these initiatives, the Vietcong stepped up military operations, infiltration accelerated, and the Diem regime grew increasingly unpopular. In late 1961, after visiting Vietnam, two of Kennedy's aides, General Maxwell Taylor and Professor Walt Rostow, recommended sending not only more military equipment and advisers but also American troops, ostensibly to assist in repairing flood damage in the Mekong Delta but actually to demonstrate the strength of America's commitment and provide a military reserve that could be employed if the situation deteriorated further. Secretary of Defense Robert McNamara and the Joint Chiefs of Staff supported their proposal, but other presidential advisers feared a deeper military involvement in Vietnam. Some even advocated negotiating an end to the conflict.

In the end, Kennedy rejected the idea of introducing American ground forces. He opted instead for more of the same, authorizing significant increases in aid and advisers. The number of American military personnel in South Vietnam rose from 3,205 in December 1961 to more than 9,000 by the end of 1962. Many of the Americans did more than just advise. Special Forces "Green Berets" conducted civic action programs among Montagnard tribesmen in the Central Highlands, while other U.S. servicemen flew helicopters on combat support missions and even substituted for South Vietnamese aviators on bombing and strafing runs. The massive infusion of American men and weapons improved the military situation temporarily, but by late 1962 the Vietcong had regained the initiative. Furthermore, the political situation was deteriorating toward chaos, as Buddhists mounted widespread demonstrations against the Catholic Diem, and his own generals plotted a coup. On 1 November 1963, they overthrew and murdered him.

Three weeks later Kennedy, too, was assassinated. Within less than two years after replacing him, his vice president, Lyndon Johnson, managed, as Herring explains, "to transform a limited commitment to assist the South Vietnamese government into an open-ended commitment to preserve an independent, non-Communist South Vietnam." Johnson did not set out to change his predecessors' policies. He and his advisers firmly believed, however, that the United States must stand firm in Vietnam in order to deter Chinese Communist aggression in Southeast Asia.

In late 1963 the North Vietnamese significantly escalated the war, and during the first three months of Johnson's presidency, the situation in South Vietnam deteriorated steadily. Pointing out that the United States lacked the sort of national interest in Southeast Asia that would inspire its people to bear willingly the massive costs of ever-deepening military involvement, Senate Majority Leader Mike Mansfield (D. Mont.) advocated a truce leading to neutralization of Vietnam. Intent on winning the 1964 presidential election, however, Johnson was unwilling to run the political risk that abandoning South Vietnam would entail. Rather than seek a diplomatic resolution of the conflict, he decided, after a major policy review in mid-March, to do more of the same, but to do it more efficiently.

Emphasizing that the essential U.S. goal was the maintenance of an independent, non-Communist South Vietnam, LBJ increased the number of American military "advisers" in the country from 16,300 to 23,300 during his first nine months in office and dispatched a hard-charging paratrooper, General William Westmoreland, to command them. The Johnson administration also boosted economic assistance to South Vietnam by $50 million. While most of its initiatives in the spring of 1964 were really just extensions of existing policies, it did opt for a new and more aggressive posture toward North Vietnam. Hoping to signal Hanoi that the price for continued intervention in the South would be high, the United States expanded covert operations above the seventeenth parallel. These entailed intelligence over-flights and the dropping of propaganda leaflets. They also included commando raids along the North Vietnamese coast, carried out by South Vietnamese personnel, acting pursuant to an operations plan known as 34A.

The 34A raids led to the Gulf of Tonkin incident in August 1964, which provided both a justification for stepping up the war and the occasion for congressional endorsement of Johnson's efforts to save South Vietnam from communism by military means. Having been criticized by Republican presidential candidate Senator Barry Goldwater for not taking more aggressive action to win the war, LBJ felt the need for a dramatic gesture. A number of his advisers recommended asking Congress for a resolution authorizing the president to use as much force as he wanted. A group of Vietnam experts drafted one, but Johnson did not think the time was ripe to send it to Capitol Hill. He opted temporarily for less dramatic measures.

Then, in the early morning hours of 2 August 1964, the U.S. destroyer *Maddox*, while conducting patrols in the Gulf of Tonkin in support of the 34A raids, came under attack by North Vietnamese PT boats eleven miles off the coast. North Vietnam claimed its territorial waters extended out twelve miles; according to the United States, no country could exercise jurisdiction over more than three miles of ocean. Thus, it was debatable whether the *Maddox* had been the victim of aggression in international waters or whether the vessels that shot at the destroyer were merely defending North Vietnamese territory. Two nights later, and much farther off the coast, the commander of the *Maddox*'s sister ship, the *C. Turner Joy*, concluding (probably erroneously) that it, too, had come under attack, ordered his gunners to return fire. They hit nothing. Despite the ambiguities surrounding the two "attacks" in the Gulf of Tonkin, President Johnson responded with retaliatory air strikes against North Vietnamese bases.

He also seized upon the Gulf of Tonkin incidents as a justification for requesting enactment of the congressional resolution his advisers had drafted in May. Secretary McNamara told Congress that both American destroyers had been attacked. He failed to mention their involvement in the 34A commando raids against North Vietnam. Nor did he say how far off the coast the *Maddox* had been; instead, he declared it had been carrying out a "routine patrol" when it was attacked in "international waters." Deceived by the administration about precisely what had happened in the Gulf of Tonkin, Congress rallied behind the president, giving him on 7 August 1964 the show of unity in support of standing firm in Vietnam that he wanted. The House passed the Gulf of Tonkin Resolution unanimously, and only two senators voted against it. The closest thing there would ever be to a declaration of war in Vietnam, the resolution expressed congressional approval and support for the "determination of the President . . . to take all necessary measures to repel any armed attack against the forces of the United States and to prevent further aggression." Foreign Relations Committee chairman J. William Fulbright (D. Ark.), who shepherded it through the Senate, would come to regret doing so.

The Johnson administration did not immediately take advantage of this open-ended endorsement of future military action in Vietnam, for the president feared broadening the war might hurt his chances in the November 1964 election. When a Vietcong mortar attack on the Bien Hoa airfield killed four Americans on 31 October, there was no retaliation. Once the election was over, however, the National Security Council began developing plans to escalate the war. On 2 December Johnson approved a two-stage program under which the United States would start by bombing infiltration routes south of the nineteenth parallel and progress to attacking targets above that line. Code-named Operation Rolling Thunder, this sustained air war against North Vietnam commenced on 13 February 1965, six days after an artillery attack on a marine base at Pleiku destroyed ten aircraft, killed 8 Americans, and wounded 126 more. So extensive was the bombing that in April alone, U.S. and South Vietnamese planes flew 3,600 sorties. Improvements in the now perpetually unstable and incompetent South Vietnamese government were supposed to accompany the implementation of Operation Rolling Thunder, but they did not.

Anticipating attacks on American installations in retaliation for the bombing, General Westmoreland requested marines to protect the airfield at Danang, and on 8 March two battalions splashed ashore. Within weeks Westmoreland was urging deployment of two army divisions to head off what he feared was impending military disaster. In April, McNamara, Taylor, and the Joint Chiefs approved the deployment of 40,000 additional ground combat troops to Vietnam. The idea was that they would fight only within fifty miles of American enclaves along the coast, but that limitation lasted barely a month. With the NLF operating at will throughout the rest of South Vietnam, Westmoreland asked for 150,000 additional troops. After a series of meetings in late July, Johnson rejected the advice of both Undersecretary of State George Ball (who warned that the United States could not win in Vietnam and urged that this country cut its loses before the momentum of events took control of policy) and McNamara (who advocated mobilizing 236,000 reservists). Primarily concerned about securing enactment of an ambitious program of domestic reform legislation, the president was unwilling to endanger it either by putting the country on a full war footing or by changing the direction of the policy he had inherited. Convinced a compromise approach could stave off defeat without provoking a backlash in Congress, he approved the deployment of 100,000 more troops to join the 90,000 already in Vietnam. In mid-November the American First Cavalry Division fought a fierce battle with the North Vietnamese in the Ia Drang Valley, losing over 300 men. By indirection and deception, and without ever really subjecting his policies to either public discussion or a meaningful congressional vote, Johnson had plunged the United States into a major war in Asia.

His escalation of the American military role in Vietnam provoked rumblings of discontent at home. During the twenty months ending in the late summer of 1965, an antiwar movement sprouted and began to grow. At first, protest against U.S. policy in Vietnam was almost entirely the work of pacifists and radicals. By the end of this period, however, these groups had been joined by college professors and students not known for their radicalism, as well as by numerous clergymen, lawyers, and journalists, some union leaders, and a number of liberal Democrats. Three thousand students and faculty members at the University of Michigan staged an antiwar "teach-in." Their innovation spread rapidly across the country; by the end of the 1964–65 academic year, there had been teach-ins at 120 schools, the largest a thirty-six-hour marathon at the University of California's Berkeley campus, in which 20,000 students participated. That spring several young men set fire to their draft cards during a demonstration at New York City's Whitehall Street induction center, igniting a form of protest against conscription and the war whose frequency and visibility soon inspired an outraged Congress to pass a law making it a federal crime. By the fall of 1965, opponents of the Vietnam War could mount sizable demonstrations on both coasts.

Yet those who participated in these protests spoke for only a small minority of the population. A May 1965 Gallup poll disclosed that 52 percent of Americans thought the United States was handling affairs in South Vietnam well, while only 27 percent believed it was handling them badly. An August survey found commitment to the war particularly strong among young respondents (aged twenty-one to thirty), 76 percent of whom endorsed it. On many campuses where teach-ins occurred, those who supported America's military role in Southeast Asia staged demonstrations to express their approval for what their classmates were condemning. At the University of Wisconsin, 6,000 students signed a petition supporting the president's policies; one-quarter of Yale students did the same thing. Meanwhile, politicians ranging from former President Eisenhower, a Republican, to California's governor Edmund G. "Pat" Brown, a liberal Democrat, condemned antiwar demonstrators.

Although Johnson's war enjoyed overwhelming popular support, there were ominous signs that this could easily erode. In late January and early February 1966, the increasingly disaffected Senator Fulbright held televised hearings, which he hoped would discredit the war. Numerous academic, military, and diplomatic experts who were considered architects of America's Cold War foreign and military policy filed before his Foreign Relations Committee to express doubts about the importance of Vietnam to the United States, concern about the magnitude of this country's commitment there, and reservations about the strategy it was employing. Most of the mail the committee received supported the critics of administration policy. It suggested the existence of substantial anxiety about the course the United States was following. Yet, the Foreign Relations Committee hearings failed to generate any concrete alternatives.

Despite the growing doubts about where the Johnson administration was headed, it continued to muddle deeper into a military morass. The number of American troops in Vietnam climbed steadily, rising from 23,000 at the beginning of 1965 to 184,000 only one year later. By the end of 1966, the number had climbed to 385,000. Early in 1968 it reached 535,000.

Like the number of American troops stationed in Vietnam, the air war grew and grew. The number of sorties that American aircraft flew against North Vietnam rose from 25,000 in 1965 to 79,000 in 1966 and 108,000 in 1967. In 1965, U.S. warplanes dropped 63,000 tons of bombs, a figure that climbed to 136,000 in 1966 and 226,000 in 1967. McNamara believed that American airpower could be used most effectively to interdict traffic along the "Ho Chi Minh Trail," the jungle route down which North Vietnam infiltrated men and equipment into the South. Giant B-52 bombers, carrying 58,000-pound payloads, relentlessly pounded approaches to this logistic pipeline. During 1965 the favored targets for American aircraft were military bases, supply depots, and infiltration routes in the southern part of North Vietnam. Beginning in early 1966, the air war shifted northward into more heavily populated areas, increasingly targeting that country's transportation and industrial systems. By 1967, along with vast property damage, American bombs were inflicting 2,800 casualties a month, many of them civilians, who were considered "collateral damage" of attacks directed at targets of military significance.

Meanwhile, an increasing number of Americans were returning home from South Vietnam in plastic body bags. As the ground war escalated, the United States sought to minimize casualties among its own forces by capitalizing on its vast superiority in firepower and technology. From 1965 to 1967, more than twice the bomb tonnage being dropped on the North rained down on South Vietnam. Americans also made heavy use of artillery and of "Puff the Magic Dragon" (C-47 transport planes converted into gunships that could fire an awesome 18,000 rounds per minute). To deprive the enemy of natural cover, the United States sprayed hundreds of square miles of South Vietnamese forests with herbicides.

But more than a million tons of bombs, over 100 million pounds of chemicals, and billions of artillery and aerial cannon shells could not keep GIs from dying in Vietnam. Westmoreland was determined to take the war to the enemy. He and other top military leaders realized that the Vietnamese, who had been fighting foreign invaders for centuries, possessed infinite patience, but Americans did not. Military strategists viewed a reasonably quick victory as essential. Hence, Westmoreland opted for a "search-and-destroy" strategy. Rather than working closely with the South Vietnamese population and protecting secure enclaves from the Communists, American troops, taking advantage of the tremendous mobility provided by their helicopters, would plunge into the bush to hunt down and wipe out Vietcong and North Vietnamese units. Westmoreland contemplated a war of attrition, but one in which enemy casualties would be high, while those of his own forces, because of their superiority in technology and firepower, would be low. He tested the effectiveness of his strategy in a series of major search-and-destroy operations in the fall of 1966 and the first half of 1967. In the area northwest of Saigon, 22,000 American and Army of the Republic of Vietnam (ARVN) troops went after the enemy in Operation Attleboro, as did 40,000 in Operation Cedar Falls and a similar number in Operation Junction City. Americans reported killing 700 of the enemy in Cedar Falls, 1,000 in Attleboro, and 1,776 in Junction City.

These large operations were exceptional, however. Ninety-six percent of battles with the Vietcong and the North Vietnamese involved units of company size (around 200 men) or smaller. Although guerrilla warfare tactics would probably have produced the best results in such engagements, U.S. forces generally eschewed those in favor of the same reliance on firepower and helicopter mobility that characterized the major operations. That held down American casualties, but with so much fighting going on and so many U.S. Army and Marine Corps troops involved, it did not eliminate them. During 1967 the number of U.S. personnel killed in action rose to over 200 each week, while the number wounded neared 1,400.

Despite escalating casualties, the American military effort in Vietnam did not seem to be making much progress. As Herring writes, "Within two years, the optimism of 1965 had given way to deep and painful frustration." By 1967 the war was costing the United States in excess of $2 billion per month. This country paid a high price for an air war that hit Vietnam with more bombs than America had dropped in all theaters during World War II, losing 950 aircraft, valued at approximately $6 billion. According to one estimate, the air war cost the United States $9.60 for every dollar of damage it inflicted on North Vietnam. Besides not being cost-effective, it had no demonstrable impact on the war in the South. Through ingenuity and determination, North Vietnam blunted the bombing's effectiveness. That country moved much of its civilian population out of cities into the countryside and dispersed its industries and storage facilities, often hiding them in caves and underground. It built 30,000 miles of tunnels in heavily bombed areas. North Vietnam replaced bombed-out concrete and steel bridges with ferries and pontoon bridges, and its "Youth Shock Brigades" repaired craters in roads within hours after the bombs stopped falling. Although the air war inflicted a great deal of damage on North Vietnam, increased aid from the Soviet Union and China offset the losses in equipment and raw materials. Furthermore, bombing failed utterly to curtail the movement of men and equipment down the Ho Chi Minh Trail. Official American estimates conceded that infiltration actually increased from around 35,000 men in 1965 to as many as 90,000 in 1967.

The ground war in the South was nearly as ineffectual as aerial bombardment of the North. By the end of 1966, the military commitment the United States was making had stopped the deterioration of South Vietnam's government, and when main-force units fought a major battle, American troops almost always won. After the Ia Drang Valley battle, however, such engagements were rare. The North Vietnamese relied heavily on ambushes and hit-and-run operations, seeking to initiate small fights at close quarters, in which the Americans could not make much use of their artillery and airpower. Their strategic objective was to draw U.S. forces away from populated areas, where the Vietcong could then operate freely.

Westmoreland's search-and-destroy strategy played into the enemy's hands. It also gave American operations a dubious objective. The mission was simply to kill people. In the war of attrition Westmoreland was fighting, there were no "front lines" to be advanced, and the seizure of territorial objectives was at most a means to the end of annihilating the enemy. The measure of success became the "body count." Those numbers, however, were hopelessly unreliable. The sheer destructiveness of the combat, especially when air strikes and artillery were used, often made it impossible to determine precisely how many human beings were represented by the body parts scattered around a battlefield. Furthermore, the guerrilla-fighting Vietcong did not wear military uniforms, dressing instead in the black pajama garb of Vietnamese peasants. That made it difficult to tell whether a dead body was an enemy soldier. Marine Lieutenant Philip Caputo reported that for troops in the bush, the rule of thumb was "If it's dead and Vietnamese, it's VC." Their superiors had no incentive to demand greater accuracy. Since the body count was the standard by which everyone's success was measured, officers anxious to obtain good efficiency ratings and promotions had an incentive to inflate the figures still further. Estimates on the extent of the padding range as high as 30 percent. Official figures placed the number of enemy killed by late 1967 as high as 220,000, but these numbers were largely worthless.

Even had they been accurate, they would not have proved, as the American military command contended, that the war was being won. The Vietcong continued to recruit South Vietnamese peasants, and 200,000 North Vietnamese men reached draft age every year. As long as the enemy remained willing to feed manpower into Westmoreland's meat grinder, he could not win his war of attrition. The best America could hope for was a stalemate.

The methods it was employing to achieve a battlefield impasse were hurting the country the United States was supposedly fighting to protect. Civilian casualties in South Vietnam rose from an estimated 100,000 per year in 1965 to 300,000 in 1968. American military operations turned many parts of South Vietnam into combat zones, forcing about 25 percent of the residents from their native villages into a swelling stream of refugees that flowed toward the cities. The sudden infusion of hundreds of thousands of American troops and advisers and billions of dollars of American money into the country triggered rampant inflation. Seeking to curtail this by sopping up the money, the United States flooded South Vietnam with consumer goods, thereby destroying the country's few native industries, retarding its economic development, and rendering it ever more dependent on foreign economic assistance and catering to the desires of Americans for alcohol, sex, and other pleasures. The disruption of Vietnamese society caused by the U.S. war effort was not likely to build popular support for the South Vietnamese regime it was intended to keep in power. That government was now controlled by generals, who schemed constantly against each other, and its subservience to the United States kindled complaints from Buddhist leaders.

Although incapable of producing victory on the battlefield and quite harmful to South Vietnam, the American war effort did hurt the North. What it did not do was persuade the enemy to end the fighting on terms acceptable to the United States. Believing the American public would tire of the war long before their own people did, North Vietnamese leaders spurned proposals for peace talks. Between 24 December 1965 and 31 January 1966, the United States halted bombing of the North and substantially curtailed it in the South, a gesture some of Johnson's advisers hoped might lead to negotiations. North Vietnam was willing to discuss only the manner in which American troops would be withdrawn from Vietnam. In June 1966 the president postponed attacking petroleum depots in North Vietnam so the Canadian ambassador to the United States could visit Hanoi to explore the possibility of peace talks. The ambassador found North Vietnam's position unchanged: America must pull its troops out of South Vietnam, end its support for the Saigon government, and recognize the NLF before it would even begin to negotiate. In the fall of 1967, the Johnson administration sent Harvard professor Henry Kissinger to Paris for secret talks aimed at getting negotiations started, but although he offered some sort of curtailment of the bombing as an inducement and was even willing to let North Vietnam keep its troops in the South, Hanoi's suspicious representatives demanded a complete bombing halt before going forward. Like its predecessors, this initiative failed.

Diplomatically as well as militarily, the United States was getting nowhere. By the end of 1966, McNamara had become convinced the war was stalemated. He had concluded that no matter how much military pressure it applied, the United States could never break the will of the North Vietnamese. Throughout 1967 he pressed quietly for basic policy changes. The secretary of defense was not alone. During 1966, opposition to further escalation of the war increased among Johnson's civilian advisers. Eventually, some of them, such as Bill Moyers at the White House and George Ball at the State Department, became so alienated that they quietly resigned. By the spring of 1967, some presidential advisers were openly advocating the abandonment of policies they had become convinced were completely bankrupt.

Concern about the war was growing outside as well as inside the government. More Americans (61 percent) worried about Vietnam than about crime and juvenile delinquency (51 percent), inflation and the cost of living (46 percent), race relations (32 percent), or air and water pollution (27 percent). Public opinion polls conducted in 1966 found that a majority of Americans approved of Johnson's handling of the situation in Vietnam, although the percentage expressing approval varied substantially from one survey to another, falling as low as 43 percent in a September Gallup poll (versus 40 percent expressing disapproval). A May 1967 Gallup poll produced similar results. Responses to other questions suggested that there was trouble ahead for the administration. Half of those who answered a question in the May 1967 survey concerning whether they had a clear idea of what the Vietnam War was all about said no. The percentage of Americans who gave a negative response when asked "In view of developments since we entered the fighting in Vietnam, do you think the U.S. made a mistake sending troops to Vietnam?" moved rather steadily downward, falling from 61 percent in August 1965 to 44 percent by October 1967.

A Harris survey from February 1966 suggested disaffection with the course of the war was greatest among those who thought the United States ought to be doing *more* in Vietnam. Such hawks tended to be right-wing Republicans and conservative Democrats, who viewed the war as an essential part of the global struggle against communism. They thought Johnson was not doing enough to win. On the other side of the debate over Vietnam were the doves, a diverse group whose ranks included everyone from Senator Fulbright to student radical Tom Hayden, from civil rights leader Dr. Martin Luther King Jr. to actress Jane Fonda, and from pacifist A. J. Muste to heavyweight boxing champion Cassius Clay (who changed his name to Muhammad Ali). A study published in the *American Political Science Review* in June 1967, but based on interviews done more than a year earlier, found strong evidence that doves were even more likely than hawks to oppose the president. There were far fewer of them, however. A May 1967 Gallup poll found that even among college students, hawks outnumbered doves 49 percent to 35 percent.

Although less numerous, the doves were more vocal. As Robert Schulzinger reports, "In 1966 and 1967 the antiwar movement became a major element in American political and social life." By the end of 1967, it included groups such as Clergy and Laymen Concerned About Vietnam and Business Executives

Move for Peace. To protest the war, hundreds of Americans refused to pay their taxes. Others resorted to fasting, hunger strikes, and prayer vigils at the White House. By the end of 1967, seven people had set themselves on fire to dramatize their opposition to the war. Demonstrations against it, involving first tens of thousands and later hundreds of thousands of protesters, erupted across the country. Antiwar agitation reached a peak during "Stop the Draft Week" (16–22 October 1967), which began with nationwide protests against conscription that featured the burning and turning in of many draft cards, the picketing and disruption of Selective Service System offices, urban guerrilla tactics, and violent confrontations with police. The climax of Stop the Draft Week was a gigantic march on the Pentagon. Most of the tens of thousands who participated were peaceful, but some of the protesters tried to storm the building and battled soldiers and federal marshals.

The chaos at the Pentagon evoked widespread condemnation. Although the public disagreed with the tactics of the antiwar activists, many Americans shared their dissatisfaction with what was going on in Vietnam. According to Schulzinger, "By the end of 1967 a consensus [had emerged] that the war had lasted long enough." Yet American soldiers would continue to fight and die in Vietnam for five more years.

Among the hundreds of thousands who would be sent off to Southeast Asia to risk their lives in this long, futile, and increasingly controversial military struggle was Lieutenant William Calley. On 15 September 1967 Calley completed OCS at Fort Benning. Now pinned on each shoulder of his uniform was the single gold bar that identified him as a second lieutenant. His new rank insignia required enlisted men to salute him. It was the army's certification that he was qualified to lead them into battle. The gold bar lied. Lieutenant Calley was not ready for the hell that awaited him in Vietnam.

CHAPTER 2

Lieutenant Calley

Rusty Calley should never have been a lieutenant. He might have served the army well as a clerk, but nothing about his life before he enlisted suggested he should be made an officer. Nothing he did before or after he became a soldier suggested he was capable of commanding others in the often bewildering small-unit fighting in Vietnam. That Rusty Calley became a lieutenant and an infantry platoon leader says a great deal about the army in which he served. It also says something about why America lost the war it sent him to fight.

Like many junior officers who served in Vietnam, Calley had been born during an earlier and very different war. His life began in Miami, Florida, on 8 June 1943, right in the middle of World War II. Fifteen million American men and women wore military uniforms during that conflict, among them Calley's father, who served in the navy. For members of this previous generation, service in the armed forces was a source of pride. Most of them wanted to fight for what they viewed as a great national cause. Some even lied and bent the rules to get into the military. The rich and famous went off to war along with the poor and the disadvantaged (Winthrop Rockefeller volunteered to be among the first 10,000 men inducted, and baseball star Ted Williams flew fighter planes). While fewer African-Americans than members of other racial groups served in combat units, blacks were the ones who complained most loudly about that situation, which they viewed as a form of invidious racial discrimination.

The attitude of Calley's generation was very different. For most of these young people, military service was something to be avoided if at all possible. The Vietnam War was fought largely by those who could not get out of going. Of the 26.8 million men in the Vietnam generation (those who reached age eighteen between 4 August 1964 and 28 March 1973), only 10.93 million served in the military. Some of these were true volunteers, but most either were drafted or enlisted to avoid conscription. According to Lawrence M. Baskir and William A. Strauss, "The draftees who fought and died in Vietnam were primarily society's 'losers,' the same men who got left behind in schools, jobs, and other forms of social competition." Ronald Spector disputes that characterization, depicting the Vietnam army as composed of "solid hard workers . . . to whom society had given no special advantages." Although insisting it is wrong to consider these soldiers dregs and castoffs, he acknowledges they "were not the social and intellectual cream of American youth."

The reason they were not was Selective Service. The Selective Service System had been created in 1940, and with the exception of a brief period following World War II, it had been conscripting men into the American military ever since. The manpower demands of World War II were so great that it inducted virtually every man eligible for military duty. Because of the limited scope of the Vietnam conflict and the vast expansion in the number of men of draft age caused by the post-1945 baby boom, however, Selective Service needed only a fraction of the available manpower for that war. By law all men had to register for the draft at age 18. A man was liable for service from 18 $\frac{1}{2}$ to 26, unless he accepted a deferment, in which case his liability for induction theoretically continued until age 35. In fact, Selective Service did not take anyone who was over 26, so once a man reached that age, he was safe.

What determined whether he could expect to be drafted before then was a classification system that entitled those in certain categories to exemptions or deferments. For example, ministers, divinity students, and those opposed to war for reasons of conscience did not have to serve at all. Agricultural workers were entitled to have their induction deferred. As the armed forces shrank after the Korean War and inductions fell from 472,000 in 1953 to 87,000 in 1960, the percentage of draft-age men receiving deferments rose substantially, and increasingly Selective Service came to view itself as a personnel management agency, whose function was to channel men into those occupations and activities in which they would make the greatest contribution to the nation. The law authorized the president to defer men in key jobs, deemed essential to the national welfare, a provision that protected scientists, engineers, and even schoolteachers from the draft. Fathers, married men, and college students also received deferments. As the war in Vietnam escalated and the armed forces expanded from 2,655,000 to 3,500,000, draft calls soared, and some of these deferments had to be eliminated. After August 1965 a man could no longer qualify for one by getting married, and in 1968 Selective Service stopped deferring graduate students. Undergraduates retained their 2-S deferments until 1970, however, and college enrollments increased an estimated 6 to 7 percent because of the presence on campus of men who were there mostly to avoid the draft.

By piling occupational on top of student deferments, young men could often postpone induction until reaching the magic age of twenty-six. If called before then, a man might be able to stay out of the army by qualifying as a conscientious objector, faking a medical condition that would enable him to fail his draft physical, or mounting a successful legal challenge to the procedures Selective Service used in his case. Yet another way to escape the draft was to join the reserves or the National Guard. Both were subject to mobilization in time of national emergency, but because the Johnson administration feared the political reaction that calling them up would provoke, fewer than 40,000 reservists were ever summoned to active duty. Only 10,000 went to Vietnam. In 1968 a commission, headed by former Assistant Attorney General Burke Marshall, warned that the National Guard and reserves were becoming refuges from the draft. A 1966 Pentagon study found that 71 percent of all reservists were draft-motivated, and in 1970 the president of the National Guard Association claimed 90 percent of those who joined the Guard did so to avoid conscription. At the end of 1968 the Army National Guard alone had a waiting list of 100,000.

The war was fought largely by those who lacked the combination of skills, foresight, connections, and luck that would enable them to find a safe haven in the Guard or the reserves, get a draft deferment, or avoid being inducted when called. A disproportionate number of the losers in the Selective Service sweepstakes were African-American. The reasons were complex. One was that less than 1 percent of the million men in the reserves and the National Guard were black. Also, African-Americans did not volunteer as frequently as whites, and thus failed to get their proportionate share of the many safe assignments in the navy and the air force. A higher percentage of qualified blacks than whites was drafted (30.2 percent versus 18.8 percent by 1968), although the reason appears to have been that, because of poor health care and education, fewer draft-age African-Americans passed the physical exams and mental tests that determined who was qualified to serve, leaving a smaller pool from which to draw those conscripted. Once in the military, African-Americans often found that educational deficiencies kept them from qualifying for the technical and skilled jobs in "the rear." In addition, attracted by the better pay, faster promotions, and higher status of combat units, they volunteered for those in larger numbers than did whites. African-Americans also reenlisted at a higher rate than whites. Both of these patterns enhanced their chances of being exposed to hostile fire and killed or wounded. At the start of the war, 31 percent of all combat troops were black, and in 1965 they accounted for 24 percent of all army combat deaths. After that, the Pentagon undertook a concerted and successful effort to reduce the share of the fighting done by minorities, which dropped from 16 percent in 1966 to only 9 percent by 1970.

The most serious inequities were social and economic rather than racial. "Blacks were overrepresented in line companies and in casualty lists not because they were black but because they were poor," Spector explains. As Baskir and Strauss point out, "Poorly educated, low-income whites and poorly educated low-income blacks together bore a vastly disproportionate share of the burdens of Vietnam." A survey conducted by Notre Dame researchers determined that men from disadvantaged backgrounds were about twice as likely as their better-off peers to serve in the military, go to Vietnam, and see combat. Another study determined that Chicago youths from low-income neighborhoods were three times as likely to die in Vietnam as ones from high-income neighborhoods. Surveys of communities in Wisconsin, Long Island, and Utah yielded similar results. It was not the very poorest who were most likely to become casualties, however, because physical and mental exams kept many of them out of the military. It was men from the lower middle class who were most likely to serve, fight, and die.

Education was the key to avoiding those fates. Youths from neighborhoods with low educational levels were four times as likely to die in Vietnam as were those from better-educated ones, and the higher a man's level of education, the less likely he was to fight at all. A 1965–66 survey discovered that college graduates made up only 2 percent of draftees. For the entire war such men had only a 23 percent chance of serving in the military, a 12 percent chance of going to Vietnam, and a 9 percent chance of being in combat. For high school graduates the figures were 45, 21, and 17 percent, respectively. (Because so many of them failed to qualify for service, the numbers for those who dropped out of high school were actually slightly lower, at 42, 18, and 14 percent, respectively.) Once in the military, if an enlisted man was a college graduate, he had a 42 percent chance of being sent to Vietnam. The chance was 64 percent if he was a high school graduate and 70 percent if he was a high school dropout.

William Calley was among those whose lack of educational achievement made him a loser in the great generational contest to stay out of the fighting in Vietnam. Neither race nor class explains why he eventually found himself under fire with an infantry platoon. Calley was white, and he was born into a comfortable middle-class family in Miami. His father was a successful businessman who ran a company that sold heavy construction machinery, and he and his wife raised their son in an upper-middle-class suburban neighborhood. Rusty (a nickname inspired by his reddish brown hair) and three sisters led a relaxed, easy childhood, dividing their time between the family's home in the Miami area and its vacation retreat in Waynesville, North Carolina. He considered his family a "stable" one, although it was not especially close-knit. According to a psychiatrist who testified at his court-martial, Rusty felt closest to his older sister. "Things went all right—as far as he was concerned," although he always considered himself something of a loner.

Young Rusty attended elementary school in Hialeah, Florida. A pleaser, he always tried to anticipate what his teacher wanted and to place himself where he could help her. He turned the pages of the music when she played the piano for class singing and volunteered to pass out erasers to other students. Calley enjoyed the recognition and approval he received for performing these small tasks. His elementary school grades were ordinary— not outstanding, but not really bad either.

The pattern of academic failure that would make him a loser in the Selective Service sweepstakes began in junior high school. Calley failed the seventh grade for cheating. According to him, he gave rather than received improper assistance, writing down answers to some final exam questions and passing them to another pupil. Calley was not a good student, though. He characterized his junior high grades as "generally poor." Before repeating the seventh grade, he switched schools. Two years later, after he was suspended for arguing with a teacher, his parents pulled him out of Miami Edison Junior High in the middle of a term and enrolled him in the private Florida Military Academy in Fort Lauderdale. He transferred to the Georgia Military Academy for the tenth grade. At his court-martial Calley testified that he had done "very well" in military school. He had told the psychiatrist earlier, however, that his grades were good at first but gradually dropped off as he became "a bit more social" and studied less.

Calley returned to public school for the eleventh and twelfth grades, and his academic performance deteriorated. Of his grades he recalled, "I went to military school and they came up. I came back to public school and they declined." The reasons were, as he explained, "I didn't study and social life." He was bored and not "too crazy about suburbanite-type living." Calley admitted to graduating from Miami Edison High School in the bottom one-quarter of his class. He ranked 666th out of 731.

Despite his unpromising academic record, he decided to attend junior college. The only reason seems to have been lack of any real occupational goals. The results were predictable. He dropped some of his courses. In those he completed, Calley received two Cs and a D. He failed the rest.

Forced by failure in the classroom to make his way in the world of work, he continued the pattern of inadequate performance that had made him a loser in school. While attending Palm Beach Junior College, Calley supported himself with a variety of what he himself characterized as "menial jobs." He was employed as a busboy, dishwasher, hotel bellman, short-order cook, and car wash worker and also had "an assortment of small jobs." Asked why he changed positions so often, Calley explained that the work was all seasonal.

After leaving college in 1963, he signed on with the Florida East Coast Railroad—which was then the target of a job action by its employees—as a strikebreaker. Starting as a switchman, Calley soon received a promotion, becoming the road's youngest freight train conductor. The pay was good because the railroad paid those it hired as strikebreakers a higher hourly wage than its regular employees. As a conductor Calley made over $300 per month. According to journalist Richard Hammer, he also made serious mistakes, twice blocking automobile traffic by stalling his train during the rush hour. The Fort Lauderdale police arrested him in connection with one of these incidents, although he was acquitted after he explained that the brakes on his train had failed. In addition, Hammer reports, "Calley was late to work often, failed to complete paperwork correctly, and even once got fifteen demerits for permitting several cars on his train to break free from his idling engine." Once the strikers began returning to work, their greater seniority soon made it impossible for him to bid successfully for regular jobs, and he found himself working only one or two days a week. Feeling he did not have much of a future with the railroad, Calley quit in December 1965.

He went home, intending to spend the Christmas holidays

with his family, then return to school. His father's business had gone bankrupt, and his parents were now living year-round in North Carolina. When he got there, Calley discovered that his mother, who had cancer, was terminal. "There wasn't much money coming in so I stayed up there and supported the family," he recalled. Unable to find "any real work" in North Carolina in the winter, he soon exhausted his savings.

Calley then left for New Orleans, where he got a job with the Hooper Homes Corporation as a commercial investigator. The company worked for insurance companies, checking out houses for underwriters to ensure that they were worth what those seeking coverage claimed and making sure applicants for automobile insurance had fully reported all relevant information. Hooper Homes moved him to Baton Rouge. Dissatisfied because he felt it would be years before he could rise any higher in the company, Calley "went off on my own, working directly for underwriters." He did not flourish as a "freelance agent." Sometime later he found himself in Mexico, looking for certain individuals he had been sent there to check on. "I just realized very rapidly that I just didn't have any mental capacity to try to figure out where a person would be hiding," he testified at his court-martial. "I just wasn't really adequate at that job."

Concluding that private investigation "wasn't really my thing," Calley left Mexico "and went up to San Francisco." There some forwarded mail caught up to him, including "a couple of draft notices." Calley had tried to enlist in the military back in 1964, while he was working on the railroad, but he had failed the physical exam because he was tone-deaf. As the American military commitment in Vietnam escalated and draft calls rose, however, local boards moved relentlessly to conscript childless married men, college dropouts, and finally "1-Y types" (men classified as physically and mentally qualified to serve only in time of war). Calley, a 1-Y college dropout, was now a prime candidate for conscription, and his board wanted him to report for reevaluation. When he failed to show up at the induction center, it wrote to inform him that he was delinquent and in violation of the law.

He climbed into his car and headed for Miami to report to his draft board. Calley's "finances were not that hot," however, and by the time he reached Albuquerque, New Mexico, he had run out of money. Stuck there, Calley looked up a local army recruiter and asked him what someone in his situation could do. "You enlist," the recruiter told him. Calley called Miami to ask his draft board if the advice he had received was correct. Informed that if he enlisted, the board would not conscript him, he signed on the dotted line.

Rusty Calley thus became, like most of those who served in the military during America's longest war, a "draft-induced volunteer." According to George Q. Flynn, a historian of the Selective Service System, "During the entire Vietnam War only 25 percent of the army and 16 percent of the total armed forces in Vietnam were draftees." Yet while most of those who served, and even most of those who went to Southeast Asia, enlisted, a 1964 survey found 40 percent of all volunteers were motivated by the draft. That figure rose to over 50 percent after 1965. As Flynn observes, and Calley could attest, "Armed forces recruiters began to have a field day."

After the one in Albuquerque signed up Calley, the army sent him to nearby Fort Bliss, Texas, where he spent eight weeks undergoing basic training. Then it shipped him to Fort Lewis, Washington, for advanced individual training at the Adjutant General's School. The Adjutant General's Corps is the branch of the army that performs many of its administrative tasks and much of its paperwork, and when he enlisted, Calley had asked to be trained as a clerk-typist. He did well at Fort Lewis. "That job, it seemed, was meant for him," Hammer writes. "He graduated in the top half of the clerk's school . . . and readily fell into the work." Calley recalled finishing "second or third in that school."

Had he remained a clerk, he might well have been successful in the army. He would probably also have avoided combat. By the 1960s warfare had become so complex and technical that military organizations needed huge logistical and support staffs to sustain the soldiers who performed the traditional infantryman's mission of closing with the enemy by fire and maneuver to kill or capture him. During the Spanish-American War, only 13 percent of all troops had been trained for noncombat roles. By World War II the primary job of 61 percent of military personnel was to do something other than fight, and by 1968, at the height of the Vietnam conflict, 88 percent of all servicemen were assigned to noncombatant occupational specialties, such as clerk-typist.

The men who did these jobs were far less likely than those in combat arms, such as infantry and armor, to be ordered to Vietnam. That was one of the principal reasons why more draftees than volunteers served in Southeast Asia and why more of them found themselves under fire. Army recruiters used the promise of specialized training as an inducement to get men to sign up, suggesting to those who were vulnerable to being drafted that by enlisting they could avoid the risks of combat. Although self-serving, this was sound advice. At the peak of the war, army draftees were being killed at almost twice the rate of volunteers.

Even if sent to Vietnam, someone with a technical specialty was likely to avoid combat. The increasing importance of technology in warfare, the fact that military bases and modern supply and transportation facilities had to be created from scratch in Vietnam, and the determination of Americans to enjoy there as many of the creature comforts of home as possible generated vast amounts of work that did not involve fighting. In April 1968 only 29 percent of army personnel and 34 percent of marines were serving in maneuver battalions. Saigon was full of soldiers performing staff jobs, who were in only slightly greater danger than if they had been doing the same work in the States. Throughout Vietnam there were rear-echelon support units, whose members faced the danger of an occasional rocket or mortar attack or an assault on their base by an enemy sapper unit, but who were otherwise unlikely to be killed or wounded. Even clerks in infantry units, because they rarely went out on operations, had comparatively safe jobs. Had he remained a clerk-typist, Calley might never have participated in actual combat.

But he did not. Apparently, someone examined his personnel records and, discovering that he had once attended a military school, concluded Calley was officer material. It is not surprising that the army should have made so much out of so little. It was desperate for junior officers. During the years before the fighting in Vietnam escalated, it had depended on West Point and college ROTC programs to meet most of its needs. Although the army expanded the size of classes at the Military Academy by 25 percent and sought to increase ROTC enrollment with an advertising campaign and scholarships, these traditional sources fell far short of meeting the greatly increased demand for officers that the war created.

To make up the difference the army had to rely heavily on OCS. The Officer Candidate program had been the principal source of commissioned officers during World War II, but in the 1950s and early 1960s OCS had been used only to develop a few promising enlisted men, many of whom had attended college before joining the service, into lieutenants. When Vietnam multiplied the number of junior officers it needed, the army vastly expanded OCS. The output of its Officer Candidate Schools increased sixfold during the first year of the buildup, from 300 second lieutenants per month to more than 1,800. During the second year, from July 1966 to July 1967, the monthly average climbed to 3,000. During the first three-quarters of fiscal 1967 alone, Officer Candidate Schools turned out more new lieutenants than in the entire 1958–66 period. The army tried to find college graduates for OCS, and ultimately its recruiting efforts and the pressure of the draft (which encouraged them to volunteer to become officers in order to avoid conscripted service as enlisted men) were surprisingly successful; by the fall of 1967, three out of every four men entering the program had a degree. During 1966 and early 1967, however, about three out of four were nongraduates. That, of course, was when the army tapped Rusty Calley to become an officer.

It was asking him to take on an extremely challenging responsibility. The troops the army wanted Calley and his fellow officer candidates to lead were very young; the median age for draftees in 1966 was 20.3 years. The army the United States sent to Vietnam was substantially younger than the ones with which it had fought both World War II and the Korean War. Nor could its youthful enlisted men look for guidance to older and wiser non-commissioned officers (NCOs). In peacetime it had taken five years or longer for a soldier to acquire the requisite experience and seniority to attain the rank of sergeant (E-5). Now, desperate for NCOs, the army created the equivalent of OCS to manufacture them, and it promoted the top graduates of these schools (whose only other military experience consisted of basic and advanced individual training) all the way to staff sergeant (E-6).

Calley would be asked not only to lead men who were young and inexperienced but also to do so in ground combat. He was accepted for OCS at Fort Benning, which was home to the Infantry School. The combat arms (infantry, armor, and artillery) had the greatest need for junior officers. Although trained for clerical and administrative work, Calley would have to become a warrior in order to become a lieutenant. His most vivid recollections of his time at Fort Benning involved the "pogie bait parties," during which the officer candidates scarfed down unauthorized civilian food, such as pizza, but he also remembered, "One thing we were taught at OCS . . . was . . . [to] kill." That is hardly surprising, for the mission of Fort Benning's OCS was to turn enlisted men into combat platoon leaders.

Rusty Calley was not one of its more distinguished graduates. He survived the physical rigors of training at Fort Benning, and he had a medal to prove he was competent with a rifle. Calley thought he did well in OCS. Actually, he finished in the bottom 23 percent of his class, ranking 120th among the 156 officer candidates in his company who completed the program. For him OCS was, in Hammer's words, "a bitter struggle." Calley had to be counseled several times for what the officers charged with molding him into a combat platoon leader considered a lack of "command presence." Only five feet three inches tall, he was not an imposing figure, but they also found his voice insufficiently authoritative. Later in Vietnam his troops would mock their lieutenant.

Besides failing to develop the sort of "command voice" that would demand instant attention and respect from enlisted men, Calley never mastered map reading. That was one of the basic skills of an infantry lieutenant, who had to use a map and compass to move his men across roadless terrain and call in artillery fire and air strikes on locations identified only by their grid coordinates on a topographic map. Lack of skill in these areas could get his platoon lost or, worse yet, subject it to "friendly fire" by gunners and aircraft that he had misdirected. "I wondered sometimes how he got through OCS," Roy L. Wood, a rifleman who served under Calley in Vietnam, remarked to journalist Seymour Hersh. "He couldn't read no darn map and a compass would confuse his ass."

Despite his ineptitude with a map and compass and his lack of command presence, Calley graduated from OCS. In peacetime he might not have received a commission, but in the summer of 1967 the army needed "cannon fodder" for infantry combat in Vietnam. In 1965, before the buildup necessitated by the war began, the attrition rate at all of its Officer Candidate Schools was approximately 42 percent. By late 1967, when Calley completed his training at Fort Benning, it had fallen to 28 percent. "When one takes account of the fact that a much smaller number of candidates was admitted in 1965," says Spector, "the picture that emerges is one of less selective admission standards and less 'selecting out' of candidates during training." Small wonder that there were persistent complaints about the quality of OCS graduates. The army was pinning gold bars on the shoulders of the marginally qualified, and sometimes even the unqualified. Isaiah Cowan, the career NCO who served as Calley's platoon sergeant in Vietnam, would later call him the worst officer for whom he had ever worked.

Now a second lieutenant, Calley was unprepared for the responsibilities that went with the commission the army awarded him on 15 September 1967. The training he had received at Fort Benning had supposedly made him a skilled warrior and a leader of men. It was supposed to have molded a soft, young civilian into a tough, proud, and self-confident commander who was competent to issue orders that would determine how others went about the deadly serious business of killing while avoiding being killed themselves. In fact, the Infantry School had accomplished none of these things. Part of the reason was probably flaws in its own training program, but the principal explanation for its failure to make Calley what he was supposed to be was what it had to work with.

Journalist David Halberstam would later write a book about the politicians, bureaucrats, and high-ranking military officers who plunged the United States into the quagmire of Vietnam, to which he gave the bitterly ironic title *The Best and the Brightest*. Unfortunately for those cocky and overconfident policy makers, there were far too few of America's best and brightest among the young men they sent into combat. Far too many of those who fought their war did so only because they were unable to take one of the many safe roads away from the battlefield that Selective Service and the armed forces had constructed for the men of their generation. Far too many of those who became "grunts" (military slang for infantrymen) were individuals who, for a variety of reasons, were not making it in civilian society.

William Calley was one of those losers. An army desperate for junior officers handed him not only a rifle but also a commission. A gold bar could not make him something he was not. He left Fort Benning with orders to report to the 11th Light Infantry Brigade in Hawaii. It was headed for Vietnam, and Lieutenant Calley was headed for a job he could not handle.

CHAPTER 3

Charlie Company's War

"The best company in Hawaii." That is what Lieutenant Calley later called the unit he joined upon reporting to the 11th Light Infantry Brigade at Schofield Barracks. It was C Company, 1st Battalion, 20th Infantry, known as "Charlie Company" because "C" is "Charlie" in the phonetic alphabet used in military communications. After a period of preparation in Hawaii, Charlie Company deployed to Vietnam in December 1967. Although Calley considered it a fine unit, his company left Schofield Barracks poorly prepared for the war that awaited it there. Infantry combat in Vietnam was hard, dirty, and dangerous, and it subjected the "grunts" who did the fighting to extreme emotional stress. Sometimes they took out their frustrations and anger on the civilians of South Vietnam. Charlie Company did that, after the enemy's 1968 Tet Offensive escalated the level of the fighting in which it was involved, and soldiers began to lose buddies to an enemy they generally could not see and often could not even identify.

The man who provided them with a way to vent their rage was their company commander, Captain Ernest Medina. He was as competent as Calley was inept. A Mexican-American, Medina had been born into poverty in Springer, New Mexico, in 1936, and his mother had died of cancer when he was less than a year old. Young Ernest went to live with his grandparents in Montrose, Colorado, and thereafter rarely saw his father, who worked as a shepherd. At the age of fifteen he joined the Colorado National Guard, in which he rose to the rank of sergeant. In 1956 Medina volunteered for the draft and entered the regular army as a private (E-2). An infantryman, he served two tours in Germany (where he married a German woman), and one tour at Fort Riley, Kansas.

During eight years as an enlisted man, Medina turned down several opportunities to attend OCS because he did not think he had enough education to be an effective officer. Finally, after taking some college-level classes at night and starting a family, he let himself be talked into pursuing a commission at Fort Benning. Medina graduated from OCS in March 1964, ranked in the top five in his class. He stayed on at the Infantry School as in instructor in the Weapons Department, teaching other soldiers how to use the 4.2-inch mortar. He even authored a paper entitled "Meteorological Effects on the 4.2-in. Mortar Shell."

In 1966 the army promoted Medina to captain and made him a company commander in the 11th Infantry Brigade at Schofield Barracks. He threw himself into the training there. Medina was anxious to get to Vietnam, for he believed in the war, and he also realized that for someone with his limited education, winning a promotion to major would be difficult unless he enhanced his credentials with some combat duty. His hustle and energy and the way he pushed his troops through difficult marches and tough field exercises earned him the nickname "Mad Dog."

Mad Dog Medina's men won intramural athletic competitions and an award as the 1st Battalion's company of the month. The battalion commander, Lieutenant Colonel Edward Beers, considered the thirty-three-year-old captain the most outstanding officer in his organization. The twenty-four-year-old Lieutenant Calley, who assumed command of Charlie Company's Second Platoon, was even more enthusiastic about Medina. He believed the army would have to commission close to half a million officers to find another who was Medina's equal. It was Medina who had made their company the best one in Hawaii, Calley believed. He was "a real leader." "I really respect him," Calley wrote later.

The members of Calley's platoon (Medina switched him from command of the Second to the First after they got to Vietnam) did not feel the same way about him. "Everybody used to joke about Calley," rifleman Allen Boyce informed journalist Seymour Hersh. Machine gunner Charles Hall told Hersh that their platoon leader "reminded me of a kid, a kid trying to play war." Calley was far less popular with the rest of the company than were the other lieutenants who shuffled in and out of it and from one platoon to another, such as Stephen Brooks and Jeffrey LaCross. He was constantly endeavoring to impress Medina, but many of the enlisted men believed the captain really did not have much respect for Calley, whom he often addressed as "Sweetheart." Certainly, they did not. Although Calley conceded later that he "was a very inadequate leader," at the time he repeatedly announced, "I'm the boss." His platoon sergeant thought nothing other than his rank entitled him to any authority. "[He] was my superior officer and I had to follow him whether I wanted to or not," Cowan told Hersh. That did not keep Cowan from arguing with Calley in front of their men.

Strangely, the lieutenant later described Cowan as "a beautiful human being" and said he "couldn't want a better platoon sergeant than him." Calley was at least smart enough to recognize that, because his second-in-command had been in the army for thirteen years, he could pass along some valuable tips. The fact that he was African-American apparently was not a problem for the white southern platoon leader. Not only was Cowan, a native of Columbia, South Carolina, black, so, too, were the key squad leaders in the understrength First Platoon that Calley commanded in Vietnam. Staff Sergeant David Mitchell, placed in charge of the First Squad after Medina relieved him as platoon sergeant of another platoon, was a high school graduate from Saint Francisville, Louisiana, with seven years of service. His fellow enlisted men considered Mitchell arrogant. Staff Sergeant L. G. Bacon headed the Second Squad. Calley claimed to be fond of all three of these African-American NCOs. "I am not a prejudiced person," he insisted. Although the racial makeup of the First Platoon's leadership was problematic, it was not unusual. Many army officers were white southerners, and a disproportionate number of the NCOs in combat branches were African-American.

In that respect as in numerous others, Charlie Company was rather typical. Like many rifle companies in Vietnam, it was about evenly divided between whites and blacks. Although most of the men tended to hang out with others of their own race, the company's ethnic composition made it the sort of marching melting pot often depicted in 1950s movies about the World War II army. "Negroes, Mexicans . . . , Filipinos, Puerto Ricans, Italians, Poles. . . . We had them all in Charlie Company," Calley recalled. Most of the enlisted men were between eighteen and twenty-two years of age, and most had graduated from high school. Indeed, Charlie Company had a somewhat higher percentage of both NCOs and enlisted men with high school diplomas than did the average unit in Vietnam. Only 13 of its 130 soldiers were products of Secretary McNamara's Project 100,000, which accepted into the army men who had not done well enough on basic intelligence tests to qualify for service (unfortunately, none of them had yet received the remedial education soldiers in that program were supposed to get). Members of Charlie Company hailed from cities, such as Portland, Oregon, Fort Worth, Texas, Columbus, Ohio, and Richmond, Virginia, as well as from small towns, such as Bradley Beach, New Jersey, and farms in the rural South. They were religiously as well as ethnically and geographically diverse. The Peers Commission, which investigated the My Lai massacre, concluded that these soldiers represented the cross section of American youth typically assigned to army combat units in Vietnam. For an outfit that would become infamous, Charlie Company was remarkably unremarkable.

Nevertheless, in trying to ready it for combat, its tough but fair "hard-core" commander faced an almost impossible task. When Medina assumed command on 19 December 1966, Charlie Company, which was supposed to consist of three rifle platoons and one weapons platoon, actually had one rifle platoon and part of a weapons platoon. New men were coming in constantly, but many of these had just completed tours of duty in Vietnam and were merely marking time until their release from the army.

"It was really difficult to establish a training cycle," Medina testified at Calley's court-martial. He started with squad-level instruction and had managed to get as far as platoon-level work when the army decided to send the 11th Brigade some soldiers who had completed basic training but had not yet received their Advanced Individual Training (AIT). Medina had to reorganize his partially trained men into a cadre-type unit that could provide the new arrivals with the instruction they needed. Around March or April 1967, "the training program started out again at squad level," with emphasis on skills such as fire and maneuver and the use of rifles and machine guns. Charlie Company finally managed to do enough platoon-level work so its platoons could complete an Army Training Test, but effective company-level training was impossible because it still had only two rifle platoons. Medina eventually acquired enough replacements to put together a third one, only to have it snatched away by the battalion commander, who was assembling a new company.

His unit somehow managed to pass an Army Training Test, administered by the 11th Brigade, but after the brigade received word that it would soon deploy to Vietnam, "a tremendous influx of equipment" hit Medina's company. This included the new M-16 rifle, a weapon significantly different from the M-14s with which its men had trained. As the deployment date approached, Charlie Company began hemorrhaging officers and senior NCOs, as those who had already served in Vietnam and had not been back in the United States long enough to be sent again and those who did not have to go because they were the sole surviving sons in their families departed. Specialists fourth class (SP-4s) or even privates first class (PFCs) assumed squad leader positions that were supposed to be held by sergeants. When Charlie Company moved out, it had only one platoon sergeant with any combat experience. It was, according to Medina, "up to full strength, approximately 176 people or 180 people." That was, however, only because of a last-minute deluge of replacements, many of them drawn from other units (such as a headquarters company, whose long-range reconnaissance platoon had been disbanded) that had been cannibalized to fill out rifle companies. Medina estimated there was an "approximately 60 to 70 percent changeover in the company prior to our departure for the Republic of South Vietnam."

The company he took to Vietnam lacked cohesion, experienced leadership, and (because of the disruptions caused by constant personnel turnover) adequate training. Its preparation for dealing with prisoners of war and Vietnamese civilians was particularly inadequate. These matters were governed by international law. The Geneva Convention on the Laws of War (1949) provided that persons taking no active part in hostilities (including soldiers who had laid down their arms) must be treated humanely, and the even older Hague Convention on Land Warfare (1907) prohibited attacking or bombarding undefended towns and villages. A 1956 army field manual informed soldiers that the fundamental human rights of persons who fell into their hands, "particularly prisoners of war, the wounded and sick, and civilians," must be safeguarded, that the law of war required refraining from the use of any kind or degree of violence not necessary for military purposes, and that the "prohibitory effect of the law of war is not minimized by 'military necessity.'"

Every soldier bound for Vietnam received two pocket-sized cards, which he was supposed to carry with him at all times, that contained instructions on how to treat civilians and prisoners. The "Nine Rules" admonished American troops to remember that they were guests in South Vietnam, to make friends with the people, to treat the women politely and with respect, and to avoid "loud, rude or unusual behavior." "The Enemy in Your Hands" informed soldiers explicitly that "mistreatment of any captive is a criminal offense" and that "all persons in your hands, whether suspects, civilians, or combat captives, must be protected against violence, insults, curiosity, and reprisals of any kind."

Army training, however, did little to reinforce the directives and noble sentiments contained in field manuals and on wallet cards. Calley testified that he had received some instruction on the Geneva Convention, but "I can't remember any of the classes." According to Medina, the indoctrination on the handling of prisoners that Charlie Company received in Hawaii dealt with the "Five S's" (search, silence, safeguard, segregate, and speed). Herbert Carter, a First Platoon enlisted man, recalled this training but also remembered the instructor laughing when he said they were supposed to hold prisoners until some-one from intelligence came to interrogate them. Calley charac-terized as "a farce" a class he himself taught just before Charlie Company deployed, entitled "Vietnam Our Host." "I read off an SOP of 'Do's and Don't's' that the Pentagon sent us. Items like . . . Do not insult the women. Do not *assault* the women." He had to keep yelling "Wake up" at the obviously bored troops. What the men of Charlie Company remembered far better than occa-sional dull classes on the Geneva Convention and how to treat their Vietnamese hosts was the emphasis on following the orders of their superiors—absolutely and without reservation—that permeated their training.

That message—rather than lessons on the law governing the treatment of prisoners and civilians—is what they would recall when subjected to the pressures of living and fighting in South Vietnam. The men of Charlie Company were bound for a land where their lives would be hard and unpleasant. For grunts the Vietnamese environment was squalid, harsh, and demanding. The climate was miserable. During the dry season the tempera-tures often exceeded 100 degrees, and the sun turned a soldier's steel helmet into a bake oven. In some units as many as one-third of all casualties were caused by the heat. It abated during the monsoon season, only to be replaced by torrential downpours that produced flooding and endless mud. "The sun scorched us in the dry season, and in the monsoon season we were pounded numb by ceaseless rain," Marine Lieutenant Philip Caputo re-calls. "Dust, filth and mosquitoes filled our hooches at night." Sometimes, of course, the grunts' living quarters were flooded or buried in mud instead.

Often they had no water with which to shower. Sometimes they did not even have enough toilet paper. Their fatigue uni-forms became white with dried sweat, and not even they could stand the way they smelled. Hot meals were a treat, all too often replaced by the cold contents of C-ration cans. "The time came when I could not look at those tin cans without gagging," Caputo remembers. The only thing he could stomach was peaches and pears, which were "about all we could eat in that climate." Grunts developed dysentery, malaria, and blackwater fever. Many also got trench foot from slogging through swamps and flooded rice paddies. Because of the pus that oozed from ulcers on his feet, whenever Caputo took off his boots to change socks, he had to hold his breath against the stench of his own rotting flesh.

Grunts also got bitten by insects. Caputo recalls the "sheer misery" of one ambush. "No enemy soldiers entered the ambush, but thousands of insects did. We lay awake eight hours, enduring bites of mosquitos and stinging fire ants." On other nights they lay in foxholes, waiting to be attacked and "picking off the leeches that sucked our veins." Grunts were also bitten by rats, which were a constant nuisance in most forward areas. Then there were the snakes, most of them poisonous, that infested certain regions and invariably washed out of their holes during the monsoon rains.

Through all of this grunts walked, and walked, and walked. Walking itself was often torture. It meant slogging through waist-deep water in flooded rice paddies and humping over the dikes that surrounded them. It meant hacking through razor-edged elephant grass, fifteen feet high and so thick that it was impossible to see more than a yard ahead. One Ranger in the division to which Charlie Company would eventually be assigned remarked that anyone who walked more than fifty feet through elephant grass should automatically qualify for a Purple Heart, the medal awarded to men who were wounded in action. As if just walking around were not tough enough, soldiers in Vietnam had to do it with outrageously heavy packs on their backs. Although studies had shown that the absolute maximum that even the strongest, best-conditioned infantryman could be expected to carry on active combat operations was fifty pounds, GIs in Vietnam regularly moved out loaded down with sixty pounds of gear and ammunition. Sometimes they carried more.

Their equipment imposed other burdens. Some of it did not work well. The aging radios that infantry platoons and companies used to communicate often failed at crucial times. When first introduced, the new M-16 rifle was prone to jam and otherwise malfunction. Sometimes GIs died because when the enemy shot at them, they could not shoot back.

That enemy was formidable. Caputo and the marines with whom he landed at Da Nang in 1965 quickly discovered that "the men we had scorned as peasant guerrillas were, in fact, a lethal, determined enemy." The Vietcong were organized into a coordinated hierarchy of forces, at the bottom of which were guerrilla squads and platoons, composed of part-time fighters controlled by village and hamlet Communist Party leaders. These units received support from unarmed self-defense and militia organizations, usually made up of younger teenagers, old men, and women. Above them were the full-time fighters of the Regional and Local Forces, organized into companies, and the Main Forces, organized into battalions, regiments, and sometimes divisions. Young men joined the Main Forces only after gaining training and experience in the guerrilla units. After the Vietcong suffered heavy casualties in early 1968, these local recruits were increasingly supplemented with infiltrators from the North. Some Main Force regiments became as much as 70 percent North Vietnamese. In 1967 the rate of infiltration was 7,000 men a month; during the first six months of 1968, it rose to 29,000. Although lacking the coordination and artillery support needed to carry out successfully attacks of larger than company size, these Communist forces were masterful and tenacious defensive fighters who repeatedly lured aggressive American troops into locations where carefully aligned weapons could chew them up.

Between January and July 1968, the rate at which U.S. troops were killed in action (KIA) in Vietnam exceeded KIA rates in Korea and in the Mediterranean and Pacific theaters during World War II. Thousands of GI's got "wasted" (their slang for dying) despite excellent medical care and the extensive use of helicopters to evacuate casualties from the battlefield, which enabled many men who would have perished in earlier wars to survive. The problem was that during 1968 and 1969 GIs were being wounded at a far higher rate than in World War II and Korea. The firefights between company-, platoon-, and squad-sized units that made up the vast majority of the battles in Vietnam were generally brief but extremely bloody. In 1967 a company of the 2nd Battalion, 503rd Infantry lost seventy killed and twenty-five wounded within a half hour after being ambushed by a Communist battalion.

Ambushes killed and wounded many American soldiers in Vietnam. So did mines and booby traps. "We were making history," says Caputo, "the first American soldiers to fight an enemy whose principal weapons were the mine and the booby trap." He recalls the anxiety of patrolling trails where "one misstep, and you were blasted to bits or crippled for life." For a grunt the consequences of letting his eyes wander even for a moment or of failing to notice a thin strand of wire stretched across a trail could be disastrous. Often referred to as "ground pounders," infantrymen normally felt a strong attachment to the earth on which they walked and fought and into which they dug the holes that sheltered them from hostile fire. Knowing the ground could erupt at any moment to kill or maim them turned their world upside down. Instead of slugging it out with an opposing force for control of some important piece of terrain, they patrolled for days on end, seldom fighting a real battle but losing a steady stream of men to booby traps, mines, and unseen snipers.

Westmoreland's search-and-destroy strategy deprived them of the sense of accomplishment that might have come from winning a major battle or capturing territory. Caught up in a war where the measure of success was the "kill ratio" (the ratio of enemy to American KIA), and where ground they seized at great cost one day was likely to be abandoned the next, soldiers soon concluded that their only real objective was to survive. According to Spector, in a war "where the conventional military measures of success . . . were largely or wholly absent, survivalism came to assume an almost exclusive place in a combat soldier's evaluation of success."

The military's policy of sending men to Vietnam for a one-year tour of duty reinforced this emphasis on just surviving. During World War I a popular song had proclaimed that the Yanks would "not come back till it's over over there," and World War II GIs knew that for them the road home ran through Berlin and Tokyo. For those who fought in Vietnam, on the other hand, there was no connection between victory and their own return to "the world." Getting home from "'Nam" required only personal survival for a fixed period of time. It took about six to eight months "in country" for a soldier to gain sufficient experience to become really effective, but soon thereafter he began thinking of himself as a "short-timer," counting the days until he could board a plane that would whisk him back to America. Cool, steady fighting men who caught "short-timer's fever" became cautious and timid. Nobody wanted to die with just a few days left in Vietnam.

Furthermore, nobody wanted to see his friends die. Because platoons and companies so often operated independently, the men who fought in Vietnam felt an even stronger attachment to the other members of these small units than did soldiers in other wars. The captains and lieutenants who commanded them viewed keeping their men alive as their primary responsibility. As for the troops themselves, they were, according to one company commander Spector quotes, "fighting for each other and for their unit. . . . They were fighting to survive."

Anything that threatened their survival was an object of fear and hostility. That is the way many GIs came to view the Vietnamese people. "The average soldier finds it hard to tell the difference between a civilian and the enemy," psychiatrist Dr. Wilbur Hamman testified at Calley's court-martial. Charlie Company's Fred Widmer found it impossible to pinpoint who the enemy was. The Vietcong did not wear traditional military uniforms, making it difficult to distinguish them from noncombatant peasants. Besides, old men, women, and even some children assisted the VC in a variety of ways. In areas such as Quang Ngai Province, where Charlie Company would operate, a majority of the people probably supported the enemy. Calley viewed killing babies in a place like that as eliminating enemies who would be taking American lives in ten years. Every soldier who fought in Vietnam heard stories about children who had supposedly supplied GIs with Coke containing ground glass or blown them up with hand grenades. The list of dead on the Vietnam Memorial Wall in Washington includes the names of men who lost their lives "because they didn't realize a woman or a child could be carrying a gun," former navy SEAL and U.S. Senator Bob Kerrey has observed.

After the war Vernado Simpson, a rifleman in Charlie Company, asked plaintively how one was supposed to distinguish the good Vietnamese from the bad ones when they all looked alike. Unable to do so, many GIs came to distrust and dislike all "gooks." Prevented by a language barrier from communicating with those they also called "dinks" and "slopes," American soldiers often developed an us-against-them mentality, tinged with substantial elements of racism. The frustrations and fear generated by the war itself exacerbated these feelings. Caputo recalls, "Some men could not withstand the stress of guerilla fighting: the hair trigger alertness constantly demanded of them, the feeling that the enemy was everywhere, the inability to distinguish civilians from combatants." These things "created emotional pressures which built up to such a point that a trivial provocation could make [them] explode with the blind destructiveness of a mortar shell."

When that happened, they sometimes committed war crimes. There were 122 convictions for such offenses, but far more atrocities went unpunished. Among them was a massacre of unarmed women and children by Kerrey and his men in the village of Thanh Phong. Lieutenant Caputo was prosecuted for murdering two Vietnamese civilians. Although those charges were dropped as part of a plea bargain, he did not consider himself innocent. At the same time, he believed it was the war itself that was really responsible for such crimes.

Atrocities were common in Vietnam, and neither side had a monopoly on barbaric behavior. The VC executed marines they had taken prisoner. "We paid the enemy back, sometimes with interest," Caputo reports. One of his enlisted men shot a captive in the face at point-blank range. Another cut the ears off a dead VC. Everything corroded quickly in Vietnam, he recalls, including morals. Charlie Company's Michael Bernhardt found you reached a point where you just snapped; it was as if someone flicked a switch, and you became a totally different person. In a war in which the measure of success was dead bodies, it was all too convenient to adopt the "If it's dead and Vietnamese, it's VC" rule.

Nor is it surprising that, as Caputo puts it, "some men acquired a contempt for human life and a predilection for taking it." "It was generally believed that you did what you had to do to protect your men," Kerrey recalls. Grunts had little respect for rules of engagement that prohibited them from burning down a village that had been used as an ambush site with white phosphorous grenades but allowed a jet to do the same thing with bombs dropped from the sky. To Caputo, "Ethics seemed to be a matter of distance and technology."

He wanted to kill VC personally, not because they were Communists but because he hated them for taking the lives of his friends and comrades. "At times, the comradeship that was the war's only redeeming quality caused some of its worst crimes—acts of retribution for friends who had been lost." After a particularly vicious engagement, Caputo's enraged platoon rampaged through a village, torching thatch huts and lobbing grenades into concrete houses, all the while closing their ears to the anguished screams of the villagers. Later he recalled what a veteran NCO, who had fought in Korea, told him: "Before you leave here sir, you're going to learn that one of the most brutal things in the world is your average nineteen-year-old American boy."

Charlie Company would soon prove the old sergeant correct. Medina's men shipped out for Vietnam at the end of November 1967 as an advance party for the 11th Brigade. Like most of those who fought this war, they rode into battle on a civilian airliner, carried into Da Nang on 1 December by Pan American Airways. Calley came off the plane expecting to plunge into a war. Instead he plunged into the Third World. His first memorable encounter was not with an armed enemy but with a Vietnamese woman defecating by the side of the road. Charlie Company spent a night as guests of the marines before being airlifted south to Landing Zone (LZ) Bronco in Quang Ngai Province. Like most newly arrived infantrymen, they were probably struck by the sharp contrast between the primitive conditions in the places where grunts lived and fought and those in the large rear-area installations where they had gotten their first glimpse of Vietnam.

At LZ Bronco Charlie Company received an orientation on the war by instructors from 4th Infantry Division NCO academy.

Lasting one day, it covered everything from how to call in fire support by helicopter gunships to how to put batteries in a radio. The new arrivals also learned a few words of Vietnamese (such as *dong lai*, meaning "stop"). In addition, they got another dose of the "Five S's." That was all that was said about the treatment of prisoners and civilians.

Later Charlie Company received some additional instruction from an Australian adviser to an ARVN division on how to tell Vietcong and their sympathizers from noncombatants. He cautioned the Americans that it was difficult to identify VC because they did not wear uniforms; everyone should be regarded as a potential enemy. Calley recalled being told that Vietnamese women were better shots than their menfolk and that the two sexes were equally threatening. Also, "because of the unsuspectedness of children, they were even more dangerous."

After its orientation at LZ Bronco, Charlie Company moved out to establish an 11th Brigade fire base at LZ Carrington, near Duc Pho in the southernmost part of Quang Ngai Province. That area had once been among the most dangerous in Vietnam, but by December 1967 marine firepower had turned it into a wasteland. Consequently, according to Calley, "We didn't fire in anger all of December, 1967." Charlie Company spent much of its time preparing LZ Carrington for the rest of the brigade, policing up the area, moving latrines around, and digging bunkers. As for fighting, "We just simulated." The company practiced patrolling (conducting five-to ten-day missions in the mountains west of Duc Pho) and carried out mock search-and-destroy operations in deserted hamlets. The only real action was provided by someone firing at vehicles on a road that ran down to the beach. Medina put out night ambushes, but Charlie Company never caught the sniper. Nor did "search-and-clear" operations in various directions produce any significant contact with the enemy.

On 3 January 1968 the company conducted its first combat assault. Only three of the eight helicopters that were supposed to carry it into the mountains west of Duc Pho showed up, and the LZ was "cold" (i.e., the troops encountered no enemy opposition where the choppers landed). Medina did spot fifteen VC running down a hill, and a helicopter gunship accidentally flushed three of those from cover with a smoke grenade. After hastily engaging them, the Third Platoon wasted one. That, recalled Medina, "was our first Vietcong killed."

Over the next few weeks Charlie Company conducted daily missions out of its firebase, rounding up civilians in hamlets that were considered hostile and moving them into resettlement camps. This was the men's first significant contact with any Vietnamese, other than the prostitutes, beggars, and thieves who plied their trades around American bases. According to Hersh, "After many weeks of no combat, the company began to systematically beat its prisoners, and it began to be less and less discriminating about who was—or was not—a VC." One GI even cut an ear off a dead Vietcong who had been killed by artillery fire. Frustration caused by a lack of real action may have contributed to such behavior.

Charlie Company's "phony war" ended on 26 January, when it was detached from its parent battalion and assigned, along with two other rifle companies and an artillery battery, to the newly formed Task Force Barker. Named for its commanding officer, Lieutenant Colonel Frank Barker, this 500-man strike force was part of the new Americal Division, which also had been cobbled together out of bits and pieces of other units. Many of the best men from the companies that constituted Task Force Barker had been reassigned, and it lacked adequate logistic support. Medina could not even take most of Charlie Company's headquarters personnel with him to its new base at LZ Dottie. He considered very appropriate the name men assigned to the new unit gave themselves: "Barker's Bastards." "We were really very illegitimate," he felt.

The area of operations assigned to Barker's Bastards would have challenged any unit. Code-named Muscatine, it was a chunk of northern Quang Ngai long controlled by the Vietcong's 48th Local Force Battalion. A tough, disciplined unit that enjoyed the general support of the villagers in the area, the 48th harassed Americans and their South Vietnamese allies with small but effective operations, while avoiding battles that could result in its own destruction.

Just as Task Force Barker was swinging into action against it, on 30–31 January, the Vietcong and North Vietnamese launched attacks all across South Vietnam, timed to take advantage of the lunar New Year holiday, Tet. Within twenty-four hours they struck 5 of the country's 6 major cities and 36 of its 42 provincial capitals, along with 64 district capitals and 50 hamlets. They seized control of the Citadel in Hue, the ancient imperial capital, and attacked Saigon's Tan Son Nhut Airport, the presidential palace, and the headquarters of South Vietnam's general staff. Nineteen Vietcong sappers even managed to blast a hole in the wall surrounding the U.S. embassy in Saigon and pound the embassy itself with rockets before being subdued after a six-and-one-half-hour firefight.

The Tet Offensive proved to be the turning point in the Vietnam War. Militarily the Americans and their South Vietnamese allies won a major victory. In intense fighting, which lasted about two weeks, they killed as many as 43,000 Communist troops, while losing only about 3,400 of their own. The enemy lost approximately one-fifth of its forces, and the Vietcong, who bore the brunt of the fighting, were so badly mauled that their regular units never recovered. Yet, while the enemy's Tet Offensive delivered a battlefield victory to the United States, it was a political disaster for the Johnson administration. Televised pictures of grisly fighting turned opinion leaders and the public against the war. In January hawks had outnumbered doves 60 percent to 24 percent. By March the doves had a 42 to 41 percent edge. Eighty percent of Americans had become convinced that the United States was not making progress in Vietnam. General Westmoreland seemed to confirm this. While calling Tet a great victory, he asked for another 206,000 troops. The Joint Chiefs of Staff supported his request, but most of the top civilians at the Pentagon did not, and Clark Clifford, who had replaced McNamara as secretary of defense, sided with them. On 12 March Senator Eugene McCarthy (D. Minn.), running as an antiwar candidate, nearly won the New Hampshire presidential primary, and Senator

{ *The Vietnam War on Trial* }

Robert Kennedy (D. N.Y.), who also opposed the war, promptly announced that he, too, would challenge Johnson for the Democratic nomination. During the last week of March the president assembled a group of elder statesmen, known informally as the Wise Men, to discuss Vietnam; to his surprise, they urged him to pursue a negotiated settlement and to take steps to disengage from the conflict. The president sent Westmoreland only 13,500 men, and on 31 March, in a dramatic appearance on national television, he declared a bombing halt over most of North Vietnam, called on the enemy to negotiate, and announced that he would not be a candidate for reelection. It was the beginning of the end of the Vietnam War.

The end was a long time coming. The war dragged on for five more years, and more American servicemen died after Tet than before. The fiercest fighting of the entire conflict occurred during the nine months following Johnson's televised speech. The rate at which American soldiers were killed in action reached its peak, attaining a level that exceeded those for Korea and the Mediterranean and Pacific theaters in World War II. "This was," writes Spector, "truly the bloodiest phase of the Vietnam War."

Charlie Company found itself swept up in the bloody fighting triggered by the Tet Offensive. In Quang Ngai City, just twelve miles from its base camp, the enemy hit the airfield, an ARVN headquarters, a military training center, and the provincial jail. At Chu Lai an American airbase and the headquarters of the Americal Division came under attack. "Even from 60 miles away, you could see it and get a little bit of the concussion off of the tremendous explosions going on in there," Calley recalled later. The realization that its division base camp, "your home where you get all your supplies," was under attack convinced Charlie Company that the enemy was very strong and increased greatly the combat stress its men had been feeling. They also experienced a sense of chaos and confusion, as the company, reacting to enemy attacks at first one place and then another, bounced back and forth across its area of operations, sometimes covering as much as twenty kilometers per day. To one of them, Michael Bernhardt, it appeared they were just walking around, trying to draw enemy fire.

Operations that bewildered Charlie Company devastated its enemy. Crippled by massive U.S. and South Vietnamese fire-power, the 48th Battalion retreated down the Tra Khuc Valley toward the coast, through a region designated "Pinkville" on American maps that included the village of My Lai. During the days and weeks after Tet, Task Force Barker attempted to locate and destroy what was left of this once crack enemy unit. Its rifle companies patrolled endlessly, their objective to locate, trap and engage the 48th Battalion.

For Medina's men this meant long stretches away from their base camp, days that began at dawn and ended only after they had dug in for the night, K ration meals, and lots of dirt and in-sects. Life in Charlie Company became a hot and thoroughly un-pleasant grind that, according to Bernhardt, wore the men down to nothing. It also became very dangerous. Casualties mounted. In early February, while returning from a night ambush, Danny Ziegler stepped off a trail onto a mine, triggering an explosion that left him with twenty-one puncture wounds and a collapsed lung. On 11 February, just north of the Diem Diem River, the Second Platoon came under rifle fire from well-hidden Vietcong, then a barrage of mortar shells that showered it with shrapnel, wounding several men.

The next afternoon Calley led the First Platoon back into the same area and called in artillery fire on the enemy. As his men pulled back from the river, snipers opened up on them. They avoided injury by crawling through muck and mud. When the sniper fire subsided and they moved back to the river, however, Calley allowed them to walk single file atop a four-foot dike. A perfect target, his radioman, William Weber, "caught a round in his radio harness." The bullet "just took his entire kidney out," Calley remembered. "He died within a matter of minutes." Two other soldiers went into shock from the stress of losing a buddy. The enlisted men blamed Calley's stupidity for Weber's death, and he later concurred. "I admit it," he told author John Sack, "I was stupid that day."

But Weber was not the only sniper fire casualty. One man was shot through the shoulder while standing right next to Medina.

Charlie Company could never identify the snipers, and the villagers would not tell them who they were.

It also continued to live with the terror of mines. On 25 February, while Calley was enjoying a brief respite from the horrors of the war—spending three days of in-country R and R (rest and recuperation) with a prostitute in the resort city of Vungtau—Charlie Company walked into a large minefield near LZ Uptight. As mines began exploding, some men panicked and tried to flee, triggering additional explosions. Surrounded by screaming and carnage, Medina kept his cool. He bravely threaded his way through the minefield to rescue several of the wounded and led the rest of his men to safety, displaying heroism that earned him the army's third-highest decoration, the Silver Star. Three members of Charlie Company died, however, and twelve more were seriously wounded. One of the dead had a brother who was also serving in Vietnam and was going to be sent home as soon as the operation ended. Calley returned from his dalliance in Vungtau to find panic and the helicopters that had evacuated the casualties. "There must have been six boots there with the feet still in them, brains all over the place, and everything was saturated with blood, rifles blown in half," he told a court-martial later. While the company was pulling back from the minefield, the Third Platoon's point man detonated a 105-mm artillery shell that had been rigged as a booby trap, killing him and wounding a couple of other men.

When Calley saw what that day had done to Charlie Company, for "the first time it dawned on me that we weren't playing games." He felt fear, anger, and hate. When he rejoined his unit, "it seemed like a different company." Almost everyone seemed to have had it. Mounting casualties had infused Charlie Company with a thirst for revenge. Some took out their hostility on the Vietnamese women. A few men in the company seem, from the beginning of their tours of duty, to have treated patrols and search-and-destroy missions as opportunities to commit rape, but sexual assaults apparently increased after mid-February. Certainly, more soldiers became aware that their comrades were committing them. Yet unit leaders did nothing to check the abuse of women.

When Weber became Charlie Company's first KIA, hostility toward the Vietnamese increased. From the beginning Medina had made clear his own dislike for the locals, repeatedly rebuking GIs who exhibited kindness toward prisoners. After losing his RTO, Calley decided he now knew who the enemy was: "Everyone there was VC. The old men, the women, the children—the *babies* were all VC or would be VC in about three years."

The minefield incident further heightened his animosity, and that of the rest of Charlie Company, toward the civilian population. There had been a village just a few hundred meters away, but the people who lived there had not warned them about the mines or even expressed sorrow over the deaths of the men who died when they exploded. Charlie Company felt a desire for revenge against every villager, regardless of age or gender. All of them were part of the problem.

Having gotten mad, the GIs got even. Men who had once liked the Vietnamese children now pushed them away when they begged for gum or money. The beating of suspected Vietcong quickly escalated into more serious violence. After one soldier questioned an old farmer and concluded he was not VC, Herbert Carter nevertheless knocked him into a well. Then Calley shot him. Prisoners were forced to serve as human mine detectors. Eventually, Charley Company stopped even taking prisoners. According to enlisted man Fred Widmer, "There was one guy Medina had to shoot the prisoners. . . . [T]hey would walk them down toward the beach, or behind some sand dunes, and shoot them." Far from checking the men's passion for revenge, Charlie Company's officers encouraged it, and even participated in the abuse of civilians. According to witnesses, Medina himself beat suspects during interrogation. There was a moral vacuum in Charlie Company. The whole unit was drifting into a culture of violence in which anything seemed permissible.

On 14 March a squad from the Third Platoon ran into a booby trap that killed the patrol leader, Sergeant George Cox. Another GI lost his eyes, and a third lost his arms and legs. "We were good and mad," remembers Michael Terry, who was on that patrol. On the way back to LZ Dottie, the angry soldiers stole a radio from a woman in a hamlet. Explaining their action, Gary Garfolo told Seymour Hersh, "We figured 'What the hell, they're gooks, they caused Cox's death.'" Members of the patrol also shot and wounded a woman they saw working in the fields. Then they kicked her to death and emptied their magazines into her dead body. In addition, GI Gregory Olsen reported in a letter home, "They slugged every little kid they came across."

The following day, an angry Charlie Company held an impromptu funeral for Sergeant Cox. After getting themselves "halfway decent" by putting on shirts and tucking their trousers into their boots, the grunts assembled at an old artillery emplacement, sitting on fifty-five-gallon gasoline drums and sandbag bunkers while a chaplain the captain had run into conducted a brief memorial service. It was an emotional occasion. Cox had been popular with his comrades, and they could not help but think about the wife he had left behind in Hawaii. Medina amplified the high voltage in an already charged atmosphere. After the chaplain finished, the captain reminded his men of the casualties the company had suffered, listing all the men it had lost. Everybody was surprised by how many of them there were, even Calley, whose own platoon had shrunk from forty-five men to only twenty-seven. Charlie Company was at about half strength, Medina reported. He told his men that "we'd have to unite, start getting together, start fighting together, and become extremely aggressive and we couldn't afford to take any more casualties," Calley testified later.

After this pep talk, Medina explained that at 0730 the next morning, they would be conducting a combat assault into the village known as My Lai (4), where, according to intelligence reports, the 48th Battalion was now located. By the time they got there, he told them, all innocent civilians and noncombatants should have left to go to market. Using a shovel, Medina drew in the dirt a map that depicted the area where the assault would take place and the concept of the operation. He informed them that the 48th Battalion had approximately 250 to 280 men, so they could expect to be outnumbered approximately two to one. Fire support from artillery and helicopter gunships would help make up the difference, but "I told them . . . that we could expect a hell of a good fight and that we would probably be engaged," Medina testified at Calley's court-martial. He added, "I told the members of my company to destroy the village by burning the hooches, killing the livestock, by closing the wells, by destroying the food crop."

What he did or did not say about killing villagers is a matter of intense dispute. Medina testified that when asked, "Do we kill women and children?" he responded that they should use common sense; if a woman or child was trying to engage them, they could shoot back; otherwise, they were not allowed to kill them. Since he did not even remember conducting his briefing immediately after the memorial service, Medina's recall is suspect, but Olsen supported his version of what he said. Others had a different recollection. Calley testified that the captain told them to "make sure there was no one left alive in My Lai." According to Bernhardt, "The instructions given to the entire company by Captain Medina was [sic] that the village was to be destroyed along with its inhabitants." Sergeant Cowan also remembered being told to kill everything in My Lai (4), as did two other senior NCOs, Staff Sergeant Martin Fagan and Sergeant Charles West.

Of course, they might have misinterpreted Medina's words because of their preexisting anger toward the Vietnamese and the Knute Rockne–style pep talk with which he had pumped them up prior to the briefing. To most of those who heard him, the company commander's main message was that they should remember all the buddies they had lost. It was time to settle the score with those responsible for the misery and death Charlie Company had suffered. For what was left of "the best company in Hawaii," it was time for revenge.

CHAPTER 4

Massacre at My Lai (4)

As Calley sat in the helicopter, the adrenaline started pumping. The air was thick with smoke, and the rat-a-tat of machine gun fire and the whop, whop, whop of the chopper's rotor blades combined to produce a deafening racket. The young platoon leader felt like an automobile racer who at any moment might hit or pass the edge of disaster. The men with him were scared. It was just before 0730 hours on 16 March, and the First Platoon, which had lifted off from LZ Dottie about seven minutes earlier, was headed southwest toward My Lai (4). Its mission was to secure a landing zone there and to make sure that no enemy troops would be left to shoot at the helicopters that would soon deliver the rest of Charlie Company.

Calley and his men had been told the landing zone would be "hot" (under enemy fire), and infantrymen participating in helicopter assaults on a hot LZ generally felt trapped. Confined in a tiny space far above the ground, they were powerless to protect themselves. Forced to endure unbearable tension, they found themselves devoured by uncontrolled fury, directed at those who had made them powerless. The grunt's "blind rage then begins to focus on the men who are the source of the danger—and of his fear," Caputo recalls. "All a soldier can think about is the moment when he can escape his impotent confinement and release this tension."

Calley and his men leaped from the choppers and began releasing theirs, along with the anger that had been building up inside them for weeks, on the inhabitants of My Lai. They hit the ground firing, and during the four hours that followed, Charlie Company proceeded to perpetrate one of the worst massacres in the annals of American warfare. Lieutenant Calley himself allegedly slaughtered over 100 Vietnamese civilians.

That was not supposed to happen. What became known as the My Lai massacre was designed as a routine search-and-destroy mission, and its focus was a different community from the one that Charlie Company devastated. The helicopter assault was part of Task Force Barker's Operation Muscatine, whose objective was to annihilate the 48th VC Local Force Battalion, destroy its weapons and supplies, and wipe out its fortifications. Task force intelligence had concluded that the base camp of the 48th Battalion was in a coastal fishing settlement east of Quang Ngai City. This hamlet, located within the village of Son My, was known to those who lived there as My Khe, but it was designated on American military maps as My Lai (1). Because it was colored pink on those maps, GIs often referred to the place as "Pinkville."

On the morning of 16 March, Task Force Barker's Alpha Company established a blocking position north of Pinkville, while navy "swift boats" screened the coastal area to the east and an aero scout company prevented the enemy from escaping to the south. Bravo and Charlie Companies were to act as a hammer that would crush the 48th Battalion against the anvil created by these blocking forces, with the former carrying out a helicopter assault to the southeast of My Lai (1) and Medina's men landing west of the VC base camp at the hamlet of My Lai (4) (called Tu Cung by those who lived there). My Lai (4) contained a bunker line that protected the western approaches to My Khe. Charlie Company was supposed to advance through the hamlet from the west to the east side (where the bunkers were located), then move on toward My Lai (1). Calley's First Platoon would be on the right (south), and Lieutenant Stephen Brooks's Second Platoon on the left (north). The Third Platoon would follow behind them, evacuating casualties and serving as the company's reserve force.

As it moved through My Lai (4) and the rest of Son My, Charlie Company was supposed to neutralize the village. There was a great deal of confusion in the ranks about precisely what that

{ *The Vietnam War on Trial* }

meant. Part of the problem was bad intelligence. The Peers Commission, which investigated the My Lai Massacre for the army, concluded that the plan for the operation "was based on faulty assumptions concerning the strength and disposition of the enemy and the absence of noncombatants from the operational area." On the basis of the briefing he had received from Lieutenant Colonel Barker, Medina testified later, he informed his men "that the 48th VC Battalion was located at the village of My Lai (4), and that the intelligence reports also indicated that the innocent civilians or noncombatants would be gone to market by 0700 hours in the morning." That information did not square with what many army intelligence officers, including some assigned to Task Force Barker's parent organizations, the 11th Brigade and the Americal Division, believed. They thought the 48th Battalion was nowhere near My Lai. Having been decimated during the Tet Offensive, it was rebuilding in the mountains far to the west. Medina believed what he was told, however, and consequently instructed his platoon leaders to have their men carry triple loads of ammunition. Calley went into My Lai expecting "to do sustained battle" with a battalion-sized military force.

Another source of confusion was the less than clear orders that Medina received from Barker. During an aerial reconnaissance of the objective the day before the attack, the task force commander informed him that they had permission to destroy villages, burn hooches, kill livestock, close wells, and destroy food crops. When Barker briefed his company commanders that afternoon, he told them that once contact was made, they were to pursue the enemy aggressively and overrun the area. According to both Colonel Oran Henderson, the acting commander of the 11th Brigade, and Captain Eugene Kotouc, an intelligence officer on Barker's staff, who were present at this briefing, he said nothing about slaying civilians. The Peers Commission found "no evidence that [Barker's] plan included explicit or implicit provisions for the deliberate killing of noncombatants." On the other hand, the task force commander failed to discuss at all how prisoners should be handled. In addition, Barker asserted that if they came under fire in My Lai, they were going to level the village. The Reverend

Carl Edward Cresswell, an Americal Division chaplain, objected, "I didn't know we made war that way." "It's a tough war," Barker replied. It is hardly surprising that the Peers Commission found "widespread confusion among the officers and men of TF Barker as to the purpose and limitations of the 'search and destroy' nature of the operation."

Barker's already ambiguous instructions were distorted further as they were passed along to the grunts who would execute them, compounding the confusion. The Peers Commission found clear evidence that as "orders were issued down through the chain of command to the men of C Company . . . they were embellished and, either intentionally or unintentionally, were misdirected toward end results presumably not foreseen during the formative stage of the orders." Robert T'Souvas, a member of the Third Platoon, walked away from Medina's briefing on the evening of 15 March convinced that everyone in the hamlet they were going to attack was North Vietnamese Army (NVA), VC, or a Vietcong sympathizer, and that their mission the next day was to shoot anything that moved, animal or human. When he testified at Calley's trial, Medina admitted telling his men they had permission to destroy the village by burning it, to kill livestock and food crops, and to close the wells. Michael Bernhardt recalled hearing more. According to him, Medina instructed them to destroy the village and all of its inhabitants. Perhaps Bernhardt's understanding of what he heard was distorted by the fact that "Medina was very passionate." Like Barker, Charlie Company's commander did not, he acknowledged later, bother to issue any instructions concerning "the capture or collection of noncombatants." Indeed, Charles Hall remembered being told not to take any prisoners.

Besides Medina's briefing, the First Platoon received one from Calley. According to Dennis Conti, it covered "relatively the same thing." They could expect strong resistence, the soldiers of the First Platoon were told. The men in the village would be armed, and the women would assist them. After listening to Calley, his troops were "'psyched up'" and "ready for battle."

The choppers carried them into something far different from

the fierce firefight for which they had been primed. Before the First Platoon touched down, an artillery battery bombarded My Lai (4) for several minutes with 105-mm howitzers. It was trying to "prep" the landing zone by shooting at paddy fields 400 meters northwest of the hamlet, but instead its poorly aimed fire rained down on the village, destroying houses, chewing deep craters into the ground, and terrifying residents. Many of the inhabitants, whom the soldiers expected to be away at market, were instead just beginning breakfast. They quickly fled into bunkers and tunnels that the Vietcong had forced them to dig throughout the hamlet. As villagers dived for cover, helicopter gunships and door gunners on troop-carrying choppers sprayed the area with deadly cannon and machine gun fire, intended to suppress any hostile threat to the disembarking infantrymen.

There was no such threat. The LZ was "cold," as Medina quickly recognized when he did not hear the familiar sound of incoming fire or the crack of rifle shots over his head. Aero scouts spotted several armed men in black pajamas running away and moved to engage them. When Medina reported that the LZ was cold, he received a radio call from a helicopter, informing him (apparently erroneously) that his men were receiving small-arms fire. Medina passed along to his platoon leaders the pilot's report that "the LZ is hot." A forward air controller had given Calley the same erroneous information just before the chopper carrying him into battle touched down. It added to the chaos created by the fact that the First and Second Platoons got switched around during the landing, and Medina had to order them to reverse positions before they could begin their assault. While all of this was going on, the troops were laying down "a heavy base of fire" on My Lai (4).

No one was shooting back. When Charlie Company finally got itself straightened out and commenced its assault, the GIs found themselves attacking an undefended village. There were no enemy soldiers left in My Lai (4), only old men, women, and children. Asked during Calley's court-martial if any of these people had weapons, the First Platoon's Thomas Turner replied unequivocally, "No, they didn't." Asked if at any time during

Charlie Company's sweep through My Lai (4), American troops had received hostile fire, Sidney Kye, a First Platoon rifleman, answered, "I don't think so."

It was difficult to be sure. The heavily armed Charlie Company was doing a tremendous amount of shooting. "We was firing into suspected enemy locations and bunkers, any bushes or anywhere that we would think that a VC would be hiding," Sergeant Cowan recalled later. Hearing this gunfire, GIs could not be sure whether it was coming from their buddies or the enemy. The physical environment made it difficult for them to know what other participants in the assault were doing or to get a complete picture of what was going on. My Lai (4) was not a group of houses clustered in an otherwise open area. It was compartmentalized by vegetation that included bamboo and banana trees and thick bushes. These limited what each soldier could see, as did the tall elephant grass growing near the LZ. As the First and Second Platoons moved into the hamlet, they split into squads, which soon broke down into smaller groups. Men wandered around My Lai (4) in pairs and even alone. Occasionally, they crossed paths with each other. Squads from different platoons became intermingled. Confusion reigned.

Conti recalled getting cut off from the company command group because of the elephant grass and not being able to figure out which way the others had gone. A machine gun opened up to his right. He turned, saw a farmer and some cattle running, and fired at them with an M-79 grenade launcher. Cowan offered a good explanation for such behavior. "We started firing knowing there was elements of the 48th Battalion in there," he testified. "Having a small element on the ground, we didn't want to be overrun. So, we started firing." "I guess you could say the men were out of control," Conti admitted to the army's Criminal Investigation Division (CID).

An out-of-control Charlie Company devastated My Lai (4). Houses were blown apart by grenades. Cows, water buffalo, pigs, chickens, and ducks were slaughtered. So were hundreds of human beings. GIs running through the hamlet screamed orders at the frightened villagers in a mixture of English and Vietnamese and gunned down those who failed to respond promptly in the way they desired.

Off to Calley's left, the Second Platoon was massacring civilians. "We started to move slowly through the village, shooting everything in sight, children, men, women, and animals," one of Brooks's men, Thomas Partsch, recorded in his diary. Another member of the Second Platoon, Vernardo Simpson, admitted later having personally killed about twenty-five people that day. On orders from Lieutenant Brooks, he shot a woman who was running away. He also killed her two-year-old boy. Simpson described later what he did to the inhabitants of My Lai (4): "I cut their throats, cut off their hands, cut out their tongue [sic], their hair, scalped them. I did it. A lot of people were doing it, and I just followed. I lost all sense of direction." Other soldiers from the Second Platoon tossed fragmentation grenades into houses and sprayed them with automatic weapons fire. When villagers emerged from hiding with their hands up, grunts gunned them down. When the Vietnamese huddled together for safety, GIs blazed away at them with rifles and automatic weapons. One machine gun team saw an unarmed middle-aged woman climbing out of a tunnel thirty feet away. They chopped her down with their M-60. Another team killed so many people that the gunner, Charles Hutto, grew weary from his labors and swapped his machine gun for his partner's lighter M-16 rifle. Dennis Bunning refused to murder women and children, and Partsch did not even fire his weapon; Gary Crossley, though he could not bring himself to kill, shot off an old man's arm, just to see what it would feel like to shoot somebody. "We almost wiped out the whole village, a whole community," a horrified Simpson recalled later.

Platoon Sergeant Jay Buchanon realized the assault was becoming a complete mess. He began yelling at the troops to keep moving, stay on line, and fire only when fired upon. Unfortunately, his attempts to restore order did not accomplish much. Medina had commanded the Second Platoon to move toward the far north edge of the hamlet to check out reports from helicopters of dead Vietcong in that area and to guard against an attack from hedgerows there. Brooks's troops found the bodies of two young Vietnamese men, armed with rifles and carrying American military packs, pistol belts, and ammo pouches. Although successful, their search for VC dead put Buchanon on the extreme left flank of the entire company, almost to the tree line, and thus out of position to direct effectively the rest of the Second Platoon. Lieutenant Brooks had totally lost control of their men. Medina called him on the radio, demanding to know, "What the hell is going on over there?"

Soldiers far closer to the company commander than Brooks's men were also out of control and waging war against civilians. Precisely where Medina was that morning is disputed. He claimed to have entered the hamlet only once and to have spent most of his time moving back and forth around the perimeter, checking out reports from helicopter spotters and trying to maintain contact with all three platoons. Jay Roberts, a military reporter from the army's 31st Public Information Detachment who accompanied Charlie Company on 16 March, insists, however, that he saw Medina in My Lai (4) most of the morning. Wherever he may have gone later, it does appear that he and his command group advanced from the LZ toward the hamlet with Lieutenant Geoffry LaCross's Third Platoon.

Thus, Medina probably witnessed at least some of the destruction that unit wrought. Acting pursuant to instructions from him, some of LaCross's men set fire to the homes in the village. According to Roberts and his associate, photographer Ronald L. Haeberle, who were following along behind, ten or fifteen Third Platoon soldiers methodically pumped bullets into a cow until it keeled over. When a woman, who had perhaps been hiding in a bunker, poked her head out from behind a bush, they redirected their fire at her. Soon chips of her bones were flying into the air. Haeberle photographed the woman's dead body. He also took a color picture of eight or nine women, children, and babies who had been rounded up by elements of the Third Platoon in the western part of the hamlet. When Haeberle and Roberts turned away from these people for a moment, they heard M-16 fire. When they looked back, all of them were dead. As they moved to the southern edge of the hamlet to join Medina and his command group, they saw a pile of bodies on the road. Haeberle photographed that, too. He and Roberts also witnessed a toddler being blown apart by a burst of rifle fire and saw GIs cut down a Vietnamese man and two small children who were walking toward them. The Third Platoon killed most of the Vietnamese it found alive, including several women whom William Doherty and Michael Terry (the latter a devout Mormon) found badly wounded and decided to finish off to save from a lingering death.

It is not clear how much of this mayhem Medina authorized. Like his location, the extent of his personal involvement in the killing that day is disputed. PFC Herbert Carter, who was evacuated by helicopter after he shot himself in the foot, claimed Medina ordered members of the Third Platoon to shoot approximately fifteen Vietnamese men, women, and children, saying he wanted none of them left standing. A machine gunner opened fire on this group, and one of the company commander's radio operators then finished off any who were still alive. Carter also claimed that a radio operator borrowed his pistol and used it to shoot a boy in the neck, and that Medina stopped a male in his late teens, ordered the youth to make a run for it, and shot him when he would not do so. Richard Pendleton accused Charlie Company's commanding officer of killing a young boy who was searching through a pile of bodies, apparently looking for his mother. Medina denied involvement in most of the killings others blamed on him. As journalist Richard Hammer writes, given "the passion of that morning, it is almost impossible to know who is telling the real truth."

The company commander did accept responsibility for one death. At Calley's trial he reported receiving a radio call from the task force operations officer, Major Charles Calhoun, who said a helicopter had marked with a smoke grenade the location of a VC with a weapon and demanded that someone go pick up this gun. Medina moved out toward the location Calhoun identified. As the company commander approached it, he saw a woman lying on her side just off the trail, facing away from him. "Her arm appeared to be under her." As Medina started to turn around, "I caught movement from the corner of my eye. Her hand started to move, her eyelid . . . her chest started moving." Because he had been told there was an armed VC in the area, his immediate reaction was, "She's got a weapon or a hand grenade, my God you've had it." Medina turned and fired twice. He assumed he killed the woman. He never bothered to verify that she had been armed and acknowledged that when he looked around after she was dead, "I did not see any weapons." PFC Michael Bernhardt, who was with Medina at the time, gave a quite different account of this killing. According to him, the captain spotted the woman about 100 meters away, pretending to pick rice, and shot her from long range. He then walked up to within six feet of her and pumped a couple of additional rounds into the body to finish her off. The difference between Bernhardt's version and Medina's, of course, is that between murder and justifiable homicide.

Even if he did not personally commit any crimes in My Lai (4), Medina clearly failed to maintain control over men under his command who were committing scores of them. As his troops stormed through the hamlet, some assaulted women. According to Michael Bilton and Kevin Sim, several members of Charlie Company became "double veterans," GI slang for raping a woman and then murdering her. One female died when someone penetrated her with the muzzle of a rifle, then pulled the trigger. "Many women were raped and sodomized, mutilated, and had their vaginas ripped open with knives or bayonets," Sim and Bilton report. A Vietnamese man who survived the massacre reported seeing one woman raped after GIs killed her children. Several members of the Third Platoon (one of whom announced, "Jesus, I'm horny") pulled open the blouse of a slender girl in her early teens, attempting to fondle her breasts. When an older woman (probably the girl's mother) intervened, one of the GIs struck her with the butt of his rifle. After some children became involved in this altercation, a grunt spotted Haeberle with his camera, and the soldiers quickly wasted all the Vietnamese with automatic weapons. In the Second Platoon, which included Charlie Company's most notorious rapists, a squad leader, Sergeant Kenneth Hodges, took a young girl into a hooch, from which she emerged fifteen minutes later wearing no pants and with her blouse unbuttoned. At least three other men also attacked this girl, who was about sixteen, one penetrating her and another having oral sex with her, while she fondled the penis of the third. Calley and one of his defense attorneys accused Conti of opening his pants in front of a woman and threatening to shoot her baby if she did not give him a blow job.

Conti denied that any such incident occurred at My Lai (4). Even if it did not, Charlie Company committed numerous other atrocities there. Multiple observers witnessed soldiers shooting small children for no apparent reason. Charles Gruver remembered observing a boy of about three or four standing by a trail with a wound in his arm. Gruver told journalist Seymour Hersh, "He just stood there with big eyes staring like he didn't believe what was happening. Then the captain's RTO put a burst of 16 [M-16 rifle fire] into him." James Bergthold told Hersh he had seen an old man who had been shot in both legs and, figuring the wounded Vietnamese was going to die anyhow, decided "I might as well kill him." Bergthold placed the barrel of a .45 pistol against the man's forehead and blew off the top of his head. Roberts watched some GIs interrogate another old man, then shoot him when it became apparent he did not know anything. Carter told the CID he had seen Paul Meadlo, a soldier from the First Platoon, shoot another male Vietnamese and then throw his body into a well.

Charlie Company seemed to be in a killing frenzy. Bernhardt watched as one of his fellow soldiers shot at everything in sight, blazing away indiscriminately with his rifle on full automatic, never taking his finger off the trigger until he had exhausted all the bullets in a clip. Reloading as quickly as possible, this grunt resumed firing, all the while laughing maniacally. Mass hysteria swept over Charlie Company, and soldiers became executioners and indiscriminate butchers.

The soldier responsible for killing the most Vietnamese was Lieutenant Calley. At his court-martial Sergeant Cowan denied having seen him shoot any civilians in My Lai (4), and while Calley acknowledged killing two Vietnamese men, he described both as enemy soldiers. According to him, as he entered the hamlet, he glanced into a concrete house, where he saw what appeared to be six to eight dead bodies on the floor. A man dressed in black "was going for the window. I shot him," Calley testified. He also claimed to have seen a man in a bright green uniform standing in a fireplace. Concluding that this individual was an NVA regular, who had just come down out of the chimney, Calley wasted him, too. It is doubtful whether the men he admitted shooting in the concrete house were actually enemy soldiers.

Even if they were, Calley killed other people who were clearly noncombatants and ordered men under his command to kill more. As the First Platoon moved through My Lai (4), it rounded up scores of civilians. Meadlo and Conti collected about twenty or thirty, whom they ordered to squat down beside a rice dike next to a trail on the eastern edge of the hamlet. Carter and PFC Joseph Dursi gathered up slightly fewer. According to Dursi, both groups consisted mostly of old men, women, and small children. When he and Carter ran into Meadlo, they directed their prisoners to stand in the same area where he was holding his while they waited for further orders. "It was normal in an operation that we moved all the people that we came across to one point," Dursi testified. While they waited, Meadlo played with the children and gave them treats from his C rations. Calley appeared on the scene and asked him and Conti if they could take care of the whole group. Meadlo assured the lieutenant that they could.

Calley returned about fifteen minutes later. He had received a radio transmission from Medina, who was upset that the First Platoon was not making more rapid progress and wanted him to get it moving. The harried lieutenant explained to his boss that his troops were being slowed down by the large number of Vietnamese they had apprehended. "He told me to hurry up and get my people moving and get rid of the people I had there that were detaining me," Calley would testify later. According to him, his company commander told him to waste the Vietnamese. Medina confirmed that he ordered Calley to hurry up, but not that he instructed him to kill or otherwise dispose of the prisoners.

There is similar disagreement about what Calley told Meadlo. According to the lieutenant, he yelled at Meadlo that if he could not move all those people, he should "get rid of them." Meadlo testified that Calley asked him "'How come they are not dead?'" implying that what he had meant by his earlier directive to "take care of" the prisoners was to kill them. According to Meadlo, his platoon leader said, "I want them dead." Dursi, Conti, and Calley's RTO, Charles Sledge, all confirmed Meadlo's version of this conversation. According to Conti, the lieutenant said that when he had instructed them to take care of the Vietnamese, he meant he wanted them killed. Sledge and Dursi both maintained that Calley instructed Meadlo to waste the prisoners, and under cross-examination, Calley acknowledged: "I told him to 'waste' them. . . . If he couldn't move the people, to 'waste them.'" According to Calley, after issuing this order, he walked away. Conti insisted, however, that Calley got on line with Meadlo and both began shooting at the Vietnamese, firing single shots and bursts with their M-16s. Meadlo claimed Calley "burned four or five magazines," while he himself emptied about three into the help-less prisoners. The victims began screaming, and Meadlo started to weep. Saying he could not kill any more people, he tried to hand his weapon to Conti, hoping to get his comrade to do the shooting for him. Conti gave the gun back. If Calley wanted the prisoners killed, he could do it himself, he told Meadlo. In a few minutes the slaughter was over. Calley, according to Sledge, "went on walking down the trail."

The platoon leader was looking for Sergeant Mitchell to tell him where he wanted him to move his squad and position a ma-chine gun. Around a bend he and Sledge overtook Dursi, who had moved out with about fifteen prisoners just before the shooting started. This group, along with a number of other old men, women, and children between the ages of one and five, was now standing next to a three- or four-foot-deep drainage ditch that ran north-south along the eastern edge of the hamlet, about fifteen feet from the tree line. Mitchell was also in the vicinity of this canal. So was Meadlo, who had wandered around the hamlet for some time after the shooting spree, gathering up more Vietnamese, and now had seven or eight new prisoners. To Dursi he looked "shook up. He was crying." Calley conversed with Mitchell. He also talked to

Meadlo. According to Calley, all he told the distraught GI was to move the Vietnamese to the other side of the ditch. Both Dursi and Meadlo testified, however, that their platoon leader said something like, "We have another job to do."

Although Calley denied it, others who were present say he started pushing prisoners into the ditch. Dursi and Meadlo helped him; according to Sledge, so did Mitchell. Perhaps other members of Mitchell's squad joined in. The Vietnamese were yelling, and some of them began to cry. Meadlo was crying, too. Then, according to both Dursi and a Vietnamese survivor of the My Lai massacre, Pham Phon, Calley gave an order to fire. He and Meadlo began shooting into the ditch. Conti, who wandered onto the scene after the firing began, "seen [sic] a woman try to get up. As she got up I saw Lieutenant Calley fire and hit the side of her head and blow the side of her head off." In his own testimony Calley acknowledged shooting at the people in the ditch, although he claimed to have fired only six or eight shots altogether. Both Conti and Sledge testified that Sergeant Mitchell joined him. A tearful Meadlo asked Dursi, "Why don't you fire?" "I said I can't, I won't and looked down at the ground," Dursi testified. SP-4 Thomas Turner observed this slaughter from a dike about seventy yards away, where he was joined by Conti and another soldier, Daniel Simone. As they watched, "Small groups of people were being placed in the ditch and Lieutenant Calley was firing into [it]." So drawn out was the fusillade of bullets he unleashed that several times he had to insert a fresh clip of ammunition into his M-16. Several GIs told Hersh they saw Calley run after a bloody but unhurt two-year-old boy who had managed to crawl out of the ditch, throw him back in, and shoot him. Calley denied that such an incident had occurred, but Sledge confirmed during the court-martial what Hersh's sources had reported. The killing at the ditch continued for about an hour. According to Turner, 90 to 100 people disappeared into the bottom of the irrigation canal.

After this bloodbath ended, Turner testified, Calley approached the place where he, Conti, and Simone were sitting. A young Vietnamese woman was also coming toward them. Her hands were raised, "and she was giving herself up. . . . Lieutenant Calley shot her several times." The platoon leader contradicted Turner, insisting that the only other shooting he did in this area was at a head that he saw moving through the rice, which turned out to be that of a small boy.

Witnesses also accused Calley of killing a Buddhist monk. Calley acknowledged going up to a bearded man in his forties or fifties, who was dressed in white, and beginning to interrogate him. With the assistance of a GI who spoke some Vietnamese, he asked this individual a number of questions. The monk responded that there were no North Vietnamese soldiers in the hamlet and no weapons either. He also insisted repeatedly that there were no Vietcong around. The man in white kept putting his hands together in a praying position and bowing his head. According to Sledge, Calley "then hit him with the butt of his rifle." After being struck in the mouth, the monk continued to fold his hands in front of him, "sort of like pleading." Other villagers begged for his life. Then, according to Sledge, "Lieutenant Calley took his rifle at point blank and pulled the trigger." He had the muzzle right in the man's face. When asked what happened to the monk's head, Sledge replied, "It was just blown off." Calley admitted butt-stroking the man in white but denied shooting him. According to the lieutenant, somebody kicked the monk into the irrigation ditch. Presumably, he died there along with approximately a hundred other Vietnamese.

Calley's superiors made no effort to halt that massacre, nor the slaughter of Meadlo's prisoners, nor any of the other atrocities committed by the First Platoon. Although some members of Charlie Company did refuse to participate in that morning's orgy of murder, rape, and pillage, the only person who made a real effort to stop it was the pilot of an OH-23 observation helicopter (called a "bubble" because of its plexiglass cockpit), who witnessed some of what was happening in My Lai (4) from the air. Warrant Officer Hugh Thompson was serving as an aero scout. His mission was to conduct reconnaissance in front of Charlie and Bravo Companies, locating the enemy by drawing hostile fire. Unlike many of those who were at My Lai (4) that morning,

Thompson actually saw an enemy soldier, a draft-age male with a weapon, who was running out of the hamlet headed south. He told his door gunner, Lawrence Colburn, to engage the man, but Colburn missed. "That is the only enemy person I saw that whole day," Thompson recalled years later.

He, Colburn, and the bubble's crew chief, Glenn Andreotta, saw scores of civilian casualties. At least three times they "popped smoke" to mark the locations of wounded Vietnamese who needed help. When the OH-23 returned to those areas, the individuals its crew had seen were dead. "Everywhere we looked, we saw bodies. These were infants; two-, three-, four-, five-year-olds; women, very old men; but no draft-age people whatsoever," Thompson recalls. They saw one old woman with an odd object lying right next to her; it was her brains. Thompson radioed for help and marked her position with smoke. "A few minutes later up walks a captain. He nudges her with his foot, steps back, and blows her away."

As the bubble continued "reconning around the village," the crew spotted a ditch "with a bunch of people in it." Thompson hovered over the ditch for a few minutes, then, spotting some Americans, set down to ask if they could help the wounded Vietnamese. A "colored sergeant" with whom he spoke responded that "the only way to help them was to put them out of their misery." Thompson thought he was joking, but as the chopper lifted off, Andreotta suddenly exclaimed, "My God, he's firing into the ditch."

Either before or after this shooting occurred, Thompson talked with Calley. The recollections of those involved are inconsistent, and while the two clearly had a heated discussion, it is not clear whether this happened before the chopper took off or the next time it touched down. In his memoir, Calley reports, "A small helicopter landed, the helicopter pilot left and a sergeant told me, 'He wants whoever's in charge.' I went where the helicopter was." That could have been near a bunker, where it landed after Thompson spotted a woman and a couple of children there. He also saw troops moving toward them. "I sat down and talked to the individual on the ground and told him there was some people in the bunker and wanted to know if they could get them out," Thompson testified. According to him, that individual (whom the Peers Commission thought might have been Lieutenant Brooks rather than Lieutenant Calley) responded that the only way to do that was with a hand grenade. Thompson did not agree. He walked toward the bunker and motioned for the people inside to come out. About ten Vietnamese emerged, including a couple of women, a couple of old men, a baby, and several children. "My crew and I were by that time very mad and upset," Thompson recalls. He told Colburn to train his machine gun on the American troops surrounding the bunker. Thompson called in a helicopter gunship that had been covering him, and it evacuated half of the Vietnamese, returning about five minutes later to pick up the rest. The grunts near the bunker did not interfere.

Once these civilians were safe, Thompson and his crew decided to fly back to the ditch to see if there were any survivors there. While he covered them with an M-60 machine gun, Colburn and Andreotta searched through the pile of bodies in the irrigation channel. The only person they found alive was a small child, who had been shielded from the hail of bullets by the body of a young woman, who had probably been its mother. With one of the crewmen holding this tiny survivor on his lap, Thompson flew to Quang Ngai City, where they delivered the child to a Vietnamese hospital.

Whether he encountered Calley at the ditch or the bunker, Thompson clearly had a heated discussion with the leader of the First Platoon. He was not asked to identify Calley at his court-martial, which suggests Thompson did not remember the defendant well enough to have done so. There can be no doubt, however, that they confronted one another in My Lai (4) on 16 March. In his memoir, Calley acknowledges having a heated discussion with the pilot of a small helicopter. After it was over, he told Sledge: "He don't like the way I'm running the show. . . . [B]ut I'm the boss here." Calley admits Sledge probably quoted him accurately.

He adds, however, that he promptly called Medina to report that a helicopter pilot did not like the way things were being done. His company commander's reaction, as reported in Calley's memoir, was "Get in the goddamn position. And don't worry about the casualties." Medina was focused on accomplishing what he considered to be Charlie Company's mission. To him the people of My Lai (4) were at best means to that end. When the Second Platoon apprehended ten males of military age, Medina, considering these men Vietcong suspects, ordered them held for interrogation by Military Intelligence. While they were in custody, the suspected VC were made to walk in front of Medina's troops as protection against booby traps. At Calley's court-martial Medina testified that he instructed the First Platoon's leader to use its prisoners in a similar fashion, as human mine detectors.

To him, Vietnamese who were not potential sources of information and could not be exploited to protect his men from mines and booby traps were most valuable dead. As corpses they enhanced the body count. Calley claimed that sometime in the late morning Medina called the three platoon leaders to his location, where all of them had chow together. The company commander did not make any critical comments concerning the way the operation had been carried out. What he wanted to talk about was the body count. Calley claimed that the platoon leaders just estimated off the tops of their heads, and that Medina seemed to want them to inflate their numbers. Medina denied that any such discussion ever took place.

Medina did agree with Calley that it was not until late in the morning (the lieutenant said it was around lunchtime) that he issued orders to cease firing. About 1030 hours most of Charlie Company, its work in My Lai (4) largely finished, began drifting aimlessly toward the village plaza and the command post a few yards south of there. About that time Brooks radioed Medina, asking what to do with three men the Second Platoon had taken alive. A GI overheard the company commander respond not to kill them. "There's been too much of that already," Medina said. Yet apparently he did not order the killing stopped until he received a radio transmission from Major Calhoun telling him to do so. Medina relayed to his platoon leaders instructions to cease firing and make sure that noncombatants were not being indiscriminately killed. His troops did not all comply promptly. According to Medina, he radioed the First Platoon, demanding, "Dammit, what's going on up there? I want all this firing stopped." He was dashing frantically around the hamlet, yelling at everyone, "Let's move out of here," GI Gary Garfolo told Hersh. By then, of course, it was too late. Bilton and Sim's harsh assessment of the captain's performance seems fully justified. "Medina's control over what had gone on since [Charlie Company] first landed was negligible," they write. "The tough disciplinarian, consciously or unconsciously, had quite simply allowed his men to run amok."

So had officers farther up the chain of command. Barker, Henderson, and Major General Samuel Koster, the commander of the Americal Division, were all allocated air lanes above the area of operations so they could observe activity on the ground from their helicopters. All were in the sky over My Lai (4) during the morning of 16 March. Their command choppers had multichannel radios, enabling them to monitor most conversations within the hamlet, as well as in the air above it. These transmissions included Thompson's and one from another chopper pilot, who characterized what was going on below as a "bloodbath" and asked, "What the hell is going on down there?" Those aboard the command helicopters could also see what was happening in My Lai (4).

Most of the time they flew at altitudes of from 1,000 to 2,500 feet, but at one point Henderson descended to only 100 to 200 feet above the ground. From there he observed six to eight noncombatant casualties in Charlie Company's area of operations. Henderson then radioed elements of Task Force Barker: "I don't want any unnecessary killing down there." He informed Koster about what he had seen and instructed Barker to submit a report on the number and cause of civilian casualties to the brigade tactical operations center.

The task force commander was less concerned about the deaths of noncombatants, however, than about the fact that his men were not recovering as many enemy weapons as he thought they should. Not until midday, and then only after being prodded by higher headquarters, did he complain to Medina about excessive civilian casualties. By the time Barker acted, Charlie Company's commander had already ordered his men to cease firing.

The Peers Commission concluded that "neither commanders nor staff officers checked reports of noncombatant casualties or gave substantial attention . . . to such matters." They were clearly negligent. The commission determined that the messages being transmitted over command radio nets should have alerted commanders and staff officers "that the operation of TF Barker was not a normal combat assault." Barker could have learned about the slaughter of civilians had he wanted to do so. A reasonable and prudent commander in his position would have made the inquiries necessary to find out exactly what was happening in My Lai (4). Barker also could and should have stopped the killing of noncombatants. The same holds for Koster. While Henderson exhibited more concern about civilian casualties than did either his commander or his immediate subordinate, Barker, he also could have done more to curtail the killing. The devastation of My Lai (4) was the direct result of a failure of military leadership.

The failure of the superior officers to monitor and control the conduct of the troops on the ground led to a massacre. The members of Charlie Company who assaulted My Lai (4) found three rifles, a couple of grenades, a little ammunition, and no enemy soldiers. One hundred five of them invaded the hamlet, and all but one emerged unharmed. PFC Carter was Charlie Company's only casualty, and his foot wound was self-inflicted. Although they encountered no resistance, Medina's men destroyed My Lai (4). They demolished every house in the hamlet. They polluted every well. When they departed, not an animal remained alive. Countless women had been raped and otherwise sexually abused. Worst of all, perhaps as many as 500 Vietnamese civilians lay dead. The American Division celebrated My Lai as a great victory. Seldom has any assessment of a military operation been more inaccurate. Seldom has self-promotion diverged further from reality.

CHAPTER 5

Cover-Up

Hugh Thompson was furious. "I was very upset; I was very mad," he recalled years later. When he got back to the operations area of Company B, 123rd Aviation Battalion at LZ Dottie, sometime between 1100 and 1130 hours, Thompson went immediately to see his section leader, Captain Barry Lloyd. "I told him that I was not going to be a part of this. He asked what was going on. I said, 'It's mass murder out there. They are rounding them up and herding them in ditches and then just shooting them.'" Lloyd suggested he and Thompson go see their unit's operations officer. Together they walked over to the operations van, where the fuming pilot reported what he had seen to his commanding officer, Major Frederic Watke.

"At this point there was a requirement for immediate and positive reaction to the Thompson Report," the Peers Commission concluded. Instead, "Within the Americal Division, at every command level from company to division, actions were taken or omitted which together effectively concealed from higher headquarters the events which transpired in [Task Force Barker's] operation." According to Lieutenant General William R. Peers, who headed the commission, those who joined in sweeping a massacre under the rug ranged from the men of Charlie Company to high-ranking officers, far up the chain of command. Leaders of Task Force Barker, the 11th Brigade, and the Americal Division participated. "Some actively suppressed information, others withheld it, and still others were responsible by merely not wanting to become involved."

Peers considered it doubtful that any of the soldiers involved in concealing the massacre realized its full magnitude. Grunts on the ground saw only part of what was happening and were un-aware of what had taken place elsewhere. Their superiors knew some civilians had been slain, but not how many. Peers found in-excusable, however, the failure of commanders and key staff offi-cers to do more to find out what had really happened. He considered their sins of omission, along with the deliberate de-ception in which some senior officers had engaged, part of a "coverup."

Those involved in this cover-up were hiding what had hap-pened at My Lai (4) only from other Americans. The Vietnamese already knew. "Almost immediately following the events of 16 March 1968," the Peers Commission found, "rumors, reports, and VC propaganda relating to the operation began to move from the VC-controlled Son My Village area in Vietnamese channels." On 18 March a Census Grievance cadreman reported to his chief in Quang Ngai City that 427 "civilians and guerril-las" had been killed during Task Force Barker's just-concluded three-day operation. No such ambiguity clouded the report that the Son My village chief submitted to the head of the Son Tinh District four days later. It divulged that 570 civilians had been killed and that 90 percent of the houses, animals, and property in My Lai (4) had been destroyed.

Such carnage was grist for the Communists' propaganda mill. Soon after the massacre, Vietcong cadres began disseminating the story of what had happened at My Lai (4) to Vietnamese civilians. They printed leaflets describing the massacre and dis-tributed these to thousands of peasants. The Vietcong hoped this information would persuade the Vietnamese people to reject the Saigon government and its American allies and to support them in their struggle for control of South Vietnam.

This exploitation of the My Lai massacre was somewhat hyp-ocritical, for the Vietcong and the NVA were killing plenty of civilians themselves. Robert Santos, a platoon leader in the 101st Airborne Division, recalls finding a row of bodies lying face down when his unit entered a village near Hue in early 1968. The dead Vietnamese had their hands tied behind their backs and had been shot execution-style. The NVA troops responsible

{ *The Vietnam War on Trial* }

for this massacre had also killed the water buffalo and every other living thing in the village. The Communists' campaign of terror and intimidation claimed 3,700 civilian lives in 1967 alone, the South Vietnamese government reported.

It probably exaggerated, but so did the Vietcong. During 1967 and 1968 they often sought to exploit actions in which they had suffered heavy losses by disseminating propaganda which claimed that American and ARVN troops had killed large numbers of civilians, burned houses, destroyed property, and committed other atrocities. Thus, it was easy for those Americans who became aware of the charges the Vietcong were making about a massacre at My Lai (4) to dismiss them as groundless propaganda.

There was far less justification for discounting Hugh Thompson's report that civilians had been slaughtered at My Lai (4). Thompson greatly impressed the Peers Commission, which considered him one of the few soldiers it had questioned who "maintained his basic integrity in spite of everything that surrounded him, [and] who knew right from wrong and acted accordingly." There is some disagreement about precisely what the helicopter pilot told his commanding officer when he stormed into the operations van, for he was extremely agitated. Thompson admits getting "real close to insubordination" toward Major Watke. "I said something like, 'If this damn stuff is what's happening here, you can take these wings right now. . . . I ain't taking part in this.' I was ready to quit flying," he recalls. Thompson told his commanding officer about his confrontation with Calley. He believes he also told him about seeing a captain shooting a wounded woman, a ditch filled with bodies, and soldiers firing into the ditch. Watke later claimed not to recall hearing any of these details, and others who were present supported his version of what Thompson said. They did recollect the furious pilot making very clear allegations of unnecessary killing, and one even remembered his using the word "murder." Watke thought Thompson was "over-dramatizing," but even he was convinced that at least thirty noncombatants had been killed. All who were present, the Peers Commission concluded, had "a clear understanding that a serious charge had been alleged against TF Barker."

Thompson was not the only aviator to accuse task force troops of grievous misconduct. According to the Peers Commission, "Other Aero Scout Company personnel submitted comparable reports, one of them claiming there had been 150 civilian casualties." Aviators who had witnessed the events at My Lai (4) talked with Watke about what they had seen. Besides speaking with him, Thompson filed a written after-action report, detailing what he had observed. Captain Lloyd highlighted this document and placed the word "Notice" on it in capital letters, to ensure that it would be called to the attention of his superiors.

The first move his commanding officer made was probably not what Lloyd had envisioned, and it certainly was not what Thompson wanted. Thompson desired a thorough investigation of the My Lai (4) incident. Instead, "MAJ Watke acted only to report the matter to the commander of the Task Force charged with the offense." It should have been obvious to him that Barker had a strong disincentive to verify allegations that would reflect unfavorably on his own unit. Yet, not until that evening, following a briefing in the mess hall by a division staff intelligence officer, did Watke decide more needed to be done. When the briefer referred to the reported body count, a flier interrupted him to ask in a confrontational manner, "You mean those women and children?" A raucous exchange ensued, and Watke had to intervene to calm his men. The aero scout company commander became concerned that he had not done enough. He began to worry about how his pilots' allegations might affect his own career.

Finally, at about 2200 hours, Major Watke reported to his battalion commander, Lieutenant Colonel John L. Holladay, what Thompson had told him, including the fact that the OH-23 pilot had threatened to turn his guns on American ground troops. What Watke gave Holladay, according to the Peers Commission, was only "a watered-down version rather than the complete story." Furthermore, by the time the two finished talking, it was past midnight. They decided to wait until the next morning to alert the assistant division commander, Brigadier General George H. Young. The Peers Commission believed that "Major Watke's delay in informing Lieutenant Colonel Holladay of

Thompson's allegations and the added delay in transmitting this report to the division command group may have prevented the initiation of a full and proper investigation."

When Watke and Holladay met with General Young the following morning, they informed him of the allegations that a large number of civilians had been killed at My Lai (4) and also that there had been a confrontation between a pilot and an infantry officer. It was the latter disclosure that most interested Young. The thought of an American flier threatening to shoot American troops obviously troubled him. Later that day, he met with Barker and with the commanding officer of the 11th Brigade, Colonel Henderson. Young also informed his boss, the Americal Division's commander, Major General Koster, about what Watke and Holladay had told him.

The following morning, Monday, 18 March, Young and Henderson flew to LZ Dottie to meet with Barker, Watke, and Holladay. Young reportedly began this crisis conclave by telling the others: "Only five of us know about this." The implication was that they should keep the allegations made by Thompson and his fellow fliers to themselves until the charges could be investigated. Looking into them was a job for the inspector general, but rather than informing the IG, Young and Koster encouraged Henderson to investigate the allegations himself. They did so despite the fact that, like Barker, the head of the 11th Brigade had an obvious reason for not wanting to uncover serious wrongdoing by his own men: if they had committed war crimes, this would reflect unfavorably on his performance as their commander. Young and Koster were not the only ones who relied on Henderson. So did Watke. On at least two occasions he quelled unrest within the aero scout company by telling his men that the My Lai incident was being investigated and instructing them not to discuss the matter further.

The investigation on which Major Watke relied was seriously deficient. While Henderson was at LZ Dottie, Watke's executive officer, Captain Clyde Wilson, asked him to talk with Thompson. The two met for twenty or thirty minutes. According to Henderson, the chopper pilot told him that both ground troops and helicopter gunships had been firing at everything that moved in My Lai (4) and that he had seen a captain shoot a wounded woman. Thompson claims also to have informed the colonel about the bodies in the ditch. Henderson surmised that the chopper pilot was upset and overly emotional, attributing his agitation to insufficient combat experience. Thompson, on the other hand, insists he remained calm throughout their rather thorough discussion of the My Lai incident. He was the only aviator in the company with whom Henderson talked. In a written statement that the colonel prepared, explaining his role in the My Lai massacre and the subsequent investigation, he claimed to have been advised by Wilson "that none of his other pilots had reported observing anything similar to WO Thompson's report."

Before leaving LZ Dottie, Henderson did talk with door gunner Larry Colburn, who was still wearing fatigues stained with the blood of the rescued child Thompson and his crew had delivered to the hospital in Quang Ngai City. Then the colonel flew out to Charlie Company's current location, near My Lai (1), to question Medina. "Captain Medina's response was immediate and direct," he reported. Charlie Company's commanding officer confirmed that there had been an OH-23 helicopter hovering near his position during the My Lai (4) operation and that it had twice dropped colored smoke. He insisted, however, that smoke signals had not been used during previous operations to identify civilian casualties, and that to him they indicated enemy dead. Medina admitted shooting a woman in her early twenties while personally investigating one of the locations the chopper had marked, but he claimed to have done so, after nudging her body with his foot, only because he thought he saw her move and believed she was about to throw a hand grenade. "Captain Medina assured me that neither he nor any of his soldiers had knowingly caused any civilian deaths." That is just what Henderson wanted to hear. On 20 March he reported orally to Koster at American Division headquarters in Chu Lai on the results of his brief investigation. Henderson explained in a general way what Thompson had reported and informed Koster that, except for Medina, no one had substantiated the pilot's allegations.

Henderson was not alone in failing to provide his superiors with an adequate account of what had happened. The misfeasance of Lieutenant Colonel Francis Lewis, the Americal Division chaplain, also helped to contain knowledge of the massacre. Within a day after the assault on My Lai (4), a distraught Thompson discussed what he had seen with Captain Carl Creswell, the division artillery chaplain, from whom he had been taking regular instruction regarding confirmation in his faith. Creswell advised him to make an official protest through command channels and assured him he would do the same through "chaplain channels." Creswell related Thompson's story to Lewis and recommended that an investigation be conducted. The division chaplain assured him that he would take the matter up with the appropriate authorities.

He never did—at least in a way that would have done any good. Apparently Lewis did speak with the division's chief of staff and with the head of one of its staff sections. These were not official discussions concerning a serious allegation, however, but rather requests by Lewis for information on the status of any investigation involving some "pretty bad things" about which he had heard. The chaplain was in the habit of referring during informal visits with key staff officers to rumors and reports concerning the unnecessary use of force or firepower by American troops that had come to his attention, and that was apparently the nature of his reports about My Lai. Furthermore, his conversation with the chief of staff did not occur until ten days after Creswell informed him about Thompson's allegations. Lewis professed to have spoken also with three other high-ranking staff officers, but none of them corroborated his claims. On the basis of his testimony, and that of the other witnesses it heard, the Peers Commission concluded "that Chaplain Lewis did not make any timely effort to transmit the information he received from Chaplain Creswell to the command group of the Americal Division." Unfortunately, after prodding Lewis continually about the matter for approximately three weeks, Creswell accepted his repeated assurances that an official investigation was under way. To the Peers Commission, "Chaplain Creswell acknowledged with remorse that he did nothing further."

There were, of course, plenty of other people who knew about and might have reported what had occurred at My Lai (4). The Peers Commission compiled a list of thirty individuals who, despite knowing that noncombatants had been killed there and other serious offenses committed, failed to take appropriate action. The soldiers at whom it pointed the finger "had not made official reports, had suppressed relevant information, had failed to order investigations, or had not followed up on the investigations that were made."

At the top of the commission's list was the commanding general of the Americal Division. Samuel Koster had played a key role in a cover-up that began within hours after the massacre. By midafternoon on 16 March, Colonel Henderson had seen the bodies of dead civilians in My Lai (4). Task Force Barker had acknowledged that somewhere between twelve and twenty-four noncombatants had been killed, but Henderson was suspicious of its claim that the operation had produced 128 enemy KIA. Because of his concerns, the 11th Brigade directed the task force to submit a report on the number of civilian casualties and the manner in which they had been killed or wounded. In addition, Henderson ordered Charlie Company to reverse direction and sweep back through My Lai (4) to determine the actual number of casualties the operation had produced, both Vietcong and civilian. Sometime between 1500 and 1530 hours, Major Calhoun relayed this order to Medina.

The captain objected to returning to My Lai (4). General Koster, who was monitoring these radio transmissions in his helicopter overhead, broke in to ask how many civilian dead there were and how they had died. Medina replied that the number was between twenty and twenty-eight and that the cause of death was artillery fire. That seemed about right to Koster, who did not think sending Charlie Company back into My Lai (4) was worth the risks such a mission would entail. Having seen plenty of corpses in Vietnam, he knew that one generally could not tell what had killed them. Koster countermanded Calhoun's order and instructed that Henderson be advised of this.

As a result of Koster's intervention, all Henderson's abortive effort to gain more information accomplished was to alert Medina that officers above him in the chain of command were concerned about civilian casualties at My Lai (4). Other developments reinforced that message. One was Henderson's visit to the field on 17 March to question him about the operation. According to Calley, after their brigade commander departed, Captain Medina remarked, "Well, it looks like I'm going to jail for 20 years."

The captain testified that when Charlie Company returned to LZ Dottie the following day, Lieutenant Colonel Barker informed him an investigation was being conducted and asked him to question his platoon leaders about "whether they had any knowledge of any innocent civilians that had been killed or had any knowledge of a colored person that had been seen firing into a ditch." Medina assembled Calley, Brooks, and possibly Lieutenant LaCross, informed them the My Lai (4) operation was under investigation, and told them he wanted to find out how many noncombatants had been killed and whether they knew about any atrocities or a "colored person" shooting into a ditch. By then the enlisted men were hearing rumors that all their officers were going to be "hung" and that they themselves could expect to go to prison for a long time. Medina decided to address the company. According to the Peers Commission, he advised his men "that the incidents of 16 March were to be investigated and that they were not to discuss them except in the course of the investigation." Medina added that he would back up anyone who got into any kind of trouble. As the Peers Commission pointed out, "This action, combined with the natural reluctance of many of the men to discuss the acts they had participated in, proved an effective means of containing the story of Son My within C Company."

After addressing the whole unit, Medina took Michael Bernhardt aside. Bernhardt had been talking about reporting what had happened at My Lai (4) to his congressman. He testified that Medina told him he did not think it "would be very good if I wrote to my congressman." The captain also informed Bernhardt that it would not be a good idea to make a report to the inspector general. Anything like that "wouldn't do any good." Medina told him "not to do it."

Although the admonitions of its commanding officer kept knowledge of what Charlie Company had done largely confined within the unit, they could not erase the men's memories of the devastation they had inflicted on My Lai (4). Paul Meadlo was especially disturbed by what he had done. The day after the massacre, his mind on other things, he carelessly stepped on a mine, blowing off his right foot. As he was waiting for a medivac chopper to lift him out of the field for treatment, Meadlo yelled and cursed at Lieutenant Calley. "God will punish you. If you don't get out of the field, the same thing will happen to you," he screamed at his platoon leader. Calley, who had been slightly wounded himself by flying fragments from the mine, yelled back, "Get him on the helicopter."

Although the leader of the First Platoon remained in the field, he was so detested by his men—mostly for currying favor with Medina by volunteering them for dangerous assignments—that they put a bounty on his head. That was only one indication of the total deterioration of discipline within Charlie Company. In the wake of the My Lai massacre, what had once been the "best company in Hawaii" seemed to be falling apart. The men were in bad shape, both mentally and physically. They were often ill.

To the extent that the depression and other symptoms they exhibited were caused by fear of prosecution, they were unwarranted. Their superiors had no interest in punishing them; they were bent on concealing their crimes. "Within Task Force Barker headquarters several actions were taken to cover up the incident," the Peers Commission found. At that level the careerism that characterized many Vietnam era professional officers (often called "lifers" by draftees and short-term volunteers) created a powerful incentive to suppress the truth. For them a combat assignment was essential to advancement. To get ahead, a lifer had to have his "ticket punched" in Vietnam. If he did, and if he returned from his tour of duty with some good efficiency reports and one of the medals routinely awarded for little more than satisfactory job performance, he could achieve promotion to higher rank. If there was something negative in his personnel file, however, he would fail to advance, and since the army operated under an "up or out" rule, being passed over for promotion meant forced retirement. Information about war crimes committed under his command was just the sort of thing that could soil an officer's service record sufficiently to prevent advancement and end his military career. It is hardly surprising that the Peers Commission should have found that "some of the most significant acts of suppression and withholding of information concerning the Son My incident involved the commanders and certain key staff officers of TF Barker and the 11th Brigade." Nor is it surprising that several of these individuals lied and/or refused to testify fully to the commission.

Their conduct during the investigation continued a pattern of concealment and deceit that began on the morning of 16 March. During the seventy minutes after Charlie Company touched down, Task Force Barker reported a total of ninety VC killed in its area of operations. After 0840 hours neither the task force nor the 11th Brigade recorded any additional VC casualties in that sector. Nor were any reported to the headquarters of the Americal Division. Although the Peers Commission was unable to establish conclusively the reason for this sudden silence, it thought the explanation was probably either Colonel Henderson's order to stop the "unnecessary killing" or a desire "to avoid attracting undue attention to C Company's operations in My Lai (4)." It seemed possible that Henderson had "either ordered or condoned" the concealment of subsequent civilian casualties in the hamlet.

"Perhaps the most blatant of all Task Force Barker's deceptions," General Peers believed, "was to change the location of where . . . sixty-nine VC were reportedly killed by artillery." At about 0830 hours Lieutenant Colonel Barker, while circling over the battlefield in his helicopter, received a radio transmission, advising him that Charlie Company's body count was eighty-four. At 0840 hours someone made an entry in Task Force Barker's journal to the effect that sixty-nine VC had been killed at grid coordinates that corresponded to the location of My Lai (4).

When Barker returned to the Tactical Operations Center (TOC) at LZ Dottie, he met with Henderson, Calhoun, Lieutenant Colonel Robert Luper, and Major Robert McKnight. "Inexplicably" and suspiciously, the brigade TOC was not notified of the sixty-nine enemy KIA for almost an hour after that figure was recorded. In the interim, the Peers Commission concluded, someone decided to attribute those deaths to artillery fire and "to shift the location at which the VC were reported killed from inside the hamlet to a point 600 meters outside the hamlet." The commission considered it a "reasonable inference" that the report had been altered to lessen the attention that the original version might have attracted when it reached division headquarters.

Although Peers considered this action "the most blatant of all Task Force Barker's deceptions," he also condemned the task force's failure to pass along Thompson's allegations. Major Watke had communicated these to Barker by noon. Yet three hours later the task force commander recorded in an official journal that only ten to twelve women and children had been killed in Charlie Company's area of operations. Nor did Barker ever inform higher headquarters that men under his command had violated "strong prohibitions against the destruction of homes and property."

Barker continued on a course of calculated deception when he prepared and submitted what the Peers Commission considered a "deliberately false and misleading" after-action report on the My Lai (4) operation. That document contained a narrative description of operations on 16 March that the commission characterized as "pure fabrication." It stated falsely that task force troops had engaged two Local Force companies and two or three guerrilla platoons. It described an artillery preparation on enemy combat positions that killed sixty-eight VC but made no mention of Charlie Company killing noncombatants. Barker included a deceitful assertion that infantry on the ground had joined helicopters in assisting civilians to leave the area and in caring for and evacuating the wounded. In the opinion of the Peers Commission, his after-action report could "only be considered an effort by LTC Barker deliberately to suppress the true facts and to mislead higher headquarters into believing there had been a combat operation in Son My Village on March 16 involving a hotly contested action by a sizable enemy force." By the time the commission published this assessment, Barker could not contest it. In June 1968 he had died in a collision between his helicopter and an air force observation plane.

That crash, ironically in the skies over My Lai (4), eliminated the key figure in the cover-up and rendered some questions about it forever unanswerable. Clearly, though, many others shared with Barker responsibility for confining knowledge of the massacre to those closely associated with the 16 March operation. General Peers was critical of three individuals assigned to the 11th Brigade who were present in My Lai (4) that day and, because they were not part of the task force, could have reported what they saw there without fear of reprisal by Barker.

One was First Lieutenant Dennis Johnson of the 52nd Military Intelligence Detachment, who accompanied Charlie Company on its assault. While moving through the hamlet with Medina's command group, he and his Vietnamese interpreter interrogated an old man, who told them the VC had left early that morning. They also saw the dead bodies of as many as thirty-three civilians and, according to the Peers Commission, "observed numerous killings in and around My Lai (4)." Yet when he returned to LZ Dottie, Johnson did not report what he had seen to Barker, Major Calhoun, or Captain Eugene Kotouc, the task force intelligence officer. He remained silent despite being urged to speak up by the interpreter, who was horrified by what he had observed, and despite the fact that, as an intelligence officer, he was specifically charged by a Military Assistance Command, Vietnam (MACV) directive to report war crimes.

Peers also censured Sergeant Haeberle and SP-5 Roberts, the military photographer and reporter who accompanied Charlie Company on its rampage through My Lai (4). They had not informed their immediate superior, the brigade information officer, of what they had observed. Instead, Haeberle wrote a glowing account of the operation for the 11th Brigade newspaper, which credited Task Force Barker's "Jungle Warriors" with crushing an enemy stronghold. According to this story, Medina's company had killed fourteen Vietcong. Haeberle turned in the black-and-white photographs he had taken with his army camera to the public information office, but he kept the color ones snapped with his personal camera. These included a picture of a pile of bodies on the road outside the hamlet. Roberts knew Barker, and he and Haeberle actually talked with the task force commander at his command post soon after the massacre. They did not mention the many civilian dead they had seen or the atrocities they had witnessed but instead listened while Barker crowed about the success of the operation. The two military journalists attributed their failure to speak up to a belief that what they had witnessed at My Lai (4) was just the way war was fought. "If either Haeberle or Roberts had told their superiors what they had seen—and if Haeberle had turned in his color film to brigade headquarters . . . ," Peers lamented, "the tragic events of the Task Force Barker operation might have been uncovered at that time."

That they were not was something for which Johnson, Haeberle, and Roberts all bore some responsibility—but not as much as their brigade commander. Colonel Henderson had plenty of reason to suspect that Task Force Barker's operation had resulted in excessive noncombatant casualties. For one thing, he personally observed from the air two groups of bodies that appeared to be civilians and did not seem to have been included in any casualty report the task force had submitted. For another, the fact that the task force captured only three weapons, while reporting 128 enemy KIA (a ratio far below its usual one gun for every 10 enemy killed), was suspicious. Finally, wiping out 90 Vietcong within seventy minutes after landing, as Charlie Company reported doing, would have been a phenomenal achievement, yet this claim prompted no inquiries from higher headquarters. "The minimum command reaction to the initial report of high VC casualties should have included inquiry concerning location and size of enemy force, unit identification, and the possibility of exploitation," the Peers Commission believed. There was "no evidence that any such inquiry was made."

Henderson claimed later to have been suspicious about the body count figures he received, and he did order Charlie Company to return to My Lai (4) to verify them. But the investigation the colonel conducted after Koster countermanded that order was inadequate. Henderson questioned Thompson, Colburn, and Medina, and he also talked briefly with approximately a dozen members of Charlie Company after they returned to LZ Dottie. He began this supposed interrogation by praising the grunts for their efforts, then mentioned he had heard some non-combatants might have been killed without provocation. That, Henderson pointed out, would detract from the success of their mission. He added that it was not 11th Brigade policy to kill or otherwise harm civilians. After these preliminaries the colonel asked the men if they had seen anything unusual or witnessed any unnecessary killings. Although the group he was addressing included four members of Calley's First Platoon, the only response was silence. Henderson went up to a handful of the grunts and asked again if there was anything different about this operation and if they had been ordered to shoot civilians. Most replied, "No sir." One, Jay Buchanon, said he would rather not answer that question, but Henderson did not ask him why. The soldiers did acknowledge seeing a few dead civilians but explained that these had been killed by artillery or gunships. Henderson looked each man directly in the eye and, from the fact that none turned away, deduced that all were telling the truth. He recalled the soldiers standing tall, with their heads high, looking proud. To their commanding officer, that meant his men had performed well and had done nothing wrong.

He claimed later to have confirmed that by asking Major Glenn D. Gibson, commanding officer of the 174th Aviation Company, to survey his pilots to see if any of them could provide further information. Henderson insisted he had been assured by Gibson that he had spoken to all of those involved in the My Lai operation and that none of them had seen any noncombatants being killed, but the aviator denied ever having been asked for the information he was supposed to have supplied. Henderson seems to have had no basis beyond his own cursory questioning of about fifteen witnesses for reporting orally to Generals Young and Koster that only Thompson had seen anything unusual on 16 March. "COL Henderson's deception of his commanders as to what he had done to investigate the matter and as to the facts he had learned probably played a larger role in the suppression of the facts of Son My than any other factor," the Peers Commission concluded. He "effectively choked off the full exposure of the facts . . . that would have resulted from a real investigation."

Apparently, Henderson put nothing in writing until 24 April. He claimed otherwise, and several witnesses told the Peers Commission they recalled seeing some sort of written communication about the My Lai incident before that date, but it was unable to locate one. In early April Henderson learned that the Vietcong were distributing propaganda leaflets, which alleged that U.S. forces had massacred 300 to 400 people during the 16 March operation at My Lai (4), as well as about reports, emanating from South Vietnamese officials in the Son Tinh District, that seemed to support these allegations. He conferred immediately with the commander of the 2nd ARVN Division, Colonel Nguyen Van Toan, and with the Quang Ngai Province chief, Lieutenant Colonel Ton That Khien. Khien told Henderson about the village chief's report that U.S. forces had killed 470 Vietnamese civilians, but he dismissed the source as an unreliable one, who got his information from the Vietcong. Neither South Vietnamese officer considered an investigation necessary. Henderson nevertheless forwarded the VC propaganda to division headquarters. Koster's reaction was to instruct Young to have him reduce his earlier oral report to writing. Henderson's superiors did not direct him to conduct any additional investigation. They simply instructed him to set down in the form of a letter the information he had gathered during his March investigation and recorded in a small green pocket notebook.

Although Henderson's investigation had been utterly inadequate, according to the Peers Commission, "Koster apparently accepted the 24 April report without any critical review of its content." Well aware that the allegations about the 16 March operation had dire implications, he and Young happily embraced

Henderson's finding that 20 noncombatants had been "inadvertently killed when caught in the area of preparatory fires and in the cross fires of the US and VC forces." The colonel's written report "further concluded that no civilians were gathered together and shot by US soldiers" and that the allegations that American forces had shot and killed 450 to 500 civilians were "a Viet Cong propaganda move to discredit the United States." What Henderson gave Young and Koster did not even mention Hugh Thompson's charges.

Although "Koster testified that he found Colonel Henderson's April 24 Report of Investigation unacceptable," General Peers could locate "no conclusive evidence that he made any effort to insure that a proper investigation and report were undertaken." There were many reasons why Koster and his command group should have undertaken a more searching inquiry into the incident at My Lai (4). The commanding general of the Americal Division had heard directly from Captain Medina that at least twenty civilians had been killed in My Lai (4). His deputy, General Young, had been informed about Thompson's allegations. The discrepancy between the number of VC Charlie Company claimed to have killed and the number of weapons it reported recovering was striking. "Yet," the Peers Commission noted, "General Koster still did not make sure that a complete and impartial investigation was conducted by the division Inspector General or some disinterested senior officer." Instead, he relied on Henderson.

Furthermore, he continued to do so even after receiving reports from Vietnamese sources that there had been a massacre at My Lai (4). Some of this was VC propaganda, which Koster discounted because "I just didn't feel that an incident like this was apt to have happened." Other information received by Americal Division headquarters was suspect because it had originated in areas that were controlled by the Vietcong, and South Vietnamese officials, reluctant to criticize their American allies, downplayed its reliability and significance. Also, Koster believed the claimed number of noncombatant casualties exceeded the civilian population of the area. The reports from Vietnamese sources "did not correlate with the information from Henderson's investigation," so he chose to disregard them. "The combination of a natural predisposition to discount all charges from VC-controlled areas as baseless propaganda, a natural reticence on the part of [South Vietnamese] officials to express forthrightly any criticism of US forces, the failure of US personnel to recognize the seriousness of the allegations subtly passed to them, and an apparent deception on the part of the Brigade Commander all contributed to a completely negative command response to the additional allegations that came to [the Americal] division from Vietnamese sources."

This "negative response" went well beyond merely failing to investigate further to determine what had actually happened at My Lai (4). "There was," the Peers Commission concluded, "at least a tacit decision to withhold from higher headquarters any information concerning the incident." On 20 April General William Westmoreland, commander of all American forces in Vietnam, visited the Americal Division. The 11th Brigade staff briefed him on a number of recent operations, including the one that had produced the massacre. According to Westmoreland, no one mentioned civilian casualties. Koster was there, and so was Henderson. Neither said anything to him about the disturbing reports they had received from both Vietnamese and American sources concerning what had transpired on 16 March.

The Peers Commission concluded that General Koster and Colonel Henderson, along with General Young and numerous other officers, were guilty of conspiring to suppress information about what had happened at My Lai (4). Some, such as Barker, lied deliberately about offenses they knew had been committed, but most of those who participated in this cover-up were unaware of the enormity of the crimes that had been committed. Their ignorance, far from exculpatory, was deliberate and therefore damning. They did not know what had really happened because they did not want to know. They carefully avoided conducting the sort of adequate and independent investigation that might have revealed that soldiers for whose conduct senior officers of Task Force Barker, the 11th Brigade, and the Americal Division were ultimately responsible had massacred innocent civilians at My Lai (4). To these officers, their careers mattered more than the truth.

Many men who had participated in the 16 March operation were aware of what had happened and would have been willing to testify about the massacre if asked to do so. Those who should have ensured that they were questioned fully chose not to probe deeply into allegations of horrific war crimes. One of the things his commission found most troubling, General Peers recalls, "was the lack of concern on the part of so many people." Because so few of those who could and should have done something about the massacre really cared, knowledge of what had happened at My Lai (4) was temporarily impounded within the Americal Division. Unfortunately for Rusty Calley, as Shakespeare wrote, "Truth will out."

CHAPTER 6

Charged with Murder

"Sit down, Lieutenant," the tall colonel directed. Rusty Calley, who found himself in the offices of the army's Inspector General (IG) at the Forrestal Building in Washington, did as he was told. "This is about an operation on 16 March 1968 in or about the village of Mylai Four," Colonel Norman T. Stanfield explained. "At the conclusion of this investigation, you . . . will possibly be charged with murder." Stanfield's words startled Calley, who thought he was in Washington to receive a medal.

It was 9 June 1969, and more than a year had passed since Charlie Company's rampage through My Lai. Calley had put the massacre behind him, but despite the efforts of his superiors to cover it up, the truth about what had occurred on 16 March had not stayed buried. Ronald L. Ridenhour dug it up. A former GI, who learned about the massacre from friends who had been there, Ridenhour wrote to Washington officials in March 1969, detailing what had happened at My Lai (4). His letter triggered probes by the IG and the army's Criminal Investigation Division (CID); by the end of the year, the press had the story, too. Although Calley considered Colonel Stanfield's talk of murder "the silliest thing I had heard of," less than three months later, the army charged him with that offense. By the end of November he was facing trial by court-martial.

That is certainly not a fate he had anticipated when he arrived in Washington. By June 1969 Calley had become a significantly different soldier from the one who slaughtered civilians at My Lai (4). The promotion to first lieutenant that he received soon after the massacre changed little. Replacing the gold bar on his collar with a silver one could not earn Rusty Calley the respect of his men, who continued to dislike their platoon leader. In April the long-simmering feud between Calley and Cowan boiled over when the lieutenant called for artillery fire on a location that his platoon sergeant realized was dangerously close to their own position. Calley spurned Cowan's demands that he cancel this order until incoming shells started landing just fifty meters away. When the First Platoon hooked up with the rest of the company the next day, Cowan went to Medina and announced, "It's either Calley or me." The captain dealt with this ultimatum from a valued NCO by transferring Calley from the First Platoon to the Weapons Platoon. In his new command the little lieutenant continued to exhibit the brutality toward Vietnamese civilians that had become routine for him and much of Charlie Company. According to Sergeant Thomas Kinch, Calley vented his anger at one woman by slapping her and at another by kicking her in the stomach.

Calley's relations with the Vietnamese changed dramatically after he left Charlie Company. Like most infantry lieutenants who were sent to Vietnam, Calley rotated from a platoon command to a staff job after about six months. According to him, upon reporting to battalion headquarters, he was told that the colonel planned to assign him to a platoon in Delta Company. Wanting a "tree-sitting job" in which he would not have to do "a damn thing," Calley asked for the vacant position of battalion S-5. An S-5 was a civil affairs officer whose job entailed assisting the local population with sanitation and education and helping civilians harvest crops and construct housing, roads, railways, and waterways. An S-5, according to Calley, also had "to talk, to communicate, to listen, to help: to win over their hearts and minds."

Although the officer who had led the First Platoon's devastating assault on My Lai (4) was an extremely inappropriate choice for a position that required working closely with the Vietnamese people, he became not only an S-5 but, in the opinion of his commanding officer, Lieutenant Colonel William D. Kelley, a very good one. Kelley thought Calley did a remarkable job for someone with so little relevant experience. Having once entered Vietnamese villages only "to search or destroy them," he now took an interest in helping the people who lived there. Calley gave Lifebuoy soap to children like those he had once dismissed as "dirty" and "cruddy." He showed movies, built wells, and even started a sewing class. The same lieutenant who had once slaughtered Vietnamese villagers now provided them with medicine. After an army doctor refused to enter a village because he was convinced everyone there had tuberculosis, Calley flew to division headquarters to get 400 TB tests to administer to the inhabitants.

Although he had been in Vietnam for months, only after he became an S-5 did he begin to appreciate the primitive conditions under which most South Vietnamese lived. Calley became convinced he could win over these people by making them aware of the comforts that democracy could provide. Although bent on teaching the Vietnamese about American-style free enterprise, he also grew more respectful of their customs. "As an S-5, I didn't enter a Vietnamese house if I wasn't asked to," Calley recalled later. "I didn't call a Vietnamese by his first name. . . . I showed the Vietnamese respect." He learned about and honored the traditions of his hosts. Calley found the work of an S-5 extremely fulfilling. "I felt alive now, as I never had in America," he recalls.

Rather than returning home when his one-year tour of duty ended, in November 1968, Calley extended his service in Vietnam for an additional six months. By late May 1969, he was serving with Company G of the 75th Rangers. "Then the division called." Lieutenant Calley had received orders to report to a chemical, biological, and radiological warfare school at Fort McClellan, Alabama, following "TDY [temporary duty] three days, Office of the Inspector General, Washington, D.C." The orders did not explain the reason for the TDY. Calley guessed it might be that, because of his background as an insurance investigator, he had been given an assignment at Fort McClellan that would involve the sort of investigative work the IG did.

His orders also did not provide for the thirty days of leave normally given to soldiers returning home from Vietnam. Everyone assumed this was the result of a mistake, and that although instructed to report on 30 May, he was not actually expected in Washington until 30 June. About a week later Calley learned division headquarters was very upset. The Pentagon had sent word that he was to pick up his orders and personnel records and board a plane within the hour. Calley hastily packed his bag and hopped a flight to the big American base at Camranh Bay. There, he had just ordered a bourbon at the officers club when some military police hustled him off to catch a plane that was leaving for the States ("I guess I bumped some GI who really wanted to go," he says). The next day, Lieutenant Calley was in Washington, seated before Colonel Stanfield.

The reason was Ron Ridenhour. Ridenhour knew men who had participated in the massacre. He had trained with them in Hawaii to be part of the 11th Brigade's Long Range Reconnaissance Patrol (LRRP) detachment. Just before the brigade shipped out for Vietnam, that unit was disbanded. Ridenhour became a door gunner in the aviation section, and several of his buddies were posted to Charlie Company. In late April 1968 he ran into one of them, PFC Charles "Butch" Gruver, in Chu Lai. While the two GIs were drinking beer and bringing each other up to date on what they had been doing since their LRRP days, Gruver asked Ridenhour if he had heard about Pinkville. When his friend indicated he had not and asked what they had done there, Gruver responded, "We went in there and killed everybody." Ridenhour pressed him for details. The more of these his buddy supplied, the more horrified and revolted he became. Several times Ridenhour stopped his friend to ask if they had killed *all* the people. The answer was always the same: they had killed every man, woman, and child, maybe 300 or 400 people in all. Ridenhour could not quite believe what he was hearing. Still, he left his reunion with Gruver wondering, "God, what if it is true?"

Ron Ridenhour made it his personal mission to find out. Over the next few months he tracked down a number of other GIs he knew who had been in Charlie Company. With each one, Ridenhour sought to steer the conversation around to Pinkville. Often, he did not have to bring up the massacre. Many of his friends, apparently tortured by their memories of what had happened at My Lai (4), seemed anxious to talk about it. Ridenhour had hoped his inquiries would establish that too many beers had caused Gruver to exaggerate or just plain lie. On the contrary, the other GIs he spoke with confirmed what Gruver had told him and added horrifying details of their own. For example, Michael Terry, a deeply religious Mormon who had been with the Third Platoon on 16 March, told him his squad, which followed Calley's men through the hamlet, had taken a break for chow near a pile of Vietnamese. Some were moaning and obviously not yet dead. Concluding the wounded were not going to get any medical attention, Terry and a buddy finished them off. Then they resumed eating their lunch. Larry La Croix, a sergeant in the Second Platoon, told Ridenhour that three times he had seen Calley chop down groups of Vietnamese with a machine gun. "They were slaughtering the villagers like sheep," La Croix declared.

Not long before his scheduled return to the States, Ridenhour learned Michael Bernhardt had been taken to the hospital in Chu Lai with a severe case of jungle rot. By then he was wrestling with a moral and ethical dilemma: he wanted to report what he had learned to someone, but he was reluctant to implicate comrades in criminal conduct. Ridenhour was delighted to learn Bernhardt had refused to take part in the massacre. Indeed, the hospitalized GI was so angry at Charlie Company's officers for not halting the slaughter that he proposed half jokingly to his LRRP buddy that they track them all down in the States and shoot them. Bernhardt promised his friend that if Ridenhour went public about Pinkville, he would support him by testifying openly concerning what had happened there.

Even with that encouragement, it took Ridenhour a while to publicize the massacre. Back in "the world" and out of the army, he shared the story with friends and family in Phoenix, Arizona. Ridenhour was a strong man who had been a defensive lineman on his high school football team and had led extremely dangerous long-range patrols though the jungles of Vietnam, but when he talked about how some of his buddies had committed mass murder, he often cried. Those to whom he disclosed with great emotion what had happened at My Lai offered divided counsel. One friend suggested he write the CID to ask it to look into the incident. Convinced that asking the army to investigate itself would accomplish nothing, the cynical former GI rejected that idea. Most of his friends told him to forget the whole thing and not rock the boat. Ridenhour's father agreed with them, fearing a reaction against the family if Ron spoke out. His mother and sister, on the other hand, told him to do what he had to do.

Ridenhour eventually concluded that for America to do nothing about the massacre would pervert its entire war in Vietnam, calling into question what he and the GIs who had died there were fighting for. He became convinced, as Seymour Hersh puts it, "that he had to stir the cold ashes of Son My, and the only way to do it would be to enlist powerful support." One friend suggested that he write to dovish Congressman Morris "Mo" Udall (D. Ariz.). Ridenhour decided to do that, but to also send copies of the same letter to twenty-two other members of Congress, the secretaries of state and defense, the secretary of the army, and the chairman of the Joint Chiefs of Staff.

In five single-spaced, typewritten pages his letter, dated 29 March 1969, outlined what he knew about My Lai and how he had learned about the massacre. Recounting what Gruver had told him, Ridenhour acknowledged, "I received that first report with some skepticism," but, he added, "in the following months I was to hear similar stories from such a wide variety of people that it became impossible for me to disbelieve that something rather dark and bloody did indeed occur sometime in March, 1968 in a village called 'Pinkville' in the Republic of Viet Nam." He related what each of the soldiers with whom he talked had told him. Gruver, who had estimated that 300 to 400 persons died in Pinkville, had alleged that orders to slaughter all the inhabitants had come from the commanding officer of Task Force Barker, or perhaps someone even higher in the chain of command. According to Ridenhour, Terry and others had informed him that Charlie Company's commander, Captain Ernest Medina, had issued an order for the destruction of the village. Gruver, although acknowledging he was not an eyewitness, had relayed reports of others he considered trustworthy "that one of the company's officers, 2nd Lieutenant Kally (this spelling may be incorrect) had rounded up several groups of villagers (each group consisting of a minimum of 20 persons of both sexes and all ages). According to the story, Kally then machine-gunned each group." La Croix had told Ridenhour that he actually saw "Kally" gun down at least three separate groups of villagers.

Along with such details of the massacre, the letter contained Bernhardt's allegation that Medina had told him "'not to do anything stupid like write my congressman.'" "Exactly what did in fact occur in the village of 'Pinkville' in March 1968 I do not know for certain, but I am convinced it was something very black indeed," Ridenhour concluded. Although he had considered sending his letter to newspapers, magazines, and broadcasting companies, the former GI told those to whom it was addressed, he had decided the appropriate procedure was investigation and action by the Congress of the United States. As a citizen he did not wish to besmirch further the image of America's servicemen. Yet, "if you and I truly believe in the principles of justice and equality of every man. . . ," he asserted, "we must press forward a widespread public investigation of this matter with all of our combined efforts."

Congressman Udall agreed. When one of his aides, Roger Lewis, called Ridenhour's letter to his attention, he reacted immediately, writing to Secretary of Defense Melvin Laird about it and sending a copy of this communication to Representative L. Mendell Rivers (D. S.C.), the chair of the House Armed Services Committee. That committee had also received a copy of Ridenhour's epistle. After reading it, staff lawyer Frank Starinshek took the letter to Chief Counsel John Blandford, who recognized immediately that it contained "too much of a germ of truth" to be brushed off. Blandford drafted a letter for Rivers's signature, which urged the Department of the Army to investigate the matter. The chairman signed it on 7 April, the same day he received Udall's message. By then Secretary Laird also had Ridenhour's letter, which had reached his office on 4 April. He, too, recognized that this was not routine. His office forwarded the letter to the army, which by the end of the first week in April had received six other copies via congressional referrals.

It checked with its headquarters in Vietnam, USARV, whose deputy IG, Colonel Howard Whitaker, looked into the matter. He confirmed that Task Force Barker had conducted an operation against My Lai (4) on 16 March 1968 but found nothing in the after-action report about civilian casualties and no record of any investigation into mass killings. Although Whitaker believed Ridenhour's letter must be an elaborate hoax or a sick joke, the army continued its inquiry into what had happened at My Lai. On 12 April a colonel in the office of the Chief of Staff, John G. Hill Jr., wrote Ridenhour to thank him for bringing the matter to the army's attention. Hill explained that, because it involved "events of a year or so ago, a proper investigation will take some time," but assured him, "This investigation is underway now."

It was being conducted by Colonel William Wilson, a highly decorated forty-five-year-old Special Forces officer who had jumped with the 101st Airborne Division into France and Holland during World War II and earned a Purple Heart for wounds suffered at Normandy. One day while reading through complaints referred to the Inspector General by Congress and the executive branch, Wilson encountered Ridenhour's letter, along with instructions from General Westmoreland, who was now the Chief of Staff, to check out his charges. Shocked by them, Wilson read the letter four times, then asked the IG, Major General William Enemark, to assign the case to him. Enemark agreed with Wilson that this investigation should be conducted by an officer with infantry combat experience, and that as the only one in the office who had any, Wilson was the logical choice. The IG cautioned him, however, that he must keep an open mind and remember that everything in Ridenhour's letter was hearsay.

Wilson promptly procured maps of the area where the 16 March 1968 operation had been conducted and a roster of personnel assigned to Charlie Company on that date. He then asked the Army Locator Files to come up with current addresses for the men on the list. Wilson found Ridenhour simply by calling information in Phoenix, and from him he learned the whereabouts of Bernhardt, Terry, Gruver, La Croix, and SP-4 William Doherty. Before setting out to interview those men, Wilson discussed procedure with his division chief and with Colonel Clement Carney, the Judge Advocate General's Corps (JAG) lawyer assigned to the IG's office. They decided that, because Wilson would be conducting an inquiry designed to determine what had happened rather than a criminal investigation, he should not warn witnesses of their rights before questioning them. The consequence of that approach, they realized, was that if anyone incriminated himself, his admissions could never be used as evidence against him.

After being briefed on procedure, Wilson and a court reporter, Albert F. "Smitty" Smith, set out to interview participants in the My Lai massacre and cover-up. They spent three months crisscrossing the country. Wilson started with Ridenhour, whom he found to be "an extremely impressive young man." Although "his allegations were still only hearsay," Wilson recalls, "they were depressingly convincing." Next he talked with Terry, also now a civilian, in Orem, Utah. Terry confirmed that he had "finished off" a heap of wounded and moaning Vietnamese. Wilson and Smith moved on to Fort Carson, Colorado, where Sergeant La Croix, after declining to have a military lawyer present, reiterated his claim that he had seen Calley order a private to open fire on a group of villagers with a machine gun and, when that soldier quit shooting before everyone was down, complete the slaughter himself. Some of La Croix's responses to Wilson's questions were untruthful; he tried, for example, to excuse what his squad had done by saying the Vietnamese they shot were diving into tunnels and picking up grenades and weapons; he also lied about Charlie Company giving medical care to wounded civilians. Next Wilson interviewed Gruver in Oklahoma City. While acknowledging that what he had told Ridenhour about Calley was hearsay, Gruver expressed confidence in the men who had given him this information. He added that he had personally witnessed a radio operator kill a small boy with a machine gun. At Fort Hood, Texas, SP-4 Doherty, although warned that he was suspected of war crimes, refused military counsel and "confirmed that nearly every living thing in the village had been shot." "I dream about it a lot," he told Wilson. When the IG investigator pressed him about whether he had killed civilians, Doherty asked for a lawyer. After consulting with counsel, he professed an inability to remember. He had said enough, though. Wilson realized, "This made just too many witnesses for the tale of mass murders to have been conjured up out of whole cloth; a repugnant picture was forming in my mind." Smith, too, was becoming very depressed.

When they returned to Washington, Wilson informed his superiors that Ridenhour's story had not been invented and that investigating it fully was going to take much longer. On 8 May he interviewed Michael Bernhardt, who had been summoned to the Forrestal Building from his current duty station at Fort Dix, New Jersey. Bernhardt confirmed his own refusal to participate in "point-blank murder." He also made it clear that on 16 March Charlie Company had encountered no resistance, suffered no casualties, and captured only three weapons. Although Wilson found him "an extremely cooperative witness," Bernhardt did not always carefully distinguish between what he had seen himself and what he had only heard about from others.

Realizing that Medina was a key witness, during the second week in May Wilson traveled to Georgia, where the captain was now attending the Infantry Advanced Officers School at Fort Benning. When informed that he was suspected of war crimes, Medina asked to have a lawyer present. Wilson informed Captain Edwin J. Richards, the JAG attorney appointed to represent Medina, that he could advise his client but not answer for him. Medina "was obviously upset by the questions and allegations" directed at him during a torturous four-and-one-half-hour interview. He claimed that Barker had given permission to burn My Lai (4) and, while acknowledging that he had shot a woman, claimed to have believed she was about to throw a grenade at him. Medina maintained that Colonel Henderson had already exonerated him for that killing after investigating the My Lai incident for General Koster.

The revelation that the commanders of the 11th Brigade and the Americal Division had known about allegations of atrocities that had apparently never been reported to higher headquarters in Vietnam was disturbing. Wilson had Colonel Henderson and Major Calhoun summoned to Washington for questioning. Henderson's confident answers impressed him and the other IG colonel who sat in on the interview. They should have, for the former brigade commander had refreshed his recollection. He had telephoned the current Americal Division chief of staff and persuaded him to search for the report on My Lai that Henderson had prepared. An unsigned carbon turned up in the safe of the 11th Brigade intelligence section, and a copy of that was sent to Henderson. He defended the quality of the inquiry that produced this report to Wilson, misrepresenting it in ways designed to explain and justify its failure to generate the appropriate paperwork and the required referral to the IG. Henderson denied ever being told that his troops had wantonly killed large groups of civilians and claimed to have dismissed what Thompson told him because the pilot was young, inexperienced, and weeping.

Wilson had learned from La Croix that sometime on the morning of 16 March someone in a helicopter had complained over the radio that what was going on in My Lai (4) looked like a bloodbath. Subsequent interviews had yielded Thompson's name, and the army eventually located him at Fort Rucker, Alabama. Ordered to report to Wilson's Forrestal Building office on 11 June, the helicopter pilot spent three days trying to reconstruct the entire My Lai incident. "He was not entirely successful—and I do not think any honest eyewitness could have been . . . ," Wilson recalls, "but he made prodigious efforts." The IG investigator "found Thompson immensely impressive." Wilson needed confirmation of Thompson's account, but he got that from door gunner Larry Colburn and another pilot, Chief Warrant Officer Dan R. Millians, who had also been flying a helicopter in support of Charlie Company on the morning of 16 March. Wilson also talked with Thompson's company commander. Major Glen D. Gibson disputed Henderson's claim of receiving from him a report that no pilots had heard or seen any indiscriminate shooting in My Lai (4). "I found Thompson immensely impressive," says Wilson; "he was the only hero on that awful day, and his testimony was damning."

Besides providing the IG investigator with a great deal of valuable information, Thompson picked Calley out of a lineup. On 13 June the pilot identified him as the infantry officer with whom he had argued after landing his chopper in My Lai (4) on the morning of the massacre. Calley had been in Washington since being told by Colonel Stanfield on 9 June that he was suspected of murder and war crimes. Stanfield had asked him if he wanted a lawyer. When Calley inquired about whether the colonel thought he needed one, the answer was affirmative. "I'll have an attorney," said Calley. Predictably, the JAG officer designated as his counsel advised him not to answer any questions, warning his client that he could be charged with murder, a capital offense. "Oh it's serious then," the suspect recalls remarking. "It hadn't filtered in on me, the seriousness of it." The gravity of the situation soon became apparent, even to Calley. After consulting with his lawyer, he offered to trade a full disclosure of what had happened at My Lai for a grant of immunity from prosecution. Stanfield refused this deal, making it clear there would be no grant of immunity. Calley then declined to be interviewed or to make a statement.

Seeking information from other sources, Wilson set out "to talk to more of Calley's people who had been on the ground." Ronald Grzesik of Springfield, Massachusetts, who had been a fire team leader in the First Platoon, told him he had been ordered by the lieutenant to "finish off the people" in the ditch. When he refused, Calley told him to take his men and burn the village. While doing that, Grzesik encountered a sobbing Paul Meadlo, who told him he had been compelled by Calley to shoot people.

Wilson recognized immediately that Meadlo "was possibly the crucial witness." On the evening of 16 July he interviewed him in a motel room in Terre Haute, Indiana. In physical and emotional pain, "his right foot and self-respect gone," the former grunt was "determined to relieve his conscience and describe the horrors of My Lai." He laid it all out, detailing how Calley had reprimanded him for not killing the prisoners he was guarding and then explicitly ordered him to waste them. "After telling about this, Meadlo raised his eyes to the ceiling of the motel room and began to cry," Wilson recalls. "His body shook with sobs."

Meadlo recounted how they had shot the prisoners. "I was shocked," says Wilson. Realizing Meadlo had confessed to murder without being warned of his rights, the investigator called Colonel Carney for advice. The JAG officer told him to give Meadlo his warnings and try to get him to confess again. Told that anything he said could be used against him in a court of law, the tormented Meadlo responded, "I don't care." He repeated his confession.

Wilson, who "had prayed to God that this thing was fiction, . . . knew now it was fact." The next day he returned to Washington to submit a written report of his findings. It was accompanied by transcripts of interviews with thirty-six witnesses. By then Calley was at Fort Benning, to which he had reported on 21 June, reassigned, he says, "by a colonel with the Inspector General's Office," who had led him to believe that he "would have a better chance there" because "everything was infantry." On 23 July Wilson warned Colonel Jim D. Kiersey, the chief of staff of the Infantry Center, not to allow Calley to be reassigned to another post. On 19 August he flew to Fort Benning to brief legal officers there on the case against the lieutenant.

By then Chief Warrant Officer Andre C. R. Feher of the CID had taken over the My Lai investigation. Ridenhour's allegations having been confirmed, it was now up to criminal investigators to collect hard evidence that could be used in court and take sworn affidavits from potential witnesses and defendants. Feher got the case on 4 August and on the twenty-third became the head of a three-agent team, to which four more CID detectives were added later. He personally spent the last week of August and most of September traveling around the country taking statements. Feher focused on former members of the First Platoon, who could testify about Calley's actions. He obtained seven detailed statements, which together provided sufficient evidence to prosecute the lieutenant. These established that Calley had been involved in two group executions, one at the trail intersection in the center of the village and the other at the irrigation ditch. Feher estimated that about 120 women and children had been murdered.

Two of the former soldiers he interviewed provided particularly valuable evidence. One was Charles Sledge, now out of the army and living in the small town of Sardis, Mississippi. Because he had been Calley's radiotelephone operator (RTO), Sledge had been with the lieutenant almost constantly on 16 March. He had witnessed the killing of the first group of villagers at the trail intersection, had been at the ditch when Calley ordered Mitchell to push civilians into it and then began shooting them, and had seen his platoon leader kill a Buddhist monk and throw a baby into a ditch and shoot it. Furthermore, Sledge's recollection of all of these events was graphic. He could recall so much that interviewing him and drawing up an affidavit required most of a day and part of the evening. He and Wilson took breaks to eat lunch and dinner in the motel dining room. There they attracted considerable attention, for Feher was white, Sledge was African-American, and although now illegal, segregated dining was still the rule in rural Mississippi. All the time the two men were spending closeted in the CID agent's room also aroused suspicion. Feher found himself forced to explain to the sheriff what he was doing in Sardis.

He did not have to deal with racial prejudice in Ridgeville, Ohio, but his visit to that town on 25 August was almost as eventful as his trip to Mississippi and just as productive. Feher went there to interview Ronald Haeberle because he realized that the black-and-white photos Haeberle had taken of Charlie Company's combat assault, some of which had appeared in military newspapers, might be useful as evidence if he could testify about where and when he had taken them. Out of the blue the former army photographer announced that he had some color slides of the massacre that he had snapped with his personal camera. Feher was astonished to learn that Haeberle had been showing these as part of an illustrated talk on the Vietnam War he had given to Optimist, Kiwanis, and Jaycee clubs, a teachers association, a church youth group, and even some high school students. The ex-soldier agreed to bring the slides to the CID agent's motel room, where they projected them on a bedsheet pinned to the wall. Realizing he had made an extraordinary breakthrough,

Feher took the precaution of photographing the blurred images with a Polaroid. As Michael Bilton and Kevin Sim explain, "The[se] pictures were the first hard evidence a massacre had taken place, evidence that could be used in court."

They would be used there, for on 5 September, Brigadier General Oscar E. Davis, the interim commander of Fort Benning, charged Lieutenant Calley with multiple murders of "Oriental human beings." Davis had to act then because Calley (who had been marking time in a make-work job in the office of the deputy base commander, planning a new system of car parking and working on a letterhead for the Infantry Center museum) was scheduled to be released from active duty on 6 September. Once out of the army, he would be immune from prosecution. In *Toth v. Quarles* (1955) the Supreme Court had struck down Article 3(a) of the Uniform Code of Military Justice (UCMJ), which purported to authorize the trial by courts-martial of discharged servicemen for certain offenses committed while they were on active duty. The Court ruled that a former member of the air force could not be subjected to military justice for allegedly murdering a Korean while he was stationed in Korea. *Toth* appeared to mean it would be unconstitutional to try Calley by court-martial once he became a civilian. On the other hand, no civilian American court had jurisdiction to punish crimes committed in Vietnam. If Calley were to be tried for what had happened at My Lai, he would have to be kept in the army.

Four young captains at Fort Benning, who had learned about the My Lai investigation at about the time that Calley reported to the Infantry School, realized this. They feared that, because of the case's explosive implications and the political repercussions that revelations about American soldiers slaughtering Vietnamese civilians could cause, the lieutenant would never be tried. To them it seemed likely that higher-ups would allow him to slip quietly into the sanctuary of civilian life without even being charged. One reason for their fears may have been a call that Colonel Robert Lathrop, the staff judge advocate at Fort Benning, received sometime in late August or early September from Colonel William Chilcoat, chief of military justice in the Office of the Judge Advocate General in Washington, whose office he had visited earlier to discuss the drafting of specifications and other matters. Chilcoat told Lathrop, without giving any reasons, "Do nothing until you hear from us."

The four young captains, none of whom was a career officer, decided that if a cover-up were attempted, one of them should prefer charges against Calley. Anticipating that whoever did this would face retribution, they flipped coins to determine which one would stick his neck into the guillotine. The loser was Captain William R. Hill, the assistant adjutant of the Student Brigade. He went to see its commander, Colonel Lon D. Marlow. As Calley's commanding officer, Marlow had the authority to file charges against him, and Hill urged the colonel to do so before it was too late. Afraid of offending President Nixon, Marlow refused. He would be "a fool or a jackass" to do what Hill wanted, he told him. So Hill decided to sign the murder charge himself.

On 4 September, however, Lathrop received another call from Washington, this one telling him the case was all his. This cleared the way for Marlow's executive officer, Lieutenant Colonel Henry E. Vincent, to do what his boss would not. Marlow had conducted a preliminary inquiry in the case and had discussed the possible number of victims with Hill and Captain Herbert Hammett, the chief of military justice in the Staff Judge Advocate's Office, whom Lathrop had sent to interview Paul Meadlo. Convinced there was sufficient evidence to justify such action, sometime late on the fourth or early in the morning of the fifth, Vincent decided to sign a charge sheet as the accuser.

There were allegations later that outside pressure produced the decision to prosecute Calley, but while Lathrop may have known that the president had taken an interest in the case, he did not communicate this information to Vincent. Brigadier General Davis, who ordered Calley retained on active duty so he could be prosecuted, testified that he had talked to no one from the Judge Advocate General's Section in Washington about the case and that Westmoreland had taken no action in connection with it. Although he avoided outside influences "like the plague," Davis did acknowledge reading a teletype message from the Adjutant General's office in Washington, informing him that someone could be retained on active duty beyond his scheduled date of separation from service only if he were the subject of an investigation that would lead to court-martial charges or had actually been charged. To ensure that Calley would remain on active duty, and thus subject to the jurisdiction of the military legal system, on 5 September the army formally charged him with murder in violation of Article 118 of the UCMJ.

The four specifications accused Calley of killing a total of at least 107 residents of My Lai (4) "by means of shooting them with a rifle." On 12 September, after reading more statements, Captain Hill, acting as an accuser, swore to additional charges. Each new specification accused Calley of a single murder. One was based on his alleged killing of the Buddhist monk, and the other was for shooting a baby of unknown sex and age.

These additional charges were referred to Lieutenant Colonel Duane G. Cameron, an infantry officer with two tours in Vietnam, who had been appointed on 5 September to investigate the original ones, pursuant to Article 32 of the UCMJ. That article provided that, before any case could be referred to trial, a thorough and impartial investigation must be conducted to determine if there was sufficient evidence to warrant such action. An Article 32 investigating officer performed a function similar to that of a grand jury in a civilian federal criminal case.

Cameron's investigation of the charges against Calley was delayed for seven weeks, largely because Calley's appointed military lawyer requested additional time to prepare. The lieutenant's civilian attorney sought to persuade the investigating officer to dismiss the charges on the ground that the army no longer had jurisdiction over Calley, but Cameron insisted he lacked the authority to do that. He also disputed defense insinuations that he had been subjected to pressure by officers above him in the chain of command.

Cameron reviewed statements made by key witnesses who were no longer in the army, such as Meadlo, Sledge, and Olson. A number of those who were still on active duty were summoned to a hearing, which he conducted on 20–23 October. Some of these, such as Bernhardt and Sergeant Cowan, provided useful information, but others, such as La Croix and Mitchell, facing possible prosecution themselves, invoked their privilege against compulsory self-incrimination and refused to testify. Medina, called as a witness by the defense, discussed the 16 March operation at length, but when Cameron asked him whether he had ordered Calley or his men to kill innocent civilians, he declined to answer. On 6 November the investigating officer submitted his report to the commanding officer of the Student Brigade. It recommended "that Lt. Calley should be tried by General Court-Martial."

That recommendation went to General Orwin Clark Talbott, who had taken over command of Fort Benning from Davis on 10 September. According to Talbott, he had not discussed the case at all with Cameron. When he received the report of the Article 32 investigating officer, he read it "with great care more than once from cover to cover. I thought about it a great deal," he testified at Calley's court-martial, and "discussed it at great length with the Staff Judge Advocate, making sure I understood every possible legal implication." "I was convinced that there was an alleged case . . . that was so serious that it could only be determined by a court of law," he declared.

Talbott's decision-making process may not have been as objective and detached as he claimed. On 13 November, while the commanding general of Fort Benning was pondering what to do with Lieutenant Calley, a freelance journalist named Seymour Hersh broke the story of what had happened at My Lai. When General Westmoreland went to Philadelphia eight days later to give a speech, reporters peppered him with questions about the massacre. The Chief of Staff refused to give them any information or to comment on the case, saying "it would be imprudent for me to pass any premature judgment on whether there was an offense or not, and whether or not any individual was guilty of an offense." The fact that Westmoreland was being pressured by the press at the same time that Talbott was making his assessment of the case against Calley aroused suspicions that Talbott had acted on orders from his superiors. He denied this, insisting he had received no instructions, either directly or indirectly, from higher headquarters about what to do with the alleged war criminal. He made his decision, Talbott insisted, "solely on the Article 32 investigation." That decision was to order Calley to stand trial.

Talbott took that step on 24 November. When Colonel Stanfield had told him less than six months earlier that he might be charged with murder, Calley had considered this "the silliest thing I had heard of." It was no longer a laughing matter. Thanks to the persistence of Ron Ridenhour and the investigations conducted by William Wilson and Andre Feher, the man who had led the First Platoon on its devastating sweep through My Lai (4) stood formally accused of murdering well over a hundred Vietnamese civilians. He also stood at the eye of a developing political hurricane that would make his forthcoming court-martial a focal point of the divisive debate over the Vietnam War.

CHAPTER 7

Reaction

"I'll never forget the night Ron found me on the phone," Seymour Hersh recalled years later when he and Ridenhour shared a platform during a conference on My Lai at Tulane University. It was only after the freelance journalist shocked the world with an exposé of what had happened at My Lai that he met the man who had unearthed the massacre. Ridenhour had begun "actively trying to figure out how to get in touch with the press" a couple of weeks after the army informed him it had decided to prosecute Lieutenant Calley. Hearing nothing about any additional arrests, he became convinced the military intended to make a scapegoat of a single platoon commander. Unwilling to let it downplay a massacre in which scores of soldiers had participated, Ridenhour decided to break a promise he had made to remain silent while My Lai was being investigated. Although he contacted a reporter at the *Arizona Republic*, it failed to run the story. Ridenhour hired a literary agent, but still the only publication he could interest in his story was *Ramparts* magazine, whose radical reputation might raise doubts about its credibility.

The indifference of *Life*, *Look*, *Newsweek*, and *Harper's* contrasted sharply with Hersh's reaction to a tip he received on 22 October 1969 that the army was "trying to court-martial some guy in secret at Fort Benning for killing 75 Vietnamese civilians." After a diligent three-week investigation, on 13 November he broke the story of the My Lai massacre in newspapers across the country. These articles elicited a phone call from someone he did not know existed. "Hey, I started it," Ridenhour informed Hersh. Soon the ex-GI was "help[ing] me enormously."

Hersh's story also triggered an avalanche of journalistic exposés.

With the media now training a spotlight on My Lai, the army decided to undertake its own wide-ranging inquiry into the massacre and cover-up. As a result, most of the facts were widely known well before Calley came to trial. The American people, however, did not react to them with the outrage Ridenhour had no doubt anticipated. Nor did the government. The Nixon administration seemed interested mainly in minimizing the adverse impact of the story on support for its increasingly unpopular war in Vietnam, while Congress actually interfered with efforts to punish those responsible for the crimes committed at My Lai.

Even the press initially displayed little interest in the prosecution of Rusty Calley. On the afternoon of Friday, 5 September, the public information office at Fort Benning, responding to a request from a local reporter, issued a bland news release, which announced that Calley was being retained on active duty because he had been "charged with violation of Article 118, murder, for offenses allegedly committed against civilians while serving in Vietnam in March 1968." It did not reveal that Calley was accused of killing more than 100 Vietnamese. The army hoped to dispose of his case as quietly as possible.

Although Fort Benning and the Pentagon braced themselves for a barrage of media inquiries about the case, the 5 September press release sparked little interest. The *New York Times* devoted just two paragraphs on page 38 to an Associated Press (AP) wire service report on Calley. The Columbus, Georgia, *Ledger-Inquirer*, published in a small city located adjacent to Fort Benning that was home to many of the soldiers stationed there, did run a fourteen-inch story on its front page, and Associate Editor Charles Black commenced a two-month investigation into what had led to the filing of the charges. But because he was reluctant to run anything until he had all the details, the *Ledger-Inquirer* published nothing further on the case. Five days after the Fort Benning press release, NBC included a short report on Calley by Pentagon correspondent Robert Goralski in its evening news broadcast. After that, as Hersh observes, "for weeks there was nothing more in the press about Calley."

Hersh himself broke this prolonged silence. A former Chicago police reporter, he had moved to Washington to cover the Pentagon for the AP, then given up that job to serve as a press secretary and speech writer for Senator Eugene McCarthy during McCarthy's antiwar campaign for the 1968 Democratic presidential nomination. Quitting after a dispute over campaign tactics, Hersh returned to Washington, where he was researching a book on the Pentagon when he received a telephone tip about the prosecution of an obscure lieutenant at Fort Benning. After making about twenty-five calls, he learned about the old AP report. Once in possession of the information in the Fort Benning press release, he soon located George W. Latimer, a former judge on the U.S. Court of Military Appeals, now practicing law in Salt Lake City, who was serving as Calley's civilian counsel. Hersh confirmed essential facts with an official source in Washington, then flew west to talk with Latimer.

On 11 November, hoping to speak with Calley himself, he took a plane to Georgia. The accused mass murderer was not easy to find, for his name appeared neither in the Fort Benning telephone directory nor in the file listing residents of the bachelor officers quarters. After ten hours of searching, Hersh found a warrant officer who was a downstairs neighbor of Calley at the BOQ, and he introduced them. At first the lieutenant was apprehensive about talking to a journalist, but after a few drinks at a party given by some of his friends, he loosened up, and when Hersh "wanted to leave, Calley wanted me to stay." The former platoon leader told him about Charlie Company's 16 March operation and about how many people he was accused of killing.

Convinced he had a sensational story, Hersh flew back to Washington the next day to write it up. Although his investigative reporting on My Lai would eventually win him a Pulitzer Prize, when he first sought a publisher, both *Life* and *Look* turned him down. He decided to hawk his article through the Dispatch News Service, started recently by two young men hoping to secure a wider audience for radical stories. Its general manager, David Obst, called the editors of fifty newspapers, offering them Hersh's story for only $100. Thirty-five, including the *Chicago Sun-Times*, the *St. Louis Post-Dispatch*, and the *Milwaukee Journal*, published it on 13 November. The *New York Times* ran a story based on its own research, but Hersh, who wrote and syndicated four more articles on My Lai over the next five weeks, deserved most of the credit for finally bringing the massacre out of the shadows.

The day after his first story appeared, Americal Division troops escorted correspondents from the *New York Times*, *Newsweek*, and ABC TV to My Lai. There they found a deserted village, overgrown with vegetation. The reporters also observed several mounds that appeared to be mass graves.

Ronald Haeberle, of course, had pictures of a very different My Lai, and of those who had died there. After reading about Calley in the newspaper, he called a college friend, Joe Eszterhas, who was now a reporter for the *Cleveland Plain Dealer*. Eszterhas confirmed that Haeberle had indeed been on the Pinkville operation, then approached his night managing editor about running his story. At first the editor, whose attention was focused on an impending moon landing, was not interested, but after he saw the startling images of carnage captured by Haeberle's camera, his attitude changed. "It's just a routine Moon walk," he told Eszterhas. On 20 November readers of the *Plain Dealer* found eight of Haeberle's graphic photos splashed across the front page. The world's press scrambled to reproduce pictures that one magazine editor characterized as the hottest property since the Zapruder film of President Kennedy's assassination. Eventually, Time-Life purchased the American rights for $19,550, and on 5 December *Life* ran a ten-page layout of Haeberle's My Lai photographs. The *Sunday Times* of London and West Germany's *Stern* magazine also purchased rights to his pictures. These deals, along with ancillary fees from Sweden, Australia, and South Africa, raised the total amount paid for them to $35,099.

Television also capitalized on the interest in the My Lai massacre that Hersh had ignited. On 24 November, four nights after showing some of Haeberle's photographs, CBS screened an interview with Paul Meadlo on its evening news show, anchored by the popular and widely respected Walter Cronkite. Asked by hardball interviewer Mike Wallace what he had done at My Lai, Meadlo, looking rather sad and pathetic, replied in a flat voice, "I went in a village and killed everybody." He had even executed babies, the former grunt admitted. "It was an incredible interview," Hersh recalls. Dispatch News Service had collected $10,000 from CBS for Meadlo's appearance, which Hersh had arranged. "I do not claim this as the greatest day in my professional life," the investigative journalist acknowledged later. The Meadlo interview aired the night before the army ordered Calley to face a court-martial, and the enormous publicity it generated threatened his right to a fair trial, raising the very real possibility that a military judge might have to grant him a mistrial. Criticized by Senator Peter Dominick (R. Colo.) for putting a potential witness on television, CBS responded that "there was an overriding public need for full disclosure about what happened at My Lai." Its broadcast promoted that. Meadlo's confession, which was subsequently published in newspapers around the world, stunned the nation. Three decades later, Sy Hersh himself conceded it was what had made My Lai "big in America."

Even before the Meadlo interview aired, Hersh's own disclosures had unleashed what army historian William M. Hammond characterizes as "a flood of sometimes lurid news stories." Newspapers and magazines were filled with accounts of the massacre. For example, on 5 December, *Time* devoted nine pages to My Lai, accompanied by everything from a photograph of a dead victim to a picture of Calley lifted from his high school yearbook. There was also an editorial on the massacre. By as early as 20 November, Hammond reports, "virtually every newspaper in the United States had taken a position [on My Lai.]"

The man who ignited this firestorm was soon working on a book about the massacre. In late January 1970 Hersh met with senior officers at the Pentagon, requesting information about My Lai. He warned them the army would not like his book. The military realized that preventing him from publishing it was impossible. Nevertheless, in a confidential memorandum obtained by Michael Bilton and Kevin Sim, one senior officer, who said he did not want the army and the Department of Defense to become "patsies for Hersh, Ridenhour and Co.," urged the military to "cut this guy's water off at the Pentagon end."

The Pentagon had already taken a much more constructive step to deal with what threatened to become a public relations disaster. On 24 November 1969, Chief of Staff Westmoreland summoned to his office Lieutenant General William R. Peers, head of the Office of Reserve Components. Westmoreland told Peers that he and Secretary of the Army Stanley Resor wanted a formal investigation of the My Lai affair and believed Peers should run it. In a formal memorandum two days later, they instructed him to "explore the nature and the scope of the original U.S. Army investigation(s) of the alleged [massacre]" and to determine "the adequacy of the investigations or inquiries of this subject, their subsequent reviews and reports within the chain of command, and possible suppression or withholding of information by persons involved in the incident." Peers, was, he recalls, "not exactly overjoyed with the prospects of this new assignment." He knew nothing about My Lai beyond what he had read in the newspapers until Westmoreland gave him a copy of Ridenhour's letter. It "stunned" him. At first he "found it hard to believe that an incident such as Ridenhour described not only could have happened but could have remained hidden for so long."

The next day Peers met with Colonel Wilson, who told him about the interviews he had conducted and gave him a copy of his report. The general concluded Wilson should be part of his investigating panel. Westmoreland and Resor, who wanted it to have civilian representation, suggested Peers make Bland West, an assistant general counsel of the army, his deputy, and West proposed also including someone else from his office. The uniformed military members selected were Colonel Robert W. Miller, chief of the international division of the Judge Advocate General's Office, Major E. F. Zuchowski, an experienced investigator from the Office of the Provost Marshall, and Lieutenant Colonel James H. Breen, a skilled administrative officer, then assigned to the Office of the Deputy Chief of Staff for Operations. "Very soon after the panel members were assembled, the philosophy of the Inquiry was clearly established," Peers reports. All agreed their job was simply to ascertain and report the facts. It was not "to be concerned about what effects the inquiry might have on the army's image."

Peers was concerned about appearances, though. Two days after his panel met for the first time, on Thanksgiving Day, Westmoreland asked him how he would feel about having a civilian lawyer or judge observe its proceedings. Peers did not really want one looking over his shoulder, but after giving the matter some thought, he agreed that the right civilian could serve a useful purpose. In a 30 November memorandum to Westmoreland and Resor, he noted that Congress and the American people had expressed intense interest in whether there had been a cover-up of the My Lai incident. "I believe that the public recognition of the inquiry and its effectiveness would be prompted if I had available to me a distinguished jurist of impeccable integrity," Peers wrote. The lawyer selected was Robert MacCrate, a partner at Sullivan and Cromwell, a prestigious Wall Street law firm, who had been active in the naval reserve from 1943 to 1946. At Mac-Crate's suggestion Jerome Walsh, who had worked closely with him at Sullivan and Cromwell and was now a partner in his own New York firm, also joined the panel. He, too, had prior military experience, having served as a lieutenant in the 82nd Airborne Division in 1953–54. It took Walsh and MacCrate a while to pick up current military terminology and jargon, but according to Peers "they fit right in." Both lawyers were tireless workers who had a firm sense that "right is right, wrong is wrong."

As the inquiry progressed, Peers added still more people to his team. Needing someone with tactical experience to interrogate ground troops, he obtained Colonel Joseph R. (Ross) Franklin from the Office of the Deputy Chief of Staff for Operations. Peers recruited Colonels Thomas F. Whalen and James H. Patterson to oversee the collection and handling of documents and Major Joseph Apici to head a witness section. "As the Inquiry progressed its scope was expanded, and the number of people assigned to it increased many times over," Peers reports. By the time his panel completed its investigation in March 1970, it had a staff of ninety-two.

The Peers Commission believed, "It was *not* our job to determine innocence or guilt of individuals." Although preparations for Calley's court-martial were going forward while the commission was conducting its investigation, the man who "was the focus of most of the public's attention on My Lai . . . played almost no role in that inquiry." Calley did make one brief appearance before the panel on 5 December 1969, but on the advice of Latimer, he answered only one question. "To the best of my knowledge and recollection," he testified, neither Colonel Henderson nor Lieutenant Colonel Barker had ever asked him about the My Lai operation.

While unable to question Calley fully, the Peers Commission did interrogate numerous other individuals involved in the My Lai affair. "The small number of witnesses we had anticipated calling expanded into hundreds," the general recalls. These had to be examined quickly, for the two-year statute of limitations applicable to the sorts of offenses with which those involved in a cover-up might be charged (such as false reporting and misprision of felony) would run on 15 March 1970. The panel's mandate was to check out reports on and investigations of the massacre, rather than the crimes committed by the participants, but it quickly realized that the officers on whom it intended to focus lacked firsthand knowledge of what had transpired in My Lai (4) and that their reporting of events could not be evaluated without questioning men who had been there. After lengthy discussions with the Chief of Staff and the army's general counsel, the panel received permission to seek testimony from those directly involved in the massacre. Some had left the army, and the Peers Commission was powerless to compel those men to appear. To give it that authority would have required converting the commission into a court of inquiry, which could be done only by formally designating "parties" whose conduct was being investigated. All of those parties would then have the right to be present and cross-examine other witnesses. Because of the large number of possible wrongdoers in the My Lai affair, this seemed likely to turn the proceedings into a three-ring circus.

The fact that the commission's inquiry did not target particular individuals also prevented it from giving witnesses lie detector tests, for army regulations permitted polygraph results to be used as evidence only if both parties agreed, and there was no respondent to give the required consent. The men who testified were advised of their right to remain silent and told that if they chose to talk, they could give either a sworn statement (which might be used against them later at a court-martial) or an unsworn one. After each witness finished his testimony, Peers instructed him not to discuss it with anyone. That included the press.

The man Peers would like to have heard from first was Lieutenant Colonel Barker, but he had been dead since a helicopter accident six weeks after the massacre. Hence, the commission started with Colonel Henderson, whom Wilson had found to be both knowledgeable and cooperative. He deceived Peers and his colleagues. The testimony of other witnesses, along with logs and letters that the commission unearthed, "developed a sequence of events . . . that was at considerable variance" with Henderson's version, necessitating that he be recalled for three days of additional interrogation. Sometimes the Commission encountered a witness like Hugh Thompson, who "had maintained his basic integrity . . . , who knew right from wrong and acted accordingly," but such men were bright spots in a "generally bleak and depressing picture."

The exceptional Thompson so impressed Peers that he decided to take the pilot along on a visit to Vietnam. In late December, leaving about half of his staff in Washington to continue interrogating witnesses, the general, accompanied by MacCrate and Walsh, led the other half to Southeast Asia on a mission to tour Task Force Barker's area of operations, locate pertinent documents, and find and question Vietnamese familiar with what had happened at My Lai (4). In addition, Peers admits, "We wanted to satisfy some members of Congress and the American people that we were willing to investigate in South Vietnam itself." Strangely, the South Vietnamese government did not want them to do this. Peers found it anxious "to play down the incident in order to minimize any disruptive effect it might have on U.S.–South Vietnamese relations." Nevertheless, his team talked with two ARVN enlisted men who had acted as interpreters for Charlie Company, with several officers, including two who had filed reports on the massacre, and with a number of civilians who had been in My Lai (4) on 16 March. It also interviewed some American soldiers connected with the incident, who had returned to Vietnam for second tours, and CIA personnel attached to the Quang Ngai Province advisory staff. With Thompson flying him, Peers conducted two aerial reconnaissances of the My Lai area, and on 3 January his team visited what was now "for all practical purposes . . . a dead village."

The most frustrating aspect of the team's trip to Vietnam was its failure to find most of the crucial documents the commission sought. Files pertaining to the 16 March operation were missing from the headquarters of the Americal Division, the 11th Brigade, and the artillery battery that had provided Charlie Company's fire support. So were all but two of the reports relating to Henderson's investigation. The Peers Commission never found the missing documents. Hersh later determined, he reports in his book *Cover-Up* (1972), that senior officers of the Americal Division had destroyed them sometime after May 1969, apparently to protect their predecessors.

They were not the only ones trying to hide the truth from the Peers Commission. Just before and early in its inquiry, Henderson and General Koster talked by telephone about investigations and reports concerning which they might be questioned. Peers viewed these conversations as "a continuation of the efforts to mislead and deceive." Having gathered evidence which suggested that many witnesses had engaged in such efforts, the panel recalled between twenty-five and thirty of them in late February and early March. Each was warned of his rights, advised of any suspicions about him, and given an opportunity to seek legal counsel. Approximately half asked for lawyers. Most of the recalled witnesses repeated their original testimony, but four—including both the intelligence and operations officers of Task Force Barker and the operations officer of the 11th Brigade—invoked the privilege against compulsory self-incrimination. That outraged Peers, who believed "any Regular Army officer who refuses to testify in a war-crimes situation is not worthy to hold the commission or wear the uniform."

Despite receiving less than full cooperation from many former

11th Brigade and American Division officers, the Peers Commission completed its investigation in time to get a report to the printer by 14 March. While hastening to finish that narrative, it also assembled transcripts of the testimony it had heard and six books of documentary evidence. The panel had an unwritten rule that during its inquiry no one would discuss its findings with outsiders. To soften the blow that was coming, however, in mid-February Peers sent Resor and Westmoreland a short preliminary report. An abrupt and brutal summary of atrocities, cover-up, and dereliction of duty, it hit the secretary "like a bolt from the blue."

Resor summoned Peers and McCrate to his office, and while the general insists he made no attempt to control the contents of the final report, the secretary did "have some suggestions for minimizing what might be termed emotionalism or overly strong language." For example, he urged toning down some vivid descriptions of rapes and characterizing the Vietnamese who had been shot as "noncombatant casualties" rather than women, children, babies, and old men. Concern for the army's image also inspired a request from its chief of information (acting, Peers suspected, on instructions from the secretary's office and the general counsel) to delete the word "massacre" from a prepared statement he planned to make at a 17 March press conference, called to announce the results of his panel's inquiry. Feeling "strongly that we had to inform the public or else we would be deceptive," the general responded that he "was not about to present a watered-down version, . . . and if that is what they wanted, to leave me out." Finally, Walsh suggested substituting "tragedy of major proportions," a phrase used elsewhere in the statement, for "massacre." After checking with "the top level," the chief of information agreed to that characterization of what had happened at My Lai.

No amount of Pentagon spin control could neutralize the devastating contents of the 225-page report. "During the period 16–19 March 1968," the Peers Commission concluded, troops from Task Force Barker "had massacred a large number of noncombatants in . . . Son My Village." The panel had been unable to determine precisely how many Vietnamese these soldiers had killed, but it was "at least 175 and may exceed 400." Although commanders within Task Force Barker and the 11th Brigade "had substantial knowledge as to the extent of the killing of non-combatants," only a small portion of what they knew was communicated to the commanding general of the division. Nevertheless, the panel concluded, Koster possessed sufficient information "concerning the highly irregular nature of the operations of TF Barker on 16 March 1968 . . . to require that a thorough investigation be conducted." Instead, "At every command level within the American Division, actions were taken, both wittingly and unwittingly, which effectively suppressed information concerning the war crimes committed at Son My village." In combination with "the false and misleading reports" of Colonel Henderson, these had been "successful in containing the story of Son My within the division."

The panel identified thirty individuals it believed had kept that story hidden by deliberately suppressing relevant information and/or by failing, although aware that serious offenses had been committed, to file reports about them, order investigations suggested by the circumstances, or follow up on those investigations that were conducted. Its list of wrongdoers reached from Generals Koster and Young down to Sergeant Haeberle and SP-5 Roberts. It included Lieutenant Calley.

Westmoreland designated Colonel Hubert Miller of the Office of the Judge Advocate General to draft charges against those whose conduct merited prosecution. Because war crimes were being handled by the CID, Miller was authorized to move only against soldiers alleged to have committed such military offenses as dereliction in investigation and reporting. He filed charges against eleven of the officers the Peers Commission had condemned, including both Henderson and Koster. Feeling that there were others on the list whose conduct merited courts-martial, two panel members, Colonel Robert Miller and Lieutenant Colonel Charles Bauer, each prepared charges against two additional officers. Those they targeted included General Young, Major Calhoun, and Chaplain Lewis. Unwilling to prosecute a clergyman,

Resor dropped the case against Lewis. Neither Calley nor Medina was among those charged at the conclusion of the Peers Commission's inquiry because both were already facing trial by court-martial.

Although it did not affect Calley directly, release of the Peers Commission's report added to the furor swirling around his case. According to the United States Court of Military Review, "The publicity engendered by the My Lai incident was massive and made the court-martial of Lieutenant Calley a *cause celebre*." Revelation of the massacre unleashed what Richard Hammer characterizes as a "wave of revulsion [that] seemed to sweep through the nation and around the world." Predictably, My Lai was condemned in Communist countries. A statement signed by twenty-four Soviet intellectuals, including composer Dmitry Shostakovich and Nobel Prize–winning physicist Nikolai Semenov, accused the American military of following in the footsteps of Nazi war criminals. Even in countries friendly to the United States, politicians and the press reacted with horror and revulsion. Prime Minister Harold Wilson of Great Britain found himself under intense pressure inside his own Labor Party, as well as from the Conservative opposition, to condemn My Lai and back off from his support of U.S. Vietnam policy. In The Hague, *Het Vrije Volk* viewed the massacre as proof that this policy was bankrupt. Although the criticism softened by mid-December, even America's allies remained dismayed about My Lai.

Like many of the critics abroad, American doves viewed the massacre and cover-up as evidence that America's Vietnam policy was fatally flawed. Reporters for the *Wall Street Journal* found, "To a man, the people who want to pull out of Vietnam immediately say the incident [appalls] them and reaffirms their conviction that the U.S. has no business in Vietnam." A group of dovish lawyers and law professors, headed by former Supreme Court justice and U.S. ambassador to the United Nations Arthur Goldberg, contended that My Lai raised the issue of the extent to which the war was "being conducted in a manner inconsistent with . . . minimum humanitarian standards." The *New Yorker* saw America "quietly choking on the blood of innocents." Comparisons with Nazi atrocities were common. In a book provocatively entitled *Nuremberg and Vietnam: An American Tragedy*, Telford Taylor, a law professor who had once prosecuted leaders of Hitler's Germany, asserted that "accounts of the conduct of American troops . . . at Son My in March, 1968, have stung the national conscience."

They did not sting the consciences of many hawks. Supporters of the war were inclined to regard the killing of civilians at My Lai as an inevitable by-product of warfare. Hawks also blamed the enemy for such tragedies. "If the Vietcong chooses to build its stronghold under a village, and the villagers, either through choice or coercion, continue to reside in the village, some perhaps to cooperate with the VC, does that mean the stronghold is immune from attack?" asked *National Review*. One *Newsweek* reader wrote that those who "succor the communists in their organized subversion" should not expect "treatment different from that . . . received at Pinkville." The *Birmingham News* ran a cartoon (which President Nixon liked) depicting a tiny American soldier, labeled "Alleged Village Massacre," and a vastly larger and more menacing infantryman, labeled "Communist Atrocities as Standard Operating Procedure." Many hawks went beyond minimizing the massacre to question whether there had really been one. "I don't believe it actually happened," a Los Angeles salesman told the *Wall Street Journal*.

Public opinion polls revealed that a substantial percentage of Americans shared his skepticism. A statewide survey in Minnesota, conducted for the *Minneapolis Tribune* in late December, found almost half of those interviewed did not believe the reports of mass murder at My Lai. Only 13 percent thought that, even if there had been a massacre, the GIs involved were to blame for it. Asked whether soldiers who took part in the shooting of women and children in Vietnamese villages should be punished, 48 percent of those interviewed for a Gallup poll in early December said no, exactly twice as many as answered yes.

Americans seemed inclined to assign responsibility for whatever had happened at My Lai (4) to the Vietnam War itself rather than to the men of Charlie Company. By the time Hersh exposed the massacre, the war was becoming increasingly unpopular. As Robert Schulzinger writes, "War-weariness . . . washed over the United States in 1968 and 1969." Disaffected with the Vietnam conflict, many people blamed it for the civilian casualties at My Lai (4). Senator George McGovern insisted the massacre was a result of "the futility and uselessness of this war." Only 12 percent of those interviewed by the *Minneapolis Tribune* considered the grunts who had slaughtered the inhabitants of My Lai (4) responsible. They had been forced to fight a war nobody wanted, that had no front lines, and in which identifying the enemy was often impossible. "Everyone knows a guerilla war such as is being waged in Vietnam is full of ambiguities," the conservative *National Review* observed. The United States had pulverized the Vietnamese countryside with bombs and artillery fire and dispatched infantrymen on "search-and-destroy" missions. Why should it now hold those soldiers accountable for the destruction of Son My? "There can be no doubt that such an atrocity was possible only because a number of other methods of killing civilians and destroying their villages had come to be the rule, and not the exception, in our conduct of the war," editorialized the liberal *New Yorker*. As *Time* saw it, America itself must stand in "the dock of guilt and conscience for what happened at My Lai."

On the other hand, Lieutenant Calley should *not* be standing in the dock of a military court, many Americans believed. According to a *Time* poll in early January, a majority of them felt "considerable sympathy" for the accused mass murderer. "Why are they picking on you . . . ?" a Vietnam veteran asked in a letter to Calley. He claimed to have participated in a similar incident himself. So did veterans of World War II and the Korean conflict, who also wrote to express their support. According to Calley, he received approximately 5,000 letters, and "only about 10 of them were derogatory to me." Many correspondents invited him to their homes. "I had letters from the John Birchers and the American Legion and the Civil Liberties Union," Calley reports. "All of them asking, 'How can I help?'" Mail also poured into the Pentagon, which received about 500 letters per week; by early February the total had reached 4,500. Fifty percent of these supported Calley. Twenty-five percent expressed opposition to the army's plan to court-martial the former platoon leader.

The Nixon administration had no desire to upset the people by punishing Calley. Its principal concern was ensuring that re-action to the My Lai massacre did not erode public support for its Vietnam policy. During his campaign for the presidency, Nixon had claimed to have a plan to end the war. After taking office in early 1969, he continued the Paris peace talks with the enemy that his predecessor had initiated; he also adopted a policy of "Vietnamization," which involved applying military pressure on North Vietnam, while training and equipping the Saigon government to defend itself and gradually withdrawing U.S. forces. Although popular with the public, troop withdrawals had a disastrous impact on the morale of soldiers in the field; no one wanted to be the last man killed or wounded in a futile war his country was in the process of abandoning. Military drug use increased dramatically. So did the number of mutinies (called "combat refusals" by the army). Numerous grunts simply refused to go out on hazardous search-and-destroy missions. While recognizing that the war had to be ended reasonably soon, the president and his national security adviser, Henry Kissinger, were unwilling simply to bring all American troops home immediately. Both men insisted the United States could not abandon the Saigon government and those South Vietnamese dependent on American protection. Although believing that military victory was unattainable, they were determined to pull out of Vietnam only when a negotiated settlement ended the fighting. To pressure the Communist side into a peace agreement, Nixon ordered intensive bombing of North Vietnamese sanctuaries in neutral Cambodia.

His "peace with honor" strategy was initially popular. An April 1969 Gallup poll found 44 percent of adults approved of the president's handling of the war, while only 26 percent disapproved. As the fighting dragged on, and American forces, although shrinking, continued to suffer heavy casualties, opposition to his approach mounted. By September, 52 percent of Americans were expressing dissatisfaction with Nixon's conduct of the war, while only 35 percent supported him. The percentage having no opinion was down from 30 to 13. In June a mere 29 percent of Americans favored immediate withdrawal. By September that was up to 36 percent. After dropping briefly in November, the number rebounded to 35 percent in February 1970, and by September it was 55 percent.

As the public's mood soured, the antiwar movement gathered strength. Presidents of seventy-nine colleges called on Nixon to step up the timetable for withdrawal of U.S. forces, and congressional doves accused him of pointlessly prolonging the fighting. Between 24 September and 15 October, they introduced eleven antiwar resolutions. These included proposals by Senator Charles Goodell (R. N.Y.) to cut off funding for U.S. forces by December 1970; by Senators Jacob Javits (R. N.Y.) and Claiborne Pell (D. R.I.) to pull the troops out by then and repeal the Gulf of Tonkin Resolution; and by Senators Mark Hatfield (R. Ore.) and Frank Church (D. Idaho) for immediate withdrawal. On 15 October antiwar activists staged a nationwide one-day moratorium on customary activities, which enlisted widespread support among college students and middle-class adults. There were Moratorium Day rallies of 20,000 people in New York's financial district; 30,000 on the New Haven Green; 50,000 at the Washington Monument; and 100,000 on the Boston Common. Dozens of locations witnessed massive candlelight marches, among them the street in front of the White House.

A month later, just as the My Lai story was breaking, the New Mobilization Committee to End the War in Vietnam mounted another massive protest. This one featured a "March Against Death," in which thousands of demonstrators, each carrying a candle and a sign bearing the name of a man killed in the war, trudged the four miles from Arlington National Cemetery to the White House, there to speak aloud the name on the sign. The march began on the night of Thursday, 13 November, and continued until Saturday morning. Later that day 500,000 people rallied near the Washington Monument in the largest demonstration yet against the Vietnam War. Another 200,000 protesters massed in San Francisco.

Two of Nixon's top aides—his chief of staff, H. R. "Bob" Haldeman, and his domestic affairs adviser, John Ehrlichman— spent the whole first night of the March Against Death hunkered down in the White House. It was obvious the administration was concerned about the antiwar movement, which by the fall of 1969 had become the focus of the president's attention. He believed that the more divided the country seemed, the less willing the enemy would be to negotiate an end to the war. Hence, it was essential to blunt the "attack" of the antiwar movement.

Nixon made a major effort to do that with a speech to the nation on 3 November. Entitled "The President's Pursuit of Peace," it was intended to energize the "silent majority" that he believed favored his policies. To ensure its effectiveness, the White House developed a postspeech game plan that included supportive addresses by legislators and show business personalities, newspaper ads, letter-writing campaigns, pro-war street demonstrations, and declaration of a "National Unity Week" (to begin on 14 November), as well as verbal and legal attacks on the antiwar movement. This effort to rally the country behind the president proved quite successful. The White House was deluged with supportive phone calls and telegrams. While acknowledging that Haldeman's operatives had whipped up some of this enthusiasm, Kissinger insisted the outpouring of support "went far beyond the capacities of even the White House public relations geniuses." Polls revealed that 77 percent of Americans were pleased with Nixon's speech and that approval for his conduct of the war had increased.

Just when things were going well for the president, and on the very day that the March Against Death began, Hersh broke the My Lai story. Nixon already knew about the massacre, although it is not clear how long he had been aware of it. According to Press Secretary Ron Ziegler, the president had been informed in August, but another presidential assistant, Patrick Buchanan, acknowledged in a 5 December memorandum that Nixon had actually known about it much earlier. Kissinger had recommended distancing the White House from the whole matter, however, and on 25 November Ziegler told reporters that "there is no White House involvement."

Public reaction to the flood of revelations about the massacre made that position problematic. Although the Pentagon was looking into the incident, Nixon aide Clark Mollenhoff doubted that its investigations and prosecutions would be "carried through in an effective and fully coordinated manner." While the Defense Department had "primary responsibility in this matter," he wrote in a 5 January 1970 memo to the president, "I have little faith in the Pentagon bureaucracy doing [what] . . . is essential to protect the President from mistakes of fact or misjudgments that can be highly embarrassing." The Defense Department needed to seize opportunities "to get its side of the story some publicity," the White House believed. Someone on the president's staff should be assigned to monitor all of the investigations and prosecutions and given full access to all records and the authority "to raise questions relative to any and all facts developed within the Executive branch," Mollenhoff recommended.

The problem, as Nixon himself saw it, was that My Lai threatened to "harm" public support for the war, destroying the accomplishments of his 3 November speech and the national unity offensive. "I felt that many of the commentators and congressmen who professed outrage about My Lai were not really as interested in the moral questions raised by the Calley case as they were interested in using it to make political attacks against the Vietnam War," he wrote later in his memoirs. At the time, Nixon privately condemned the press for bringing the massacre to light. In an attempt to undercut the president's critics, Ziegler reminded reporters that "this alleged incident occurred some ten months before this Administration came into office." Nixon too, while acknowledging that there had been "what appears certainly a massacre," noted that it had occurred on Johnson's watch. He insisted what had happened at My Lai was contrary to U.S. military policy and sought to minimize its significance. On 8 December, after assuring reporters that this was "an isolated incident," the president emphasized "the other side of the coin": that 1.2 million Americans had served in Vietnam, 40,000 had died there, and "virtually all of them have helped the people of Vietnam in one way or another."

Nixon also resisted calls for creation of a presidential commission to investigate the massacre and study the broader problem of war crimes in Vietnam. Buchanan advised him that the existence of such a panel would undercut his argument that the atrocities committed at My Lai were "isolated exceptions." Not all of Nixon's aides agreed. Daniel Patrick Moynihan (the token Democrat on the White House staff) endorsed the proposal of Arthur Goldberg and thirty-three other attorneys and professors for the president to "appoint a special commission of distinguished civilians and military general officers to launch a broad investigation of . . . the My Lai incident and . . . a broad range of military-civilian governmental operations and policy guidelines." Moynihan, who had been deeply moved by Meadlo's interview on CBS, feared the social consequences of an incident that could be misperceived as the product of a corrupt society. He considered it a grave error for the presidency to remain silent while the press and the army passed judgment on My Lai. Kissinger was more worried about the possible effect of further revelations on the country's ability to continue the war in Vietnam. His staff firmly opposed Goldberg's idea, and Nixon rejected it. "I do not believe that a civilian commission at this time would be useful," the president told reporters on 8 December.

His stated reason was that "the matter is now in the Judicial process," and defense attorneys might properly argue that such an inquiry prejudiced their clients' rights. Coming from a president who had announced publicly his belief in the guilt of such high-profile criminal defendants as Charles Manson and Angela Davis, it was a somewhat hypocritical justification, but one likely to win favor with the large segment of the public that believed intense publicity had irrevocably harmed those accused of crimes allegedly committed at My Lai. One expression of that sentiment was a 10 December letter from the American Civil Liberties Union (ACLU) to Secretary of Defense Melvin Laird calling for dismissal of all charges against Calley because press coverage had made it impossible for him to get a fair trial.

While the ACLU fought to protect the lieutenant's rights, Nixon went after the men who had uncovered his crimes. During a 1 December meeting with Haldeman, he apparently hatched the idea of a White House effort to discredit Ron Ridenhour. By the seventeenth an aide to the chief of staff, Alexander Butterfield, had prepared a memorandum for the president that "responds to your request for a report on Ridenhour." It disclosed that two other presidential assistants, Bryce Harlow and Lynn Nofziger, were discussing what member of Congress to enlist in an effort to discredit him. Butterfield also reported that Ehrlichman had procured an investigator, who had been "sent into the field where he remains today." He informed the president (inaccurately) that Ridenhour was incensed because Hersh had realized financial gain at his expense and was looking for a lawyer to help him sue the journalist. After reading Butterfield's memorandum, Nixon asked "whether a good news reporter shouldn't be put to work on this." He also suggested making use of "our California boy," David R. Hunter, the executive director of the Edgar B. Stern Family Fund, from which Hersh had received a $1,000 grant to support his research.

Among those in Congress whom Nixon's aides considered likely allies in their campaign to discredit Ridenhour was Representative H. Edward Hébert (D. La.), who had "recently been given the My Lai project" by Congressman L. Mendel Rivers (D. S.C.), the hawkish chair of the powerful House Armed Services Committee. The firestorm ignited by Hersh's revelations had spread quickly to Capitol Hill, where several Senate and House committees vied for the right to investigate the My Lai incident. The winner of this struggle for the spotlight was Rivers, who on 24 November announced that his committee's Investigative Subcommittee would look into the charges of a massacre. That was, of course, the same day that Resor disclosed creation of the Peers Commission. Not about to be upstaged by an army inquiry, Rivers hastily convened a hearing of the full Armed Services Committee. Between 26 November and 10 December, it took testimony from a number of individuals, including Thompson and Medina. Among those Rivers's committee questioned were General Peers and his civilian legal adviser, Robert MacCrate. During an appearance on December 9 they briefed the committee on their assignment and explained how unexpectedly large it had proved to be.

Aware that some congressmen had expressed strong reservations about the army investigating itself, Peers offered assurances that his inquiry would be conducted in a fair and impartial manner. What he promised may not have been what Rivers wanted. As Peers was leaving, the chairman asked him to come by his office two days later. During an 0700 meeting, he seemed to be trying to protect those accused of committing war crimes at My Lai. Rivers mentioned how difficult it was to distinguish Vietcong from other Vietnamese and how women and children aided the VC by doing such things as planting mines and booby traps. "While we were talking about the My Lai operation," Peers recalls, "he said, in effect, 'You know our boys would never do anything like that.'" The general "felt it had been a good meeting," but the obvious bias of Rivers, "who always supported the men and women in uniform," made it unlikely that Congress would conduct an objective inquiry into the My Lai incident.

The hearings Rivers held generated more heat than light. Although witnesses testified in executive session, they and committee members talked freely to reporters, giving statements that often contradicted one another. Disturbed by the resulting public confusion, on 11 December Rivers named a special panel of the Armed Services Investigative Subcommittee to delve further into the My Lai affair. It consisted of Samuel Stratton (D. N.Y.), William Dickinson (R. Ala.), and Charles Gubser (R. Calif.), with Hébert as chair. Like the man who picked him, Hébert was a hawk; in March 1968 he had openly advocated the use of tactical nuclear weapons in Vietnam.

In a 19 December directive, Rivers instructed Hébert's panel to "examine all pertinent documents and take the testimony of such witnesses as might be necessary to permit you to make a full report to me as soon as possible" on both the massacre and the army's investigation of it. Hébert soon found himself in a conflict with the Peers Commission that escalated into "a constitutional dispute between the My Lai Incident Subcommittee . . . and the Department of Defense." Peers asked the Armed

Services Committee to call no witnesses his team had not already interrogated, but in mid-December the subcommittee began requesting testimony from men it had not yet questioned. Resor wrote to Hébert on 19 December, 6 January, and 14 April to express his belief that "discharge of our own responsibility to execute the laws will be imperiled by such actions as your subcommittee now contemplates." The secretary furnished Hébert's group with the findings and recommendations of the Peers Commission, and he also promised to provide it with transcripts of testimony by the witnesses in whom the subcommittee was interested, so it would have "an adequate basis for . . . independent review of those conclusions." Because most of the civilian and military personnel Hébert's panel wanted to interrogate had either been charged with crimes or were material witnesses, however, Resor urged it to defer questioning them until that could be done without prejudicing defendants in court-martial cases. Saying the subcommittee was "right on the edge of revolt," the chairman refused and issued subpoenas to those it wanted to question. Hébert's panel eventually interviewed over 150 witnesses. In a report released on 15 July 1970, it lambasted the army for frustrating its investigation, citing the military's failure to cooperate as the primary reason that producing the document had taken so long.

The subcommittee's heavily edited fifty-three-page report was not the favorable assessment of its handling of the My Lai matter for which the army had hoped and that it had pressured Hébert to provide. According to the Louisiana legislator, "they" called him day after day—on Capitol Hill, at his home in Alexandria, Louisiana, at his daughter's house, and even at a Boston hospital where he spent some time recuperating from eye surgery. Despite these tactics, Hébert's subcommittee, while characterizing the massacre as "foreign to the normal character and actions" of America's armed forces, accused the military and State Department personnel of making a concerted effort to suppress evidence. It recommended that in the future the army appoint qualified investigators from outside the chain of command to look into alleged war crimes.

Although its report was critical of the way the military had handled the My Lai investigation, Hébert's subcommittee seemed more interested in discrediting those who had exposed the war crimes committed at My Lai than in ensuring that those responsible for them were punished. When its hearings began on 15 April, the subcommittee announced its intention to "studiously avoid any efforts to fix criminal responsibility for the death of any civilians at My Lai 4." It would leave "judgments in that area" to the military courts. The subcommittee also announced that it would examine all witnesses in executive session, in an "effort to avoid any prejudice to the rights" of men who had been or might be charged with criminal offenses.

Hébert's solicitude for potential defendants extended beyond merely ensuring that the subcommittee did not deprive them of a fair trial. When Congressman Stratton bore down on Medina concerning what instructions he had issued to his troops, the chairman intervened to protect the witness, insisting that subject had been covered in a statement he had given the panel earlier. The subcommittee allowed Colonel Henderson to make a prepared statement that, he acknowledged, did "not go to any of the facts involved in this matter presently under inquiry." Then it accepted his blanket refusal, on advice of counsel, to respond to any questions on the subject, allowing him to avoid invoking his constitutional rights in response to specific ones. When Stratton subjected General Koster to what his lawyer regarded as excessively rigorous cross-examination, Hébert instructed his colleague to "ask him affirmative questions, without an effort to impeach his testimony."

Ronald Haeberle and Hugh Thompson received much different treatment. The subcommittee subjected Haeberle to exhaustive questioning regarding his failure to report the My Lai incident and also badgered him about why he had been carrying two cameras and what he had intended to do with the pictures he took with the one that belonged to him. When Hébert thought the former combat photographer was being non-responsive, he informed him, "We are going to keep asking you the questions until you respond and answer." Gubser badgered Haeberle about whether the pictures he had taken with his personal camera should have been considered classified, and Stratton about whether these were government property. Hébert grilled Haeberle concerning how his photographs had come to be published in the *Cleveland Plain Dealer* and *Life* and about the financial arrangements he had made with the newspapers and magazines in which they had appeared. Counsel John Reddan accused him of publishing them "for a buck," and the subcommittee required Haeberle to turn over his tax records and return for two more rounds of questioning.

General Peers characterized the grilling of Thompson as "more of an inquisition than an investigation." Hébert interrogated him mercilessly about whether he had ordered his crew to shoot at other American soldiers. Thompson also endured extended questioning concerning the medal he had received for his actions on 16 March and those for which he had recommended his crewmen. The citations for all three stated that the civilians the helicopter crew had rescued were trapped between friendly and enemy forces, but since Thompson's handwritten recommendations had been retyped and signed by someone else, who might have altered them, it was difficult to understand why Reddan made so much of these false statements. It is also difficult to understand why Hébert excoriated the pilot for talking to Larry Colburn outside the hearing room, when their conversation seems to have been intended only to pin down the precise date on which they had talked jointly with someone else, or why the subcommittee devoted approximately one-fourth of its report to Thompson's verbatim testimony.

When the chopper pilot began his testimony, Hébert told him that the subcommittee was "not fixing blame on anybody for an illegal act. We are protecting, as far as we can, the individuals involved in the courts-martial now pending." The subcommittee was, he claimed, shielding the prosecution as well as the accused, but that did not appear to be the case. While it was holding its hearings, Representative Rivers gave a speech in which he expressed disgust with the many courts-martial of soldiers allegedly involved in the massacre, and the report issued by Hébert's panel suggested the subcommittee agreed with him. It accused the Pentagon of overreacting when it finally decided to pursue allegations that war crimes had been committed at My Lai (4) and of charging several officers prematurely. The subcommittee's report also recommended that all persons accused of war crimes be subjected to a psychiatric examination, and in a 16 July press conference, Hébert remarked that the soldiers alleged to have committed atrocities at My Lai should have been allowed to plead not guilty by reason of insanity.

In addition, he refused to turn over to the military transcripts of the testimony taken by his subcommittee. Secretary Resor asked for these after the hearings ended, but Hébert turned him down, claiming it had been possible to obtain "frank and complete" statements from witnesses only by "assuring them that their testimony would not be disclosed voluntarily to anyone outside the subcommittee." There were important constitutional and policy reasons for giving such assurances. While the Fifth Amendment protected witnesses from having to incriminate themselves, it did not insulate them from embarrassment or protect them from harassment by the media. "Now this subcommittee takes this position, that your privacy is paramount," Hébert assured General Koster. Also, as Koster's lawyer, Edward Bennet Williams, pointed out, if prosecutors obtained a defendant's answers even to questions that were not incriminating, they would gain access to "defensive materials," giving them an unfair procedural advantage. The subcommittee would in effect be doing their discovery for them.

But Hébert would not even honor subpoenas from military courts for subcommittee transcripts. He treated the transcripts as classified documents and refused to allow their release "until final disposition has been made of all criminal cases now pending which may arise from the My Lai affair." Because the government was denying defense attorneys access to material they needed for cross-examination, the military judge in Sergeant Mitchell's court-martial refused to let four key prosecution witnesses testify. That fatally weakened the case against Mitchell, leading to his acquittal. Representative Abner Mikva (D. Ill.) of the House Judiciary Committee sharply criticized Hébert, but Hébert insisted that withholding the transcripts was necessary to avoid influencing pending military cases. Of course, *not* making them available also influenced those cases, making it more difficult to convict soldiers accused of criminal conduct.

For a politician that was not a bad thing. The press and the Peers Commission had flooded the channels of communication with information about My Lai, but even many of those who were outraged about the massacre seemed unenthusiastic about prosecuting the soldiers who had allegedly perpetrated it. The Nixon administration viewed the Calley case as an embarrassment that threatened to undermine support for its war effort. Many ordinary Americans considered it unjust. An Atlanta policewoman, interviewed by the *Wall Street Journal*, probably spoke for much of the country when she declared, "I don't think it was right, what he did," but "I don't think he should be tried."

CHAPTER 8

Court-Martialed

"I'm going to ask you in the name of the United States Government, in the interest of justice, to convict the accused and find him guilty of all specifications," Captain Aubrey Daniel told the officers constituting the court that would try Lieutenant Calley. It was 17 November 1970, and the legal proceeding that many Americans believed should not take place was getting under way. "The trial will be lengthy," prosecutor Daniel warned. It would also be immensely significant. Among the courts-martial of the Vietnam era, only that of Captain Howard Levy (an army dermatologist, prosecuted for refusing to train Green Beret medics and allegedly urging enlisted men not to fight) rivaled it in importance.

What made the Calley case so significant was that it had become the focal point of the national debate over My Lai. During the spring of 1970 the Pentagon and the Department of Justice discussed the possibility of a mass trial, in which all charges against everyone accused of crimes related to the massacre would be disposed of at once. Proponents of this approach argued that, like a court of inquiry, such a proceeding would get all the facts out at one time and resolve the entire incident. While a mass trial appealed to Justice Department lawyers, the prospect of having over two dozen American soldiers, including generals, in the dock together horrified the army. Such a proceeding would be too reminiscent of Nuremberg, and it would undercut the claims of the military and the president that My Lai was an aberration. Each alleged wrongdoer had to be tried separately, the army insisted.

Calley was not the first of those to face a court-martial, but his case had received the most publicity. Hence, it would bear the full weight of a national controversy. It would become one of the longest trials in American military history. Well before it ended, Daniel would establish that U.S. troops had massacred civilians at My Lai (4) and that William Calley was a mass murderer.

Calley's historic court-martial took place in a small fifty-nine-seat courtroom at Fort Benning, decorated in patriotic red, white, and blue. The judge sat between an American flag and one emblazoned with the infantry's "Follow Me" motto. In front and to the left of the bench, at a long wooden defense table, "Calley sat like a child in [a] large cushioned chair . . . facing the judge," reported Richard Hammer, who covered the trial for the *New York Times*. "His feet seemed barely to reach the floor." The defendant sat there from "nine to four-thirty, minus a half-hour coffee break, a two-hour lunch break at the officers club, and a half-hour coffee break," Calley recalled. "A beautiful life for an army officer, really. I couldn't bitch."

He did find annoying the television crews that hovered around what some members of the media called "Calley Hall." The press also harassed the defendant's family. A TV reporter approached his sister at her high school in Hialeah and asked, "Now what do you think of your brother murdering all of those people in South Vietnam?" Calley's reaction: "What a hell of a question for a fourteen-year-old. My sister was crying then." Their father moved her to another school in Gainesville, Florida, but the incident made Calley feel like *"I'm a lousy bastard. I'm hurting my little sister."* In Columbus, Georgia, and across the Chattahoochee River in Phoenix City, Alabama, it was members of the media who felt like pariahs. Everywhere reporters went, they were condemned by people anxious to argue with them about the trial. Hammer found "most of the locals blindly and vociferously pro-Calley."

One who was especially supportive was Calley's girlfriend, Anne Moore. A slim, sharp-featured woman in her twenties, she was a Red Cross hospital worker at Fort Benning. Moore came to court almost every day, sitting through the proceedings without showing any emotion. Another courtroom regular was "Joanne," a tall, dark divorcée who had driven in from New Mexico, where she claimed to be a graduate student in anthropology, to witness and become part of the most decisive trial of the era. Her sexually provocative attire attracted the attention of both journalists and the defendant. Initially Joanne was a "press groupie" who dated reporters. Then she introduced herself to Calley. Soon she was sitting in one of the five front-row seats allocated to the defendant and controlled by John Sack, a writer who was tape-recording interviews with Calley for publication as a book and in *Esquire* magazine. Joanne also spent time with the lieutenant in his BOQ apartment and at her rented bungalow. Both insisted they were just friends and that, when they were together, all they did was talk and play with her children. Although reporters covering the trial were skeptical about that, Joanne was far from the only person to visit Calley's apartment. He often entertained well-wishers there, pouring drinks behind a padded bar and cooking elaborate meals.

While Calley had plenty of supporters, he also confronted a skilled and determined adversary. Captain Daniel was a ruggedly handsome twenty-eight-year-old blond, who had been born in Monks Corner, South Carolina, raised in the upper South, and educated in the manner of a southern gentleman at Woodberry Forest prep school and the University of Virginia. Mediocre undergraduate grades forced him to obtain his legal training at the less prestigious T. C. Williams Law School of the University of Richmond, but Daniel did well enough there to land a position at a top Richmond law firm. After only nine months on the job, he received his draft notice. Daniel immediately applied for and received a direct commission in the Judge Advocate Generals Corps.

As a new military attorney he prosecuted and defended everything from simple absent without leave (AWOL) cases to homicides. While this work earned him a solid reputation as an advocate, his gifts as a lawyer had been at least partially obscured by a lack of truly challenging cases. They burst forth when he became Calley's prosecutor. That duty highlighted Daniel's stern and unbending moral code. He was one of four young officers who reacted to what they thought were the army's plans to let Calley slip quietly out of the service by flipping a coin to see which one would file charges against him. The deeper Daniel dug into My Lai, the more he came to question the morality and legitimacy of America's military intervention in Vietnam, but despite his personal beliefs, he considered it his duty to prosecute Calley, not the others involved in the massacre or the war itself.

Driven to obtain a conviction, he pushed himself to the point of exhaustion. Both before and during the court-martial, Daniel often worked far past midnight. He and his assistant trial counsel, Captain John Patrick Partin, a twenty-five-year-old Tennessee native and graduate of the University of Virginia School of Law, personally interviewed every witness who could shed any light on the massacre and examined every relevant document. They also read everything they could find about My Lai. Daniel eschewed social contact with opposing counsel and the judge and, unlike most of the Calley court-martial lawyers, also avoided the reporters who swarmed around the trial. He was so focused that, according to Hammer, when not addressing the court or examining a witness, he "usually perched like a waiting tiger on the edge of his seat."

Despite his commitment and hard work, Daniel appeared overmatched. Heading the defense team was George Latimer, an attorney with a towering reputation in military law. Calley had retained him even though informed by a reporter that famed Washington trial lawyer Edward Bennett Williams (who had represented Jimmy Hoffa, Bobby Baker, and Senator Joseph R. McCarthy) was willing to take his case. He wanted someone who would adopt a low-key approach rather than seek headlines, and Latimer, who wrote him a supportive letter soon after he was charged, seemed ideal. Even before attending law school at the University of Utah, the Salt Lake City attorney had served in the National Guard during World War I. After seventeen years of practice, he reentered the military during World War II, rising to the rank of colonel, becoming chief of staff of the 40th Infantry Division, and participating in four South Pacific invasions. In 1947 he won election to the Utah Supreme Court, and in 1951, although a Republican, he was appointed by President Harry Truman, a Democrat, to the United States Court of Military Appeals. During his years on the nation's highest military court, Latimer often published strident dissents to rulings broadening the rights of individual soldiers. In 1961 he stepped down from the bench to become a partner in a Salt Lake City law firm that represented insurance companies and other large corporations.

Calley had heard about Latimer's defense of some Green Berets accused of murdering a Vietnamese double agent, and friends at Fort Benning told him he was a brilliant trial lawyer as well as an expert on military law. Calley called Latimer and after they had talked for a while, asked the former judge to take his case. Without even asking Calley for his version of what had happened at My Lai, Latimer agreed—and promised to work for free. He volunteered despite being nearly seventy years old and partially deaf in one ear. He thought he had "one more good case left in him," he told a friend.

Latimer was not Calley's only lawyer. The lieutenant also had a military defense counsel, Major Kenneth Albert Raby. Raby was a career JAG officer who had entered the service in 1960 after graduating near the top of his class from the University of South Dakota School of Law, where he was editor in chief of the law review. Among his previous assignments was deputy staff judge advocate of the Americal Division, a position he held from July 1968 to July 1969. A lawyer who gushed case citations like a fountain, Al Raby was regarded in military legal circles as a brilliant scholar, but he was not at his best in the courtroom, where he came across as stilted and pedantic.

His assistant, Captain Brooks S. Doyle Jr., contributed little to Calley's defense, although that was not his fault. Through much of 1970, while Latimer and Raby were preparing their case, Doyle, a Pennsylvania native who had attended law school at Wake Forest, toured the country, interviewing potential witnesses. His efforts filled several file drawers with notes, but no one ever bothered to look at those.

Calley also had a second civilian lawyer, Richard B. Kay, fifty-two, of Cleveland. Kay, who practiced mostly personal injury and real estate law, had once been convicted of bribery, although he managed to get that conviction reversed on appeal. He knew nothing about military law and had to be lectured constantly on that subject, as well as on courtroom procedure and deportment, by the judge. He became part of the defense team by volunteering his services, apparently in the hope that his association with the Calley case would lead right-wing presidential candidate George Wallace to choose him as his running mate in 1972. Kay was a publicity hound whose main contribution to the defense was to leak confidential information to reporters he was trying to impress.

His ineptitude proved surprisingly representative of Calley's legal team. Concluding that it needed help if fairness was to be ensured, on about a dozen occasions the military judge, Colonel Reid W. Kennedy, although apparently considering prosecution objections well-founded, overruled them anyhow. "If not a great legal scholar," Hammer concluded, "Kennedy was essentially a fair man." A fifty-year-old graduate of Drake University Law School, he had originally joined the army in 1943 as an enlisted man. While practicing law in Iowa after World War II, Kennedy earned a commission in the National Guard. Following his defeat for reelection as county attorney in Spencer, Iowa, he returned to active duty during the Korean War. Deciding to make the military a career, he served in legal positions with the 101st Airborne Division and the 1st Cavalry Division and attended the Command and General Staff College and the Armed Forces Staff College. After a tour as a staff judge advocate in Vietnam, Kennedy was assigned to Fort Benning in July 1967 as a military judge of the army's Fifth Judicial District. Just as the Calley trial began, he was promoted from lieutenant colonel to full colonel.

At about the same time he and his wife stopped playing bridge with Captain and Mrs. Daniel. The prosecutor thought it would look bad for him to be socializing with the judge. Kennedy was determined to ensure that no personal bias of his would influence the proceedings. He wanted to make sure Calley got a fair trial.

Kennedy went as far as he thought he legally could to protect the defendant from harmful pretrial publicity. The first "Article 39(a) session" (a type of hearing designed to dispose of preliminary legal issues not requiring participation of a jury) was the day after Paul Meadlo's 24 November appearance on the CBS evening news. Kennedy reacted to that broadcast by directing

Daniel to inform each prospective witnesses not to disclose or discuss his testimony or other evidence with anyone but prosecutors, defense counsel, and the accused. He also ordered those officers detailed as members of the court-martial (i.e. potential jurors) to refrain from talking about the case and from intentionally listening to or reading news about Calley's trial or related proceedings.

That was not enough for Raby or even Daniel, who, in what Kennedy recognized "may be . . . the only time in the entire proceedings that you two will agree," filed a joint motion asking him to prohibit the publication of massacre photographs and accounts of witnesses. Concerned that the order they wanted might violate the First Amendment, Kennedy held their request in abeyance, declaring he would grant the news media a "reasonable time . . . to act in a responsible manner." It made no effort to police itself, and CBS issued a statement proclaiming Meadlo's right "to make his story public if that was his decision." On 28 November, convinced that journalists were ignoring the Supreme Court's decision in *Sheppard v. Maxwell* and prejudicing Calley's right to a fair trial, a dismayed Kennedy agreed that "extraordinary measures" were required.

He saw this as "an extremely delicate constitutional issue," however, and expressed doubt that the UCMJ gave him the authority to enforce the sort of injunction the lawyers wanted. He directed them to "seek appropriate relief from a court within the Federal judicial system or elsewhere as deemed necessary." On 8 December, apparently believing that media interest in the case—and thus the danger posed by pretrial publicity—was subsiding, Kennedy ruled he had no authority to issue the injunction counsel wanted. He believed, however, that "the accused's right to a fair trial must be paramount." By 16 December Kennedy had become convinced that protecting this right required drastic action. He directed Daniel to request that the attorney general prosecute potential witnesses who had violated his earlier nondisclosure order and also take legal action against some media outlets, most notably the *Houston Chronicle*, which had published an interview with Herbert Carter.

Many observers believed that saturation coverage had already made it impossible to find impartial jurors to try Calley. Raby demonstrated that they were probably correct when, just a few days after the judge issued his directive, he purchased in the Infantry School coffee shop an issue of *Newsweek* featuring a lengthy story on the massacre. That article quoted Nixon as saying "under no circumstances was it justified." Although trying to keep media coverage of My Lai from influencing the court-martial was probably a futile endeavor, Kennedy did manage to exclude the press from pretrial hearings. He persuaded the defense, despite Latimer's reservations, to request that he take this action, thus ensuring it would not violate Calley's right to a public trial.

The judge thus insulated from media scrutiny a January 1970 hearing at which the principal issue was "command influence." Defense counsel alleged that officers at Fort Benning had not made the decision to prosecute Calley independently but had done so only because of pressure from others higher up in the chain of command, including the Judge Advocate General, General Westmoreland, Secretary of Defense Melvin Laird, and even President Nixon. In support of their allegations they offered stories from *Time*, *Life*, and other sources. These, Kennedy concluded, did raise the specter of command influence, imposing upon the prosecution the burden of refuting the defense charges. At his direction Daniel presented testimony by the staff judge advocate, the officers who had acted as accusers on the original and additional charges, the commanding officer of the Student Brigade (who had forwarded the charges with a recommendation for a general court-martial), and Generals Davis and Talbott (commanders of Fort Benning during the period when the case was filed). After hearing these witnesses, however, Kennedy found there was "absolutely no evidence" that Nixon, Laird, Resor, or Westmoreland had in any way communicated with commanders at Fort Benning. The defense wanted to subpoena those officials, but while suggesting that it interview people at the Pentagon, he denied its request.

Judge Kennedy also refused to preclude the prosecution from calling witnesses who had testified before Congressman Hébert's subcommittee. He did attempt to obtain transcripts of their testimony, issuing subpoenas for these in October 1970 and again in February 1971. The House refused to release to the defense, to the prosecution, or even to the judge for inspection in camera (i.e., in private) the material he requested. Kennedy believed the separation of powers precluded him from compelling its production, but a federal statute, commonly known as the Jencks Act, suggested the prosecution might have to pay a price for the House's obduracy. It provided that in any federal criminal prosecution, once a government witness testified on direct examination, the United States had to produce for in camera inspection any statements he had made previously that were in its possession. If the judge subsequently ordered one of these turned over to the defense, the government must comply, or the court was required either to strike the witness's testimony from the record or declare a mistrial. Latimer argued that this law applied to things said before congressional committees, but that it was wrong for the defense to have to wait until witnesses questioned earlier by Hébert's panel testified at the court-martial before raising an objection based on the Jencks Act. Following that procedure would require Calley's lawyers to ask for a recess so they could seek congressional transcripts and search through them for anything that could be used to impeach the witness.

Kennedy disagreed with Latimer. On 10 November 1970 he declared that he was "satisfied from the language of the statute and its legislative history and all of the cases construing it that [the Jencks Act] does not include within its framework statements or testimony given to a congressional subcommittee in executive session." Most of the witnesses Daniel planned to call had been questioned during the inquiries conducted by the Inspector General, the CID, and the Peers Commission, and all of those statements, as well as all criminal investigative progress notes, had been made available to the defense. Hence, Kennedy did not think Calley had been deprived of due process. He ruled the government might call witnesses who had previously testified before Hébert's subcommittee.

Although protesting that ruling, the defense acquiesced in

Kennedy's unprecedented approach to the problem of selecting impartial officers to try the case. Under Article 41(b) of the UCMJ, each side was entitled to one peremptory challenge, which it could use to remove someone who had been detailed as a member of the court, without giving any reason or justification for doing so. Kennedy concluded that in this case one was not enough because so many potential jurors were dismissed for cause. As Calley himself explains, picking the jury "took us three days. . . .We went through twenty-five officers, most of them prejudiced for me: not personally, but against the army for trying me." Challenges for cause reduced the number of originally detailed court members to five, the minimum allowed by the UCMJ.

Recognizing that if either side exercised a peremptory challenge, there would no longer be a quorum, Kennedy suggested a stratagem not authorized by military law: "What I propose is that an arrangement be made to obtain some more people for this afternoon and what I will do is give you each a peremptory challenge from this batch and as we get the new, I will give you each a peremptory challenge from it." Seven more officers were detailed, but again challenges for cause reduced the court dangerously close to the mandatory minimum of five members. At that point Kennedy restated what he understood to be "the agreement with counsel . . . that as each new panel of jurors was brought in, you would each have a right to peremptorily challenge one of those." Asked if that was indeed "the agreement between counsel," Latimer replied, "Yes, sir."

After both sides exercised a peremptory challenge, nine more officers were detailed. Following more challenges for cause, each exercised another peremptory challenge. Both sides used their last one to remove an officer who had been part of the first group of potential jurors. Calley's lawyers argued later on appeal that the resulting court was unlawfully constituted because the prosecution had been given more than its authorized one peremptory challenge. The United States Army Court of Review rejected that argument, holding the defense had waived whatever right it might have had to object to an admittedly novel procedure by agreeing to it in order to get extra challenges.

Certainly, Calley's counsel had little reason to complain about the membership of the court finally selected to try him. It did consist entirely of career officers, while he was a short-term volunteer, but all six of them were combat veterans, and five had seen action in Vietnam. When questioned by the lawyers, most said they believed the Vietnamese placed a somewhat different (although not necessarily lower) value on human life than did Americans and (of particular importance, given the tack the defense would take) that military men must obey orders. All professed to have only the sketchiest knowledge of the My Lai incident.

The senior member of this group of highly decorated officers, and thus the "president" of the court, was Colonel Clifford H. Ford, the deputy director of operations and training at Fort Benning. A fifty-four-year-old Tennessean, he had seen combat during both World War II and the Korean conflict. Major Charles C. McIntosh, thirty-eight, was a native of Brownsville, Pennsylvania, who had been in the army since 1951. After eleven years as an enlisted man, he won a commission in 1962. McIntosh had seen combat both in Korea, where he was wounded three times, and in Vietnam, where he was an operations officer in the 1st Cavalry Division. He was a year older than Major Carl R. Bierbaum, who had also joined the army in 1951, following his graduation from high school in Litchfield, Illinois. Commissioned in 1958, Bierbaum did two tours in Vietnam as a helicopter pilot. Major Walter D. Kinard had also been to Vietnam twice. He served with the United States Military Assistance Command (MACV) in 1964–65 and as a company commander in the 173rd Airborne Brigade in 1968–69, winning a Silver Star for heroism in action. Practically a native of Fort Benning (he had been born in Columbus), the thirty-three-year-old Kinard enlisted in 1958, become a paratrooper, and earned his commission through OCS in 1962. Gene Brown, also thirty-three, was promoted from captain to major during the trial. From Matador, Texas, he had earned a Bronze Star for valor while serving with MACV in 1965.

The junior member of the court was Captain Ronald J. Salem, thirty-five, of Dearborn, Michigan. Salem had been in the army from 1954 to 1957, then reenlisted in 1963. Like Calley, he had received his commission through Infantry OCS at Fort Benning, from which he graduated the year after the defendant. Like the officer on whom he would pass judgment, Salem had served as a platoon leader in Vietnam (with the 25th Division). He had also been both the executive officer and the commander of a rifle company.

Although this looked like a jury that would empathize with an officer caught up in the horrors of infantry warfare in Vietnam, the prosecution presented it with a strong case against Lieutenant Calley, which Daniel outlined to a hushed court during a twenty-two-minute opening statement on 17 November. He first read specifications to the murder charges against the defendant. Now reduced to a total of four, these accused Calley of the killings at the trail junction and the irrigation ditch, as well as those of the monk and the small child. Daniel acknowledged that these were somewhat unusual in that they did not identify the Vietnamese human beings Calley was alleged to have killed. The prosecutor had to admit that the government could not prove their names, ages, or even genders.

Having conceded that he did not have the sort of evidence concerning the identity of the victims generally provided by the prosecution in a murder trial, he moved on quickly to a description of the physical layout of My Lai (4). Daniel explained that much of the government's evidence would "be devoted to orienting you with this area." He then explained the organization of Charlie Company, how it fit into Task Force Barker, and the 16 March operation. "The members of the accused's platoon entered the village, and as they entered the village, they found the village to be undefended," Daniel asserted.

Endeavoring to persuade jurors that Calley had possessed the state of mind required to make him guilty of murder, Daniel argued that when the lieutenant told Meadlo and Conti to "take care of" the people at the trail intersection, although they thought he only wanted them to guard those prisoners, he had actually wanted them to kill the Vietnamese. When Calley returned and found the villagers still alive, he told the two enlisted men that. "And with a full burst of automatic fire, Meadlo and Calley shot those people," Daniel declared, turning to glare at the defendant. "Those unarmed, unresisting women and children there on the trail." Calley looked up and grinned at him.

Unfazed, Daniel proceeded to tell the court about the witnesses whose testimony would prove what he had alleged. The prosecutor then narrated the story of how Calley had instructed his men to put villagers into the irrigation ditch. "And he orders them executed and they are—men, women, and children." Daniel informed the jurors about the witnesses whose testimony would prove that allegation, discussing in considerable detail what Hugh Thompson would tell them. "Over seventy people were executed in this ditch . . . by the accused and by members, at his direction, of his platoon," Daniel asserted. In addition, the defendant had butt-stroked an old man in the face with his rifle and had picked up a small child, thrown it "in the irrigation ditch and shot and killed it."

When Daniel concluded with a plea to convict the accused and then walked to his seat, there was a long moment of absolute silence. As everyone filed out for a short recess, Hammer overheard another spectator say, "God, he doesn't look like he could do all those things, does he?"

Daniel quickly set about proving that Calley not only could but also had done the things of which he was accused. The prosecutor wanted to present his case in such a way that members of the court could see the 16 March operation unfold as if they were watching a movie about it. Besides making order out of chaos, he hoped to present facts which would convince jurors that an inexcusable slaughter had taken place at My Lai (4). Only then would he offer any evidence at all about Calley himself. Daniel wanted, as Hammer puts it, "to bring the members of the court to the point of rising in the jury box and demanding a name."

To achieve his objectives he began with witnesses who could set the scene, while also establishing that Charlie Company had encountered no resistance at My Lai (4). By the time the court adjourned for Thanksgiving, Daniel had called twenty of these, including pilots and air crewmen who had been in the sky over the hamlet on 16 March and soldiers who had viewed the action from the ground. None was a member of Calley's First Platoon. Collectively, they painted a picture of a sudden assault on a village from which, according to every witness but one, no shots were fired. Former rifleman Gene Oliver Jr. said he had heard three rifle bullets whistle past him, but when Partin asked if he had received any other hostile fire, Oliver replied, "No sir, when we got there the village was cleared."

Particularly damning was the testimony of Frank Beardslee, a rifleman who was acting as an aide and driver for Colonel Barker. When Barker said he was recommending him for the Combat Infantryman's Badge, awarded for participation in hostilities, Beardslee asked to take part in an operation so he could earn it. He tagged along with Charlie Company on 16 March but received no hostile fire. "I did not accept the CIB on this mission . . . ," he testified, "because we met no resistance and the CIB indicates combat action."

According to prosecution witnesses, despite encountering no opposition, Charlie Company destroyed the homes and crops in My Lai (4) and killed the livestock. It also slaughtered the inhabitants. Beardslee testified that he had seen two or three GIs guarding some Vietnamese women and children, but when he returned to the same area later, all of them were dead. Ronald Haeberle told about witnessing the massacre of what was apparently the same group of civilians. After several of the soldiers who were guarding them walked off, he heard automatic weapons fire. Turning, he saw one of the two remaining GIs "firing toward the people." Some of the Vietnamese tried to get away, but they fell down. "This one woman, I remember, she stood up and tried to make it—tried to run—with a small child in her arms. But she didn't make it." Haeberle had photographed the pile of murdered Vietnamese, as well as numerous identifiable members of Charlie Company.

Unable to keep Daniel from painting a picture of American soldiers inflicting wanton destruction on an unresisting Vietnamese village, Latimer resorted to several tactics while cross-examining prosecution witnesses that he hoped would reduce the impact of their testimony. One was suggesting that the dead Vietnamese had been killed by helicopters and artillery. He got Roger Aloux, a forward observer with Charlie Company, to acknowledge that that could account for the corpses he saw near a trail intersection. The impact of this admission probably would have been greater if Aloux, who was a Calley supporter, had not leaned over and wished the defendant good luck as he left the witness stand. Another Latimer tactic was to get these early witnesses to acknowledge that they had not seen Calley do anything. Asked when he had first observed the defendant, Haeberle had to admit, "I did not see a lieutenant all day." Since much of this testimony was essentially background, such admissions probably did not do much damage to the prosecution.

Latimer's final cross-examination tactic was to raise doubts about the character of the government's witnesses. He was particularly hard on Haeberle, accusing him of avoiding real military training by becoming a photographer, of stealing government property by not turning in to the army the color pictures he had taken with his own camera, of being motivated by desire for financial gain, and of violating a MACV directive by failing to report war crimes he had observed. Unfortunately for Latimer, Haeberle's pictures spoke for themselves, proving irrefutably the prosecution's contention that a large group of civilians had been killed at the trail junction. Raising doubts about his integrity could not diminish the impact of his pictures, so courtroom observers questioned the wisdom of Latimer's tactics.

Although Raby asked prosecution witnesses far fewer questions, Hammer found him more effective. He used cross-examination to try to diminish Calley's responsibility for what had happened at My Lai (4) by showing that everyone had been killing indiscriminately. Kay took a different tack, asking Oliver, over repeated objections from Daniel, questions designed to establish that Charlie Company had been on a search-and-destroy mission and that My Lai was within what was known as a "free-fire zone": an area where American troops were essentially authorized to kill anything that moved. Although Kay elicited answers tending to broaden responsibility for the killing on 16 March, unfortunately for the defense,

Oliver also revealed his bias by stopping at the defense table on his way out of the courtroom to wish Calley well.

His testimony and that of most of the other witnesses who appeared during the first week of the trial served to set the scene, portray American soldiers destroying an unresisting hamlet, and establish that some of them had killed a large number of Vietnamese civilians at a trail junction. At the end of the week, Daniel began presenting evidence concerning the massacre at the irrigation ditch. Richard Pendleton testified that he had seen a "large mound of dead Vietnamese" there, which, he estimated, consisted of forty to fifty people. Pendleton had been a rifleman in Charlie Company's Third Platoon, but most of those Daniel called to report seeing bodies in the ditch had observed them from the air. They included helicopter pilots Jerry Culverhouse, Dan Millians, and Brian Livingston and door gunners Calvin Dean Hodde and Larry Colburn. Culverhouse estimated that he had seen "seventy-five to more than a hundred bodies" in the irrigation ditch, many of them babies, and he remembered the water being stained with blood. He had observed a black sergeant standing near the ditch with his rifle near shoulder height and had heard automatic weapons fire. Millians also witnessed this individual firing into the ditch; he remembered a shuddering impact as the bullets smashed home. Millians and Livingston hurt the defense with answers they gave during cross-examination. Both described gunships firing on a group of Vietnamese refugees who were fleeing along the highway that led to Quang Ngai City, but when Kay attempted to link those killings to the ones at the ditch and trail junction and to blame the latter on helicopters, both objected, accusing him of misconstruing what they had said. About the best the defense could do in cross-examining these witnesses was to get Colburn to admit that he smoked marijuana. The door gunner insisted, however, that he never did so while flying.

Furthermore, his testimony was consistent in every detail with that of Lieutenant Hugh Thompson. Although the appearance of Thompson, who had received a commission since the massacre, was the dramatic high point of this phase of the trial, it proved somewhat disappointing to reporters, who were expecting to hear about his melodramatic confrontation with Calley. Daniel did not question him concerning that incident, instead using Thompson, like the other aviators, to prove that "there was a ditch down there with a bunch of people in it." Asked to describe what he had seen, Thompson replied, "There was just a lot of bodies in there sir, women, kids, babies, and old men." Thompson also recounted a conversation with a GI he had encountered upon landing his chopper. Told that there were wounded people in the ditch and asked if he and his buddies could assist them, this soldier said "something to the effect that the only way to help them was to put them out of their misery." Thompson also testified that, after rescuing a group of Vietnamese some GIs had trapped in a bunker, he and his crew returned to the ditch, hoping to aid any civilians there who were still alive. All they found was "a kid . . . about the size of a six year old, muddy and blood all over him." It was a gruesome story. Unable to cast any real doubt on Thompson's account, Latimer wandered through an aimless and somewhat inept cross-examination. Like the Hébert subcommittee, he sought to reduce the impact of Thompson's tale principally by heaping scorn on the medal he had received for his actions on 16 March.

That tactic could not diminish the power of the pilot's testimony. Along with the other evidence Daniel had presented, it left little room for doubt that scores of unresisting Vietnamese civilians had been massacred at My Lai (4). Now all that remained was to prove that Lieutenant Calley was responsible for those killings. Two weeks into the court-martial, Daniel proffered the first witnesses from his own platoon. Although Roy Woods, a rifleman in the Second Squad, acknowledged under cross-examination that he had not seen Calley on 16 March, Rennard Doines, also from the Second Squad, testified that after rounding up a group of unarmed and unresisting civilians, he had turned them over to the defendant and some other soldiers. Doines, who denied believing he was supposed to go through the village and kill all the people, began a parade of prosecution witnesses who tied Calley directly to the killings at My Lai (4).

Sidney Kye had seen his platoon leader standing near a group of dead civilians with smoke coming out of the muzzle of his rifle. Earl Maples, a machine gunner in the First Platoon, testified that after he and some other GIs rounded up a number of villagers and marched them through the hamlet to a big ditch on the other side, he had seen "Lieutenant Calley [herd] . . . the people he had into the hole and him and Meadlo was firing into the hole and Meadlo was crying." Maples said Calley wanted to use his machine gun, but he would not give it to him. Asked to describe those his platoon leader had shot, he answered, "It was women, babies, and a couple of elderly men." Lenny Lagunoy, who had heard shooting in the vicinity of the ditch, saw Meadlo weeping as he stood with his rifle pointing into it and observed the lieutenant standing nearby. Charles Hall had seen Calley talking to Sergeant Mitchell near the ditch, then heard slow, semiautomatic rifle fire coming from that area. Later when he crossed the ditch, he noticed dead people in it. "How did you know they were dead?" Daniel asked him. "They weren't moving," Hall answered. "There was a lot of blood coming from all over them." Gregory Olsen, who had been with Hall, confirmed the essential details of his account but said that as he crossed the ditch, "Some of the people appeared to be dead and others followed me with their eyes."

Hammer found Olsen "unshakable on cross-examination." Dennis Conti gave the defense more to work with. Calley alleged that on the day of the massacre he had prevented Conti from forcing a Vietnamese woman to perform oral sex on him, and Kay sought to highlight this incident during cross-examination. The defense attorney also got Conti to admit that he did not like his platoon leader and that he had refreshed his recollection of the events about which he was testifying by returning to My Lai in 1969 to assist the CID with its investigation. His testimony was nevertheless damning. Conti recounted how Calley had told him and Meadlo to "take care of the people" at the trail junction, then after returning to find them merely guarding the prisoners, declared, "No. I mean kill them." Conti went on to describe how the lieutenant and Meadlo "got on line and they opened fire." He had also seen Calley and Mitchell shooting at people in the ditch. One woman tried to get up. "As she got up I saw Lieutenant Calley fire and hit the side of her head and blow the side of her head off," he recalled.

After Conti left the stand, Daniel digressed briefly, calling Major Charles Lane, an army pathologist, who examined Haeberle's picture of the bodies on the trail and gave his opinion that their deaths had been caused by small-arms fire rather than by artillery or helicopter gunships. "Then," in Hammer's words, "it was back to tying the final chains around Calley." Charles Sledge was perfect for that job, since as the defendant's RTO he had accompanied him everywhere. He testified that Calley had ordered Meadlo to "waste" the prisoners at the trail junction. When the firing began, Sledge turned and walked off down the trail. Behind him he heard "firing" and "screaming." He watched as Calley and Mitchell shoved villagers into the ditch, then began shooting at them. Later he saw his platoon leader hit a Vietnamese man, who was wearing the white robes of a priest, in the mouth with the butt of his rifle, then shoot him in the face at point-blank range. "Half his head was blown off." Sledge also claimed Calley had grabbed a small child by the arms, thrown it into the ditch, and fired. Raby attempted to discredit Sledge by revealing that in 1964, at the age of seventeen, he had been convicted of being a Peeping Tom, a maneuver even Calley found distasteful. For a black man in Mississippi to be punished for being in someone's alley, he felt, "means nothing. . . . Hell, I say that's nothing but Sledge's race." The testimony of his former RTO unsettled the defendant, causing him to wonder (he reported later) if he was the one who was wrong about what had happened at My Lai (4).

It was Thomas Turner's testimony that hit Richard Kay particularly hard. He considered it "devastating." According to Turner, when he approached the ditch, he saw Meadlo and several other GIs firing into it. Calley emptied his weapon, changed clips, and started shooting again. Turner sat on a dike just north of the ditch for over an hour, watching as small groups of people were herded into it and Calley systematically executed them. He also said he had seen his platoon leader shoot a young Vietnamese woman who was coming toward him with her hands up. This allegation was a total surprise to the defense, for Turner, who had not talked to any of the investigating panels or the CID, let alone to Calley's lawyers, was something of a mystery witness. Latimer and Kay objected strenuously that the story about the woman amounted to an accusation of a new murder, outside the bill of particulars filed by the prosecution. Although agreeing with Daniel that it was admissible to prove Calley had possessed the intent to kill, Judge Kennedy nevertheless ordered it stricken from the record. Even what was left of Turner's testimony was devastating.

"If Turner had thrown the defense into enormous distress," Hammer observed, "James Joseph Dursi was to turn that distress into near panic." Dursi confirmed that Calley had told Meadlo to take care of a group of prisoners, then returned to yell at him for not having "wasted them yet." Although he had heard firing after he moved out, Dursi did not actually see them shoot those Vietnamese. He did witness the slaughter at the irrigation ditch. Along with a weeping Meadlo, he and his men had been ordered by Calley "to start putting the people in the ditch." "Some of them started to cry and they were yelling." Then the platoon leader gave the order to shoot. "Lieutenant Calley and Meadlo started firing into the ditch." Turner could not bring himself to join in the execution of "little defenseless men, women, and kids," and Calley instructed him "to get across the ditch before I got sick."

By the time Dursi left the stand, Daniel had put a noose around the neck of the former platoon leader. All he needed to pull it tight was the testimony of the man who had helped Calley commit murder at both the trail junction and the irrigation ditch. Although Meadlo had told his story on national television, he was reluctant to tell it in court; he and Calley were accomplices in each other's crimes, and in the process of giving evidence against the lieutenant, he would inculpate himself. Because the Fifth Amendment prohibits compelled self-incrimination, the government could force Meadlo to testify only by granting him immunity. General Talbott issued an order providing that "no testimony given by" Meadlo nor "any information gained as a result of said testimony" should ever be used against him by the United States "in any criminal prosecution" or any other proceeding that might result in a penalty or forfeiture.

That was not enough for either Meadlo's lawyer, John Kessler, or Major Raby. They argued that General Talbott could not prevent Meadlo's testimony from being used against him in a civilian court. Judge Kennedy was satisfied, however, that the law did not give either a U.S. District Court or any state court jurisdiction to try him for offenses committed at My Lai. Raby and Kessler pointed out that legislation had been introduced in Congress that would authorize civilian federal courts to hear such cases, but Kennedy brushed aside that argument. They also contended that, because war crimes were violations of international law, Meadlo might be tried before some international tribunal or foreign court, where his compelled testimony could be used against him. Raby submitted that this was not only possible but likely, if it were determined that the grant of immunity itself constituted "a grave breach of [United States] treaty obligation to try [Meadlo]."

Kennedy was convinced, however, that "the only tribunal that could exercise any jurisdiction over him would be [a] court-martial or some special type of tribunal . . . set up by the President of the United States." The grant of immunity would prevent either of those from trying him. Kessler's plea to give Meadlo "the right of every citizen of the United States—to invoke his rights under the Constitution" did not move the judge. "Isn't this the man that granted the interview on television . . . ?" Kennedy responded. "I didn't notice any great reluctance on his part at that point to tell everything that he knew about My Lai." Following an Article 39(a) hearing on 3 December, he ruled Meadlo must testify.

Calley's principal accomplice then took the stand, but Meadlo would only give his name and say where he lived and that he knew the defendant. Kennedy warned him that if he failed to testify fully, the matter would be referred to the local U.S. attorney for prosecution. He called a short recess so Meadlo could reconsider, but during that break Kessler told the press, "You bet your ass he's not going to testify." Meadlo remained mute, and Kennedy ordered the military police to take him away. Rather than being turned over to the U.S. attorney, however, after being held for part of a day, he was allowed to fly home to Terre Haute, Indiana.

When he returned to take the stand, two U.S. marshals, an assistant U.S. attorney, and a representative of the Department of Justice were crouching in the front row, ready to pounce if he again refused to testify. Kessler rose to address the judge, but Kennedy refused to hear any further arguments. "If you have anything to say, you can be heard in the United States District Court," he told him. When Kennedy asked Meadlo if he was going to testify this time, the former grunt answered, "Yes."

In an emotionless manner and a lifeless voice (that seemed to Hammer "almost dead") Meadlo described helping to round up thirty to fifty men, women, and children and move them to the center of My Lai (4). There Calley came up to him and said, "You know what to do with them, Meadlo?" Assuming the lieutenant wanted him to guard the prisoners, he did that until Calley returned ten or fifteen minutes later and asked, "How come they're not dead?" According to Meadlo, the lieutenant backed off twenty or thirty feet and started shooting the Vietnamese. He "burned four or five magazines," and Meadlo himself fired about three clips at them. Upset and scared, he wandered around for a while, then began gathering up more prisoners and moving them east to a "ravine." There Calley told him, "We've got another job to do, Meadlo." The lieutenant started shoving Vietnamese into the ditch and shooting them. "He ordered me to help kill the people. I started shoving them off and shooting." Asked what the victims were doing, Meadlo replied, "The people was just laying there with blood all over them. . . . They had wounds in the head, in the body, in the chest, in the stomach."

Latimer's cross-examination elicited Meadlo's opinions that Calley had only been "doing his duty and doing his job" and that he was not "raving around," but Daniel used his redirect examination to undermine the defense's contention that the defendant had simply been carrying out Medina's orders. Meadlo testified that he did not kill women, children, and other prisoners until Calley told him to do so because until then he had no orders to do it. Daniel asked him, "Did Lieutenant Calley or did Captain Medina order you to kill?" "I took my orders from Lieutenant Calley," Meadlo replied. He went on to volunteer that, because Medina had been at the ditch and had made no effort to stop what was going on there, he assumed everything was OK with him. His answer to Daniel's question was disastrous for the defense, however, for if believed, it made Calley responsible, as an aider and abettor, for all the murders that Meadlo himself had committed.

The defense's failure to discredit Meadlo's damning testimony was fairly typical of its habitually ineffective cross-examination. Calley's lawyers sometimes asked questions that raised genuine doubts about whether prosecution witnesses had actually observed what they claimed to have seen. For example, Kay got Oliver to admit he had looked at photographs of a pile of bodies about which he testified and that it was possible these had changed his ideas about what he had observed. "You know, the memory is a funny thing, especially after a year," Oliver conceded. Sometimes defense lawyers asked questions that raised doubts about whether witnesses had even been in a position to see the things they described.

Generally, however, they seemed more interested in attacking the character and motives of those who had given evidence against their client. With Conti, whom Kay grilled not only about his sexual assaults on Vietnamese women but also about several run-ins he had had with Calley, this approach was probably productive. Thrusts such as Kay's dramatic demand to know if it were true that once, when ordered to go out on a night patrol, "you refused, and you threatened to shoot Lieutenant Calley" probably reduced Conti's credibility. Attacking Sledge's morals and Thompson's heroism, however, was likely counterproductive.

Often, there seemed to be no real purpose behind the questions Calley's lawyers asked. Furthermore, Hammer thought, the defense "seemed never to know, despite its opportunities for preparation, what a witness was going to say." On one occasion Latimer questioned Dursi about his conversations with Conti and his dislike of lawyers, only to have the witness blurt out that the reason for both was that "My story . . . is damaging to Lieutenant Calley, I know this." Another time Doines responded to Latimer's question about whether it was his understanding that they were to go through My Lai and kill all the people with a firm no, directly contradicting the point the defense attorney was hoping to make. Latimer highlighted his lack of preparation while cross-examining Maples about testimony he had given the previous day, badly misstating what the record showed the witness had said and being corrected by him in front of the jury.

The only defense attorney who really seemed to know where he was going and why was Raby. He repeatedly asked questions designed to establish that Calley was just one of many soldiers who had indiscriminately killed civilians at My Lai and that what had happened there was not unusual, but part of a pattern characteristic of combat in Vietnam. Kay did try, in questioning Oliver, to establish that My Lai was in a free-fire zone and what that implied, but Kennedy admonished him: "Frankly, I think that what you're attempting to do now is lay what would be your defense. I think you have to do this with witnesses that you call."

When the defense did begin to call its own witnesses, it would face a daunting task. The composition of the jury seemed favorable, and Judge Kennedy had bent over backward to be fair to the defendant. The prosecution had presented a strong case, however. From a host of witnesses whom the defense had been unable to discredit, jurors had heard damning testimony against Lieutenant Calley. The prosecution had presented ample evidence that he was guilty of multiple murders. The challenge facing the defense was how to persuade the jury, nevertheless, to acquit him. That would not be easy.

CHAPTER 9

Defenseless

There was "a sense of electricity" in the courtroom on the morning of 10 December. Every seat was filled, and almost everyone was leaning forward as George Latimer, fashionably decked out in a trim gray suit and blue shirt and tie, rose to address the jury. His mission was to outline how the defense would establish that Lieutenant Calley was not guilty of murder. Anticipation quickly gave way to disappointment. Speaking from rough notes, Latimer droned and rambled through an often inaudible nine-minute speech that demonstrated he was not up to the task of defending Calley.

Mostly, he summarized what had happened to Charlie Company prior to its assault on My Lai (4). He did not bother to explain the legal significance of this narration. For a while Latimer seemed to be laying a foundation for claiming Calley had acted in self-defense. Then he asserted that the memorial service the evening before the operation had created a desire for revenge and reprisal in the minds of all the men in the company. If that was the defendant's motivation, the killings could not be self-defense. At times Latimer seemed to be contending that Charlie Company had been provoked into killing innocent Vietnamese, but even if Calley's actions were the product of legally adequate provocation, he would still be guilty of manslaughter. The defense attorney also suggested that Captain Medina, or even officers higher up in the chain of command, might be responsible for the deaths at My Lai (4) and that helicopters had killed some of those who died at the irrigation ditch. He said nothing about Calley's mental state. Latimer did assure jurors that the defendant would take the stand, but he added, "I am purposely not relating Lieutenant Calley's personalized testimony at this time." He wanted to avoid "having it diluted by me in a recitation." By the time Latimer finished, the jury must have been hopelessly confused about what the defense planned to prove. His opening statement left courtroom observers questioning his ability.

Unfortunately for Calley, Latimer's disappointing performance previewed all too well an inept defense that doomed him to conviction. It revealed that Calley's lawyers had no real strategy. In a review of Richard Hammer's book on the court-martial, Geoff Metcalfe characterized the defense case as "confusing and confused, rambling, directionless, contradictory, and totally ill-prepared." Calley's attorneys could not seem to decide whether they were trying to prove that there had been no massacre at My Lai (4) or that everyone who was there had killed indiscriminately. For a while their objective seemed to be to blame Medina for whatever had happened, but then the defense shifted into a totally different gear, trying to prove Calley's lack of responsibility with psychiatric evidence. When it bungled that endeavor, Kennedy summoned the lawyers to his chambers on 19 February. He told Calley's counsel, "It's becoming increasingly apparent to me that there is considerable disagreement between various members of the defense staff as to the plan of the trial." The judge expressed concern that if these differences were communicated to the jury, Lieutenant Calley could be severely disadvantaged.

Calley was hurt not only by his attorneys' lack of a coherent strategy but also by their inadequate preparation. Neither Latimer nor Kay seemed to know what his own witnesses were going to say. Kay in particular was constantly being surprised by the responses he received. "When the answer was not what he seemed to expect," Hammer observed, "his face assumed a hurt look (while Daniel donned a sardonic smile and Kennedy a look of resignation . . .)." A few sharp questions from the prosecutor often neutralized whatever evidence Kay had managed to elicit. Sometimes Daniel even managed to turn defense witnesses into government ones. For example, Captain George White, a former platoon leader in Alpha Company, who had been called to testify that civilians might have been responsible for inflicting casualties on American troops, responded to the prosecutor's question about whether there had been any orders to kill them with a firm no. White even said that had he shot an unarmed man and a teenage boy he confronted, this would have violated the orders he had received. Although, according to Latimer, Calley's testimony was to be the core of the defense case, he failed to prepare his star witness for it. Kay told reporters before the lieutenant took the stand that defense attorneys had never heard his version of events. A couple of times Calley had tried to tell them, but Latimer had held up his hand and said, "I know you're innocent and that's all I need to know. I don't want to hear the story."

An inadequately prepared defense got off to an uninspiring start by reading depositions to the jury. These presented the testimony of witnesses who were not available to testify in person, and while Raby delivered their lines, Doyle played him and Partin read Daniel's cross-examination. The deposition of Daniel Hill, a former door gunner, now confined to a Montana veterans hospital with a nervous disorder, supported the defense contention that helicopters were responsible for some of the deaths on 16 March. Hill also reported that there had been at least one Vietnamese near the irrigation ditch who was armed and running away.

The other depositions were all from ARVN soldiers Raby had questioned during an evidence-gathering trip to Quang Ngai Province. Nguyen Van Toan, the commanding general of the 2nd Division, testified that Son My was Communist-controlled, that all of the people who remained there were Vietcong or VC supporters, and that it was in a free-fire zone, filled with booby traps and mines. Linh Ta Vien, assistant director of the district census grievance committee, supported this characterization. He had not visited the village since 1959, but the other two Vietnamese deponents had been in My Lai (4) on 16 March 1968. Sergeants Nguyen Din Phu and Duong Minh, both interpreters, reported seeing houses burned, animals killed, and women, children, and old men shot. Minh recalled asking a captain, who looked Spanish, why they were doing these things and being told they had been ordered to do them. The reading of these depositions was so boring that even Calley was soon yawning visibly.

Although it created the impression that the defense was just striking out blindly in all directions, a common thread did connect much of the testimony presented during the following week. A few witnesses, such as Captain White and Chaplain Cresswell, who reported that Colonel Barker had told him they were going to level My Lai (4), discussed other matters, but most had been present when Medina addressed his troops following the memorial service. Their testimony was so similar that Kennedy eventually complained it was becoming cumulative and expressed the hope that "they don't intend to call every member of the company to testify about that briefing." All of these witnesses agreed that Medina had ordered them to kill the people of My Lai (4). Now testifying for the defense, Oliver reported being told to level the place. Asked what they were supposed to do to the inhabitants, Calley's platoon sergeant, Isaiah Cowan, replied, "Well, he told us that . . . we was to destroy everything that produced food." Charles West recalled the captain saying to "leave nothing walking, crawling, or growing." Salvatore LaMartina said Medina had told them to "kill everything that breathed." "The instructions given to the entire company by Captain Medina was [*sic*] that the village was to be destroyed along with its inhabitants," Michael Bernhardt reported. Thomas Kinch added that Medina must have known what his men actually did there, for he had followed the captain through the village, and they passed more than twenty bodies at the trail junction.

Raby wanted Kinch also to testify that orders such as those his company commander had issued were commonly given and carried out in Vietnam. When he tried to question Kinch about an order to execute unarmed civilians that he had received from a lieutenant prior to being assigned to Charlie Company, Daniel objected, and Kennedy insisted on first hearing out of the presence of the jury what Kinch intended to say. Having done that, the judge pointed out that the men involved in this earlier incident had talked their lieutenant out of what he had told them to do. Alerted that the proffered testimony might actually hurt Calley, Raby withdrew it. Kinch did, however, along with many of the witnesses who had attended Medina's briefing and then assaulted

My Lai (4), add detail to the picture of indiscriminate killing that Raby hoped to paint. Unfortunately, that portrait made Cowan's insistence, under questioning by Kay, that he had not seen Calley shoot any civilians seem highly improbable.

An internally contradictory and seemingly rudderless defense wrecked on the reef of psychiatry. Although many people thought only a crazy man could do what Calley was accused of doing, the *Manual for Courts Martial* provided that a soldier was "not mentally responsible in a criminal sense" only if at the time of the alleged offense he lacked, because of a "mental defect, disease, or derangement," the ability "concerning the particular act charged both to distinguish right from wrong and to adhere to the right." Calley insisted he was not unbalanced, and his lawyers assured Judge Kennedy that they had no intention of raising an insanity defense.

After the Christmas recess, however, Latimer revealed that they intended to call three psychiatrists. Irritated, the judge reminded him that if the defense was going to raise the issue of Calley's mental responsibility, the lieutenant would have to be examined by a sanity board at Walter Reed Army Hospital. Although Latimer assured Kennedy that all the psychiatrists were going to do was testify about how orders and the stresses of combat affected people, the judge insisted on hearing them first out of the presence of the jury.

Dr. Albert A. LaVerne of the New York University–Bellview Medical Center, who appeared before Kennedy on 18 January, averred that an especially potent variety of marijuana grown in Vietnam might have caused Calley and others to act irrationally at My Lai and that the stress of combat could result in oxygen deprivation that impaired judgment and motor abilities. An experiment LaVerne had done on the defendant indicated he was subject to "non-specific stress syndrome," the psychiatrist reported. Under questioning by Daniel (who had prepared for this cross-examination by staying up nights educating himself in psychology), LaVerne admitted there was no evidence Calley had been exposed to marijuana on 16 March. He also said the defendant had no mental illness, knew right from wrong, was "absolutely sane," and possessed the capacity to form the intent to kill. LaVerne insisted, however, that the defendant was suffering from impaired judgment, caused by the stress of combat and his relationship with Medina (whom he "revered . . . as a father figure."), and that this made it impossible for him to challenge the legality of orders he believed had been given by the captain. While Latimer squirmed, LaVerne also testified, under relentless pounding by Daniel, that Calley had been acting under a "compulsion" that deprived him of the ability to adhere to the right.

His testimony, Kennedy concluded, raised the issue of the defendant's sanity. It would be reversible error for him not to instruct the jury on this issue. Also, the prosecution now bore the burden of proving Calley possessed the mental capacity to distinguish right from wrong and to adhere to the right. Daniel was inclined to agree with the judge's assessment of LaVerne's testimony, and his rulings left the prosecutor with little real choice but to request a sanity board. Over Latimer's objections, and having issued orders that "the government should not and will not . . . have possession of anything told to the psychiatrists by Lieutenant Calley," Kennedy adjourned court for three weeks so the defendant could be examined at Walter Reed.

There he underwent a battery of tests, including neurological and physical examinations, as well as twelve separate interviews by psychiatrists (some of them attended by lawyers for the two sides). Although anxious about the outcome of his trial, Calley exhibited confidence and talked to the doctors about his plans for the future. He told them that during the My Lai operation he had been "hyper" and "psyched up." He had not felt "as if he were killing humans but rather that they were animals with whom one could not speak or reason." The doctors found Calley had a strong drive to achieve and tended to dwell on his successes, while ignoring his failures. Also evident was a tendency to solve problems in a rather simplistic fashion. "His style of thinking seems to allow him to miss finer discriminations of meaning, so he tends to reduce subtle graduations of meaning to simple 'either/or' concepts," the psychiatrists reported. They were certain, however, that Calley knew the difference between right and wrong.

Their report became the factual basis for expert opinions rendered by LaVerne and Dr. Goodrich Crane, a former army Medical Corps doctor, now in private practice in Indianapolis and teaching at the University of Indiana Medical School. Crane also had a law degree. He and LaVerne were presented with a "hypothetical" statement of fact, which actually had been lifted almost verbatim from the summary findings of the Walter Reed sanity board. The two defense psychiatrists were then asked whether, assuming everything in the statement was true, on 16 March 1968 Lieutenant Calley (1) had possessed the mental capacity "to plan, think out, or contrive" the killing of the inhabitants of My Lai (4); (2) could "fully comprehend the act of taking their lives without apparent reason or excuse"; (3) was "able to make a reasoned decision concerning the legal consequences of the orders of his company commander"; and (4) had the mental capacity to form a "specific intent to kill someone." Since the validity of the answers they gave depended on the accuracy of the statement, and since the sanity board's findings included admissions by Calley of killing civilians, the defense seemed to have changed direction. Rather than denying Calley had committed homicide, his lawyers now seemed only to be trying save him from the death penalty by establishing that he was incapable of committing premeditated murder, a capital offense under Article 118. Crane insisted the Lieutenant Calley described in the hypothetical statement had not "contemplated or taken any consideration in forming a specific intent to kill." Rather, he had acted spontaneously and without premeditation.

LaVerne expressed general agreement with Crane's conclusions. Calley, he said, had suffered from impairments of both volition and cognition and had acted like a robot, knowing but not understanding what he was doing. He was unable to formulate, plan, contrive, or carry out such a design as the government alleged. Although LaVerne purported to base these opinions on the hypothetical fact statement, he had interviewed Calley himself, and Daniel asked him about something the defendant had told him. LaVerne said he needed to check his notes, but what he retrieved from his briefcase was actually the hypothetical state-

{ *The Vietnam War on Trial* }

ment. The flustered psychiatrist could not remember any of the questions he had supposedly asked Calley himself.

Judge Kennedy quickly called a recess. During a meeting in his chambers the next morning, he opined that if LaVerne "wasn't lying [concerning his supposed notes] it was the next thing to it." Daniel wanted the psychiatrist prosecuted for perjury, and even Raby admitted he "had never seen anything like that before" and was "completely shocked." Realizing it was "almost impossible . . . to rationalize why he did it," Latimer offered to excuse LaVerne as a witness and move that all his testimony be stricken from the record. When court reconvened, with the jury absent, Kennedy observed that LaVerne had been "saved by the bell" after nearly being caught in "a complete falsehood." Latimer did what he had promised, giving as his reason for withdrawing the witness a supposed disagreement between them over strategy. Seeking to salvage a tattered professional reputation, LaVerne brought his children down from New York for an emotional press conference outside the courthouse, then sought to justify his actions to the judge. Saying he did not want to hurt the psychiatrist's career, Kennedy ordered his harsh comments about him and his testimony stricken from the record.

The LaVerne fiasco caused Kennedy to suggest in chambers that Calley's counsel might want to reconsider this whole line of defense. After all, "You are only talking about diminished mental responsibility anyhow." Raby responded that the psychiatric evidence was needed to show the defendant lacked the "mens rea" (guilty state of mind) required for a murder conviction. If it were stricken, the judge might have to grant a mistrial to prevent irreparable harm.

Instead of abandoning its psychiatric maneuver, the defense sought to salvage it with the testimony of Dr. Wilbur Hamman, an experienced court-martial witness, who was on the staff of Saint Elizabeth's mental hospital in Washington, D.C., and had also been to Vietnam. His original mission was, by answering the same four questions as Crane and LaVerne, to support their contentions that Calley lacked the capacity to premeditate and could not form the specific intent to kill someone. Latimer intended for him to base these opinions on the hypothetical fact statement. Because Hamman had interviewed Calley five times, however, he first had to verify that what was in the statement conformed to what he knew about the defendant.

On 19 February, after the LaVerne disaster, Hamman went much further than originally planned. Testifying on the basis of his own interviews, he recounted for the jury what Calley had told him about his life, his feelings, combat in Vietnam, and the My Lai operation. The psychiatrist then stated that in his opinion on 16 March the defendant "did not have the capacity to form [the] specific intent [to kill]." Factors such as the training he had received to obey orders rapidly and without question, the experiences that had conditioned him to view all Vietnamese as potential enemies, Medina's briefing and orders, the hostility aroused before the attack, and the stress and fear kindled by combat had "acted to limit his volition, his ability to make a choice, to decide. In my opinion, he acted automatically," Hamman said. "He did as he was told, and there was no element of volition." Hamman also thought Calley's ability to make complex decisions had been impaired. Told that a premeditated murder was one "committed after the formation of a specific intent to kill someone and consideration of the act intended," he stated, without providing reasons for his conclusion, that the defendant "was not able to premeditate."

Although not disgraced on the witness stand, as LaVerne had been, both Hamman and Crane were bloodied by Daniel's prolonged and relentless cross-examination. The prosecutor forced Crane to admit that he was not board-certified, was not a member of the American Psychological Association, was not familiar with recent writings on stress, and had not read relevant psychological literature. Daniel even got him to acknowledge that when Calley ordered Meadlo to kill, he knew death would result, an admission seemingly at odds with his insistence that the defendant lacked the capacity to premeditate. The prosecutor forced Hamman to admit that he, too, was not board-certified and that he did not read regularly the major journals in his field. In addition, Daniel induced him to concede that Calley not only had no mental illness but was "normal with respect to most of the men who served in Vietnam." Although Hamman claimed the defendant had told him he did not know if he had killed anyone at My Lai, Daniel extracted from him an admission that the defendant had reported telling Meadlo to "waste" some people. Hamman insisted that even though Calley wanted those individuals dead, he did not have the intent to kill them; in his mind there was a difference between killing (which Americans were told from childhood was wrong) and wasting. Besides pushing Hamman into such implausible positions, Daniel also forced him to reveal that he had contacted Latimer to volunteer his services as a witness and to admit, "I do not believe that we should hold any person responsible for [the My Lai situation]."

By the time Daniel finished with the psychiatrists, their value to the defense was problematic at best. Lieutenant Calley would have to exculpate himself. A seemingly "small, lonely figure," he took the stand on the afternoon of 22 February. Latimer walked him through his early life and his pre–My Lai military career, pausing along the way to emphasize that his army training had stressed obedience to orders while giving slight attention to the Geneva Convention.

After arriving in Vietnam, Calley said, he had learned that "everyone was a potential enemy." Men and women were equally dangerous, and because of their "unexpectedness," children were the most menacing of all. The casualties his unit suffered prior to the My Lai operation instilled in him "a deeper sense of hatred for the enemy." Calley took away from Medina's 15 March briefing the impression that the 48th VC Battalion was in Pinkville, that they "would have to neutralize My Lai (4) completely," and that there were "no civilians in the area."

He acknowledged shooting only three people. Two were men (one wearing "a bright green uniform") whom he encountered in a large concrete house, and the other was an individual he saw running away through the rice paddies, who subsequently proved to be a small boy. Calley denied having killed a monk, saying he had butt-stroked a man he was interrogating but never shot him. Although acknowledging that he had fired into the irrigation ditch, Calley claimed to have expended only about a dozen rounds all morning. He even maintained that he had not planned to waste Vietnamese during the operation and had formed neither a specific nor a general intent to kill. Calley denied having physically pushed anyone into the ditch and said all he had ordered his men to do was move people through it to the other side.

While admitting that he had ordered Meadlo to waste some prisoners if he could not get rid of them, the defendant said he had done so only once—at the ditch. He had never seen a trail junction, let alone issued such a directive there. Furthermore, the order to "waste the Vietnamese" had originated with Medina, who wanted them killed because they were slowing down his platoon. Asked directly why he had instructed Meadlo to "waste them," Calley answered, "Because that was my order . . . [from my] commanding officer, sir, Captain Medina." Latimer guided him through testimony that seemed designed to establish that Medina had been motivated by a desire to pump up his body count. To Hammer it seemed that Calley's defense had once again become "It was all Medina's fault."

Determined to establish that it was actually all Calley's fault, when the time for cross-examination arrived, Daniel loosed coiled tension. He pounded away at the defendant for four hours in a hard-edged voice that demanded immediate answers. Most of his questions traversed ground already covered and were designed simply to trip up Calley or trap him in inconsistencies. Latimer eventually complained, with some justification, that they were becoming repetitious and argumentative. Daniel did, however, raise doubts about Calley's story by forcing him to profess inability to remember details of matters about which he had testified on direct.

The prosecutor also elicited some answers that hurt the defendant. Calley acknowledged not being fired upon while landing at My Lai (4) and never receiving any information that his troops had suffered casualties, been shot at, or encountered booby traps. The accused even admitted he had not checked the men he shot in the house to see if they were armed. He had not discriminated among the Vietnamese he encountered in the village because they "were all the enemy," and consequently needed to be destroyed. His reason for ordering some of them gathered up was so they could be used as human mine detectors (as Medina had instructed). Although he now acknowledged firing "six to eight" shots into the ditch, Calley claimed not to know whether he had hit anyone. "My main thing was to . . . finish off these people as fast as possible and get my people into position." He repeatedly acknowledged telling Meadlo, "If he couldn't move the people, to 'waste them,'" and conceded he had said to Hugh Thompson that the only way to evacuate the civilians his men were holding was with a hand grenade.

Although occasionally very effective, Daniel's grilling grew increasingly less productive, and Kennedy became steadily more protective of the defendant. Courtroom observers were nevertheless a bit disappointed when the prosecutor suddenly terminated his cross-examination. Apparently so were the members of the court, for they directed a number of questions of their own to the defendant. Asked by McIntosh to define the term "civilians" as he had used it in describing the people rounded up for use as human mine detectors, Calley responded that it meant "non-regular troops, civilian VC forces." His answer made as much sense as most of the confused and internally contradictory defense case, a case that Latimer rested after his client withdrew from the witness stand.

Daniel counterattacked with two weeks of rebuttal testimony. He called three psychiatrists who had conducted the sanity board examination at Walter Reed. All agreed that Calley was sane. He suffered from no mental disease or transient mental disorder, they testified, and had experienced no greater battle strain than any of his men.

Daniel also recalled several prosecution witnesses who had attended Medina's 15 March briefing to dispute defense claims that the captain had ordered his company to kill everyone in My Lai (4). He buttressed their testimony with that of Jeffrey LaCross, the former commander of the Third Platoon, who confirmed that Medina had said everything in the village was to be destroyed but added that the captain had also remarked that if civilians in

{ *Defenseless* }   179

the area were helping the VC, it was because they had been forced to do so. During the assault, LaCross reported, "the old man" had instructed him to hold some detained civilians for interrogation. Task Force Barker's intelligence officer, Captain Eugene Kotouc, who had heard both Medina and Barker issue their orders, testified that they had given instructions to destroy houses and livestock but had said nothing about killing women and children or taking no prisoners. Major Calhoun maintained he had overheard a radio transmission in which Barker told Medina to make sure his troops were not hurting civilians.

While countering defense efforts to shift responsibility for the massacre up the chain of command, Daniel also sought to refute claims that Calley lacked the capacity to premeditate and the ability to form a specific intent to kill. He now got Turner's story about the woman the lieutenant had shot into the record, along with testimony from James Bergthold that he had seen Calley point his rifle down into a well and blow the brains out of a prisoner some soldiers had thrown in there "to see if he can swim," a story that two other witnesses confirmed. Daniel also tried to rebut Calley's testimony that Medina had ordered the use of human minesweepers, but LaCross undercut that effort by acknowledging that he, too, had used prisoners as "guides" through minefields.

The witnesses the prosecutor presented for purposes of rebuttal were not the last the jury heard. Judge Kennedy informed the members of the court that they had the right to call anyone who had not appeared whose testimony they considered vital. The court submitted a long list of names, which included Generals Koster and Peers. Informing the members that their job was simply to determine whether Calley was guilty, not to conduct a wide-ranging investigation into the My Lai incident, Kennedy pared their list down to Colonel Henderson, Captain Medina, and Sergeant Mitchell.

As one of Calley's squad leaders and an alleged participant in the massacre at the irrigation ditch, Mitchell obviously possessed relevant information, but Article 31 of the UCMJ gave him a right against compulsory self-incrimination somewhat broader than that conferred on all Americans by the Fifth Amendment. On 20 November 1970 a court-martial had acquitted him of crimes allegedly committed at My Lai (4), but on 8 March 1971 the staff judge advocate at Fort Hood, Texas, where Mitchell was stationed, received a "TWX" (teletype message) saying that the Chief of Staff had ordered him "flagged" while the army reviewed his "professional duty performance" to see if it met "the standards the nation and the army expects of one of his rank and experience." Mitchell's attorney claimed the TWX justified an assertion of the Article 31 privilege. The lawyers disagreed about whether flagging could lead to anything more than administrative action against him, and whether, if there were no possible criminal consequences, Article 31 even applied. Kennedy thought it probably did not, but to avoid any unfairness, he ruled Mitchell did not have to testify.

Colonel Henderson did appear. He was the highest ranking of 104 witnesses, but little of what he had to say bore directly on the guilt or innocence of Lieutenant Calley. Henderson reported seeing from the air a couple of corpses dressed in military uniforms. Although he had ordered Charlie Company to sweep back through My Lai (4) to get a true body count, that was only because of a "discrepancy or two" in a report he had received from Colonel Barker. According to Henderson, Barker had said nothing to him about civilian casualties.

Unlike Henderson, Captain Medina could testify from personal knowledge about matters central to the Calley case. He was anxious do so, for the defendant's testimony (communicated to Medina by his own lawyers) infuriated the former company commander. Daniel wanted to call Medina as a rebuttal witness, but his supervisor, Major William Eckhardt, forbade him to do so. Along with the Judge Advocate General and Secretary Resor, Eckhardt reasoned that if the government put Medina on the stand, it would be vouching for his credibility, and he believed polygraph results showed some of what the captain was saying was untruthful. Aware that the lie detector test indicated his client was telling the truth about his briefing and some events of 16 March, Medina's attorney, F. Lee Bailey, accused the army of trying to silence his client. Bailey filed a petition with the Court of Military Appeals, challenging its refusal to let Daniel put the captain on the stand. Before that court had a chance to rule, Kennedy told the jury it could call him as its witness.

While Medina was preparing to leave his duty station (ironically, the morgue at Fort McPherson, Georgia) to come to Fort Benning, he was formally ordered to face a court-martial. One of the three specifications in the murder charges against him in effect accused the captain of responsibility for killings for which Calley was being tried. He and his attorneys were convinced the army was trying to gag him by forcing him to invoke his privilege against compelled self-incrimination. Boiling mad, Medina insisted on telling his story anyhow.

Hammer found him "an impressive witness. Medina was articulate and had a good memory for dates, unit numbers, and other details." Guided by Judge Kennedy, he described his army career and Charlie Company's history prior to 16 March 1968. According to Medina, Barker had told him on 15 March that his unit could expect a heavy engagement at My Lai (4) and that it had permission to destroy the village. When Medina briefed his troops, he repeated what the task torce commander had told him. "I did not make any reference to the handling of prisoners," the captain testified. In response to a question, however, he had told his men they were not to kill women and children.

Medina recounted in considerable detail what he himself had done during the My Lai (4) operation. He admitted shooting a woman because he thought she had a grenade and issuing instructions to use prisoners to lead elements of the company through minefields. When asked, however, "Did you at any time on the 15th of March or at any time on the 16th of March order or direct Lieutenant Calley to kill or waste any Vietnamese people?" he answered emphatically, "No sir." Medina denied being informed by Calley that villagers were slowing him down, ordering him by radio to speed up his progress, or reprimanding him for not following orders. He had not told anyone to move civilians out of the way or get rid of them, the captain claimed. Medina also disputed Calley's contention that he had discussed body counts with his platoon leaders during a chow break. He reported observing twenty to twenty-eight bodies, apparently of civilians, at a trail junction and identified them in a photograph taken by Haeberle, but he claimed these corpses were too far away to tell if they had been killed by small-arms fire or (as he hoped) by helicopter gunships and artillery. He also insisted that he had not become aware until later (there was some inconsistency about precisely when) that his men might have killed far more noncombatants.

Latimer subjected Medina to a lengthy, sometimes venomous and even angry, cross-examination. Becoming exhausted, the captain grew less direct and articulate, but he survived the onslaught. He admitted participating in a cover-up but claimed his motivations were a desire to avoid disgracing the army and concern about the repercussions of the massacre for his family and the country, as well as himself. Since the statute of limitations had already run on cover-up offenses, this confession struck reporters as a bit too convenient. Yet, among the spectators who had heard both Calley and Medina, the consensus was that the captain's story seemed more believable.

It also strengthened the prosecution's case, which Daniel summarized on 15 March. The government had proved, the prosecutor argued to the jury, that Calley had ordered Meadlo and Conti to shoot unarmed and unresisting men, women, and children at the trail junction, had joined members of his platoon in killing people in the irrigation ditch, had butt-stroked and then shot a monk, and had thrown a two-year-old child into the ditch before shooting it. He reminded jurors that it was not their job to decide whether anyone else had committed crimes at My Lai (4). "Your function is solely to judge the guilt or innocence of the accused."

Daniel reviewed the testimony he believed proved Calley was guilty of all the killings enumerated in the specifications, stressing that, although differing on some details, the witnesses' stories reinforced one another. The biggest problem was that they disagreed about the number of victims. Daniel argued that Haeberle's photograph provided the best evidence of how many

Vietnamese had died at the trail junction. Despite uncertainties concerning the magnitude of the slaughter, Daniel submitted, "With respect to all of the specifications, we have clearly established the fact of death of the victims, and that the accused either killed them or directed that they be killed."

He devoted a great deal of attention to the testimony of the psychiatrists and to the issue of whether Calley had possessed the "mental capacity to entertain the required criminal state of mind." One did not need great intelligence to commit premeditated murder, Daniel insisted. "You've just got to have the ability to think and form the intent to kill somebody and form that intent in your mind before you kill them." Specific intent to kill existed if one's purpose in shooting someone was to bring about her death, rather than just scare or wound her. Enumerating the complex tasks Calley had performed on 16 March, Daniel declared, "If he could think about all those things, he had the mental ability to formulate the attitude that when he pulled the trigger on his weapon, he intended to kill who he shot at, or when he gave the order to Meadlo that he intended for the people to die." The prosecutor reviewed evidence relating to each specification, which, he said, "proved beyond any shadow of a doubt" that the accused had the ability to premeditate and had done so.

Daniel denied that Calley had been ordered to exterminate civilians during Medina's briefing and insisted the testimony of his own RTOs established he had received no instructions on 16 March to waste the Vietnamese he detained. If such orders had been given, they would have been unlawful, and any reasonable man would have known this.

"We have established beyond reasonable doubt every element of every offense we have charged," Daniel concluded. The jurors had listened closely as he summarized the prosecution's case "with an eloquence . . . rarely . . . heard at this trial." As he spoke, Hammer saw some of them nodding, as if in agreement.

Latimer's response, delivered ironically on the morning of 16 March, convinced Hammer the defense attorney was "no more up to this moment than he had [been] to any other." His two-hour summation was directionless, diffuse, and delivered in an often inaudible monotone. Latimer complained that infantrymen were judged by different standards than men who killed with bombs and artillery. He urged jurors not to believe the government's witnesses because their stories were inconsistent, they were seeking to avoid prosecution as accomplices, and infantrymen always exaggerate when telling war stories. He emphasized "that the intelligence information was fantastically wrong" and also attributed the My Lai (4) killings to Charlie Company's earlier experiences and to war itself.

Mostly Latimer blamed Medina. Good young men would not have become involved in such an incident "unless it had been suggested, ordered, or commanded by somebody upstairs," he contended. Furthermore, it was reasonable for untrained troops to follow their company commander's orders. Calley had become "the pigeon" because he was the lowest-ranking officer involved.

Latimer elicited an objection from Daniel and a rebuke from the bench when he suggested that either the lieutenant or the captain must receive the death penalty. Seemingly abandoning hope of winning an acquittal, he explained to jurors the definition of the lesser included offense of manslaughter. Changing direction, Latimer concluded with a hoarse appeal to distinguish between errors in judgment and criminality.

Anxious to get the case to the jury that day, Kennedy ordered Daniel to respond after an early supper break. "There was not a sound or a movement in the whole courtroom while he spoke," Hammer noted. The prosecutor was eloquent. He began by rebutting Latimer's arguments, including his contention that if Calley were guilty of anything, it was only voluntary manslaughter. "They tell you that the accused was not the only man responsible," Daniel observed. "Well, I ask you, did anyone else do any more that day than he did?" He was not ordered to round up civilians and shoot them, and if he had been, no reasonable man would have obeyed such an order.

The facts showed "beyond any shadow of a doubt" that Calley was to blame. Under American law and the laws of war, Daniel asserted, all human beings were entitled to be treated humanely, regardless of their race, nationality, or political affiliation. "The fact that the accused was an American and these were Vietnamese is irrelevant. They were human beings." Calley had summarily executed people never determined to have done anything wrong. His attempts to absolve himself of responsibility "prostitute all of the humanitarian principles for which this nation stands."

Daniel reminded the officer jurors that there were "rules governing your profession." He asked them to make those rules effective and, more than that, to serve as the conscience of the army and the nation by fixing responsibility where it belonged. "The duty is yours to find the accused guilty as charged," the prosecutor concluded.

After a short break, Judge Kennedy instructed the jury. Elucidating the law it must apply, he explained that the defendant was presumed innocent and that the government must prove every element of every offense with which he was charged beyond a reasonable doubt. They could convict Calley only if convinced killings had been committed by him or by "ground troops who acted pursuant to [his] counsel, command, or procurement." Kennedy outlined in considerable detail the elements of the four specifications and what the jury must find in order to convict on each. With respect to the two alleging multiple killings, he instructed that "two-thirds of you must be convinced beyond a reasonable doubt that the same oriental human beings are dead." If they concluded that Calley had killed some but not all of those alleged in a specification, they must modify their findings to reflect the figure on which two-thirds of them agreed.

If, as to any specification, they believed the government had failed to prove all the elements of premeditated murder beyond a reasonable doubt, they might consider the lesser offenses of unpremeditated murder and voluntary manslaughter. Kennedy explained the elements of each. Because premeditated murder required "formation of a specific intent to kill and consideration of the act intended to bring about death," he told them, they should ponder carefully all evidence showing Calley might have been suffering from a mental condition or impairment that deprived him of the ability to entertain a considered design to kill.

Kennedy explained that an intentional killing would be only voluntary manslaughter if committed in the sudden heat of passion, provided it resulted from a provocation "such as would excite uncontrollable passion in the reasonable man" and so much time had not elapsed since the provocation (he mentioned Charlie Company's previous casualties as possibilities) that a reasonable person would have cooled off.

Because there was no direct evidence that when Calley shot at the small child he was accused of murdering he actually hit it, Kennedy said they might consider convicting him of the lesser offense of assault with intent to commit murder. He also instructed jurors to think about whether the defendant had been acting pursuant to orders when he caused the deaths of his alleged victims. He added, however, that any order to kill "unresisting human beings" would have been unlawful, and that if a subordinate knew a superior's order was illegal or "a man of ordinary sense and understanding" would have known, it was no excuse. Concluding his summation at 2145 hours, he gave the case to the jury.

"It deliberated all week and the next, " Calley recalls. Except when needed in court, he waited in his apartment. Usually Anne Moore was there. Frequently, so were other well-wishers, reporters, and hangers-on, who made him feel important by listening intently to what he had to say and seemingly taking his ideas seriously. Unable to bear being alone, Calley kept his guests there late into the night, pouring them one bourbon after another. Although sometimes optimistic, he knew he would need luck to go free. Unable to sleep, the anxious defendant stayed up past dawn, making papier-mâché statues and drinking.

Meanwhile, the jurors slowly and meticulously reviewed the evidence. They pored over every exhibit and asked to have the testimony of so many witnesses reread that an angry Latimer accused them of acting "more like investigators than a jury." "We looked for anything that would prove Lieutenant Calley was innocent," Kinard told Hammer later. "We gave Lieutenant Calley every benefit of every doubt." Several days into the deliberations, Brown was rushed to the hospital with severe stomach pains, raising briefly the possibility that the court-martial might end anticlimactically in a mistrial. The problem proved to be minor, however, and the jury was soon back at work. Through nine days of "knock-down-drag-outs" it relived and argued about the slaughter at My Lai (4).

On the tenth day the jurors finally voted on the first specification, the one involving the killings at the trail junction. It took only a single ballot to find Calley guilty, although there was a dispute about the number of Vietnamese killed there. Two days later, on Sunday, 28 March, they decided to convict him of the killings at the ditch. Again, although there was a dispute about numbers, only one ballot was required. The next day the jury voted to convict Calley of premeditated murder for killing the man believed to be a monk and found him guilty of assault with intent to commit murder in the case of the small child.

At approximately 1530 hours on Monday, 29 March, the phone rang in the defendant's apartment. An hour later, Calley, flanked by Latimer and Raby, was standing before Colonel Ford. He saluted the president of the court stiffly, then waited to hear the verdict. "Lieutenant Calley," Ford announced, "it is my duty . . . to inform you that the court, . . . two thirds of the members present at the time the vote was taken concurring in each finding of guilty, finds you: Of Specification 1 of the Charge: Guilty of premeditated murder." The jury had convicted him of killing "an unknown number, not less than 1," rather than the alleged "unknown number not less than 30," but Calley could take little consolation in that, for it had also found him guilty of murdering "an unknown number, not less than 20," at the irrigation ditch. Ford went on to inform him of the jury's verdicts on the specifications involving the monk and the child. It had convicted him of at least twenty-two premeditated murders, as well as one assault with intent to commit murder. As Calley heard the verdicts, his eyes widened. When Ford finished, he tried to salute but could not get his hand all the way up to his forehead. As Lieutenant Calley walked stiffly back to the defense table, the courtroom was absolutely silent.

Kennedy ordered the members of the court to return at 1300

the next day to begin the sentencing phase of the trial. In it, the issue would be simply whether Lieutenant Calley should live or die. Under Article 118, the minimum penalty for premeditated murder was imprisonment for life. The maximum punishment was death.

The defense could have called witnesses to testify about mitigating factors, which might persuade the jury to spare the life of the convicted mass murderer. Latimer chose not to do that. The members of the court heard only arguments from Calley's two civilian lawyers and a brief statement by the defendant himself. Kay asked jurors to consider "matters in extenuation." One of these was Calley's motives. The other was whether any of his actions "had as a basis the general policies, both politically and militarily, that were being followed in the Republic of South Vietnam at the time these acts were committed."

Latimer, again rambling and almost incoherent, emphasized what he considered mitigating factors. One was that Calley had been "woefully and inadequately trained." Another was that he had been "a good boy and remained that" until the army made him a killer and sent him "into that Oriental climate in Vietnam . . . to fight." "Who taught him to kill, kill, kill?" Latimer asked. He also made an emotional appeal to the jurors' patriotism. Flourishing some of the thousands of letters of support the defense had received, he asserted that "no case in military justice, since its beginning, has ever torn America apart" the way this one was doing. Flags would fly at half-staff all over the country if parents thought their boys were going to be taken into the military, made aggressive by the army, and then punished for doing the job it gave them to do. Perhaps Latimer's most telling point, however, was that of the twelve members of Charlie Company who had participated in the My Lai (4) incident and remained in the military long enough so they could be prosecuted, only two, Medina and Calley, still faced possible punishment. "I think that it is a cruel situation [that] Lieutenant Calley is the only one who has been found guilty," he asserted. Latimer concluded by arguing his client could still "make something out of himself and his life but can't do it from a graveyard."

Calley himself declined "to stand here and plead for my life or my freedom." Looking small, lonely, and dejected, he addressed the court for just over two minutes. If he had committed a crime, the lieutenant said, it was "in judgment of my values." He had valued the lives of his troops more than those of an enemy the military had never described as anything but Communists. "Yesterday you stripped me of all my honor," he concluded. "Please, by your actions that you take today, don't strip future soldiers of their honor. I beg of you."

Daniel responded, "You did not strip him of his honor. What he did stripped him of his honor." The prosecutor did not, however, ask for the death penalty. He left that decision entirely to the jury.

It elected not to impose the ultimate punishment. At 1430 the next afternoon, Colonel Ford informed Calley that the court had sentenced him "to be confined at hard labor for the length of your natural life." In addition, he was to be dismissed from the army and to forfeit all pay and allowances. Obviously relieved, Calley slumped briefly. Then, straightening himself, he saluted and announced, "I'll do my best, sir."

"This court is closed," Judge Kennedy declared. After forty-five days, one of the longest courts martial in American history had finally come to an end. Unlike the courtroom proceedings, the public controversy surrounding the Calley case was far from over.

CHAPTER 10

An Unlikely Hero

"He's been crucified," screamed a woman outside the courthouse after Lieutenant Calley's sentence was announced. "He should get a medal," she added in disgust. Soon America's airwaves were alive with the sounds of "The Battle Hymn of Lieutenant Calley." After a voice-over about a little boy who wanted to grow up to serve his country, Nashville's Tony Nelson trolled:

> My name is William Calley, I'm a
>   soldier of this land,
> I've vowed to do my duty and to
>   gain the upper hand,
> But they've made me out a villain,
>   they have stamped me with a brand
> As we go marching on.

Within three days after the court-martial ended, the Plantation label sold over 200,000 copies of Nelson's improbable ode to a mass murderer. Three weeks later *Life* magazine observed, "The case of William Calley simply will not rub away. . . . [H]is name still crops up daily." Calley, a man a court-martial had convicted of killing twenty-two Vietnamese civilians, had become a national hero. Every measure of public opinion revealed popular outrage at his conviction. Members of Congress joined hundreds of thousands of Americans in protesting the verdict, and President Nixon intervened personally in the case. Although Captain Daniel challenged the propriety of his action, the people backed the president, for Calley was their hero. To them the little lieutenant was a victim of a war with which they had become disaffected and a government they did not trust.

Senator Robert Taft Jr. (R. Ohio) recognized that "the widespread reaction against the Calley conviction was ill-informed and in error," but his was one of only a few dissenting voices. *The Nation* maintained that "there can be no quarrel with the verdict," and the *Washington Evening Star* found it "difficult to see how the six members of the Fort Benning jury could have found otherwise." *Commonweal* warned against "deadening our abhorrence of acts like Mylai." Likewise, the *Chicago Tribune*, while pointing out that the Vietcong had also committed savage war crimes, conceded, "Two wrongs, of course, don't make a right."

While a few publications accepted the verdict, Taft's fellow politicians overwhelmingly condemned it. Governor George Wallace of Alabama, who had been the American Independent Party's presidential candidate in 1968 and was seeking the 1972 Democratic nomination, made freeing Calley a campaign theme. After asking Selective Service officials in his state to see if they could suspend the draft there, Wallace headed for Columbus to visit the lieutenant and take part in a rally that also featured Georgia's lieutenant governor, Lester Maddox. Maddox wrote to President Nixon, urging him "to immediately utilize the vast power of your office to free 1st Lt. William L. Calley, Jr." Not to be outdone, Governor Jimmy Carter of Georgia proclaimed "American Fighting Man's Day" and asked citizens to drive with their headlights turned on. Mississippi's governor, John Bell Williams, informed Vice President Spiro Agnew that his state was "about ready to secede from the union" over Calley. The Louisiana legislature and the Texas Senate passed resolutions urging Nixon to pardon the convicted killer, and the Arkansas Senate joined them in requesting executive clemency. In Florida the city commission of Plant City and the mayor and approximately 3,000 citizens of Crestview enlisted in the pro-Calley army. While support for Calley was strongest in the South, his backers included politicians from throughout the country. The elected officials of Artesia, New Mexico, protested the verdict, and that state's Representative Manuel Lujan Jr. urged the president to pardon Calley, or at least reduce his sentence. The Kansas House of Representatives and even the Guam legislature

{ *The Vietnam War on Trial* }

called for executive clemency. The county commissioners of Lancaster County, Pennsylvania, a New York assemblyman, and the mayor of Concord, California, all wrote to the president to complain about the verdict. In Pittsfield, Illinois, the entire draft board resigned "in protest of the results of the court-martial of Lt. William Calley, Jr."

Protesting politicians and public officials were only echoing the sentiments of their constituents. Polls revealed overwhelming opposition to the conviction and life sentence Calley had received. Louis Harris reported to the White House over the weekend after the court-martial ended that "a slight plurality of the American public [36 to 35 percent] disagree with the verdict of the military tribunal," and 29 percent "could not make up its mind on whether or not Lt. Calley should have been declared guilty or innocent." Indecision quickly evaporated, as did most of the support for the verdict. A telephone survey done for the president by the Opinion Research Center on 1 April found 78 percent of those interviewed disagreed with the conviction and life sentence imposed on Calley. On 7 April, the Gallup Poll reported that a special survey, commissioned by *Newsweek*, had found that only 9 percent of Americans approved of the court-martial's finding that he was guilty of premeditated murder, while 79 percent disapproved. When a Wheeling, West Virginia, radio station asked its listeners to comment on the verdict, 1,412 of them responded; only 15 agreed with it. Even Harris's polling organization eventually found 65 percent disapproval of the guilty verdict, versus only 24 percent approval. Since most Americans thought Calley should have been acquitted, it was hardly surprising that 79 percent of those surveyed by Gallup considered life imprisonment too harsh a penalty. A poll done for the president found 51 percent of the public wanted Nixon to free Calley, and another 28 percent thought the chief executive should reduce his sentence. A mere 9 percent agreed with the court-martial that the former platoon leader ought to spend the rest of his life in prison.

Opposition to the conviction and sentence was intense as well as widespread. During the trial Calley's supporters had bombarded him with fan mail. By mid-February he had already received more than 10,000 letters, only 7 of which were derogatory. After the jury returned its verdict, a stream of fan mail turned into a torrent, reaching 10,000 pieces per day. To keep up with it, Calley's girlfriend and secretary had to buy an automatic letter opener. As late as 19 April, supportive missives were still pouring into his apartment at the rate of 2,000 per day.

Support for Calley and opposition to the verdict were particularly intense among former members of the armed forces. On 1 April a group of veterans' leaders met with Nixon aide Charles Colson, demanding to see the president. An official of the Veterans of Foreign Wars (VFW) told Colson that nothing since the Kennedy assassination had gotten the country so excited. William Hauck of the American Legion informed him that his organization's telephone had "been ringing night and day for the past two days—calls from every state in the Union." John Keller of the Disabled American Veterans reported, "Getting lots of calls and mail condemning the verdict and supporting Calley." The experience of the Fleet Reserve was similar. Martin Coy of AMVETS told Colson its "membership and post representatives have been calling from all over the country condemning the verdict."

Besides communicating their outrage to the defendant and to veterans organizations, Americans bombarded the government with phone calls, telegrams, and letters. They wrote to military lawyers at Fort Benning and to the Judge Advocate General in Washington. Even the United States Court of Military Appeals, which thus far had played no role whatsoever in the case (and would not entertain Calley's appeal until late 1973), received hundreds of letters and petitions from his supporters. Most came from the Dallas–Fort Worth area, and many were exactly alike. Obviously, someone in north Texas had mounted a well-orchestrated, if somewhat misdirected, correspondence campaign on Calley's behalf. In identically-worded missives, Charlotte Maare and a number of other protesters communicated their belief that "Lt. William Calley should never have been brought to trial." "I think it's a shame and disgrace for them to have found him guilty of murder," declared Mary Mikel of Dallas.

The hundreds of pieces of mail that poured into the Court of

Military Appeals would have been barely noticed at the White House, which received tens of thousands. The deluge started immediately after the verdict was announced. By early the following evening, the White House had received 5,505 telegrams and 3,075 telephone calls. All but 5 of the telegrams expressed opposition to the verdict; callers opposed it by a margin estimated at 100 to 1. By 5 April the number of phone calls was up to 8,500 and the number of telegrams to 50,823. In addition, 21,407 letters had been received. Communications on the Calley case continued to run 99 percent against the verdict, and they kept pouring in. A Florida VFW leader forwarded the names of a thousand people in his state who wanted the president to help the convicted officer. From Dry Prong, Louisiana, where high school students were reportedly "100% behind Lt. Calley," came petitions urging his release, signed by over 4,500 persons. The mayor of Macon, Georgia, delivered a petition bearing approximately 30,000 signatures, and a disc jockey from Cayce, South Carolina, brought in a duffle bag containing 5,000 letters and "a few thousand more names on petitions." By 13 May the White House had received 260,000 letters and cards and approximately 75,000 telegrams. Over 99 percent of correspondents continued to oppose the verdict. A White House aide noted that the "flood of communications about Calley has been exceptionally intemperate in nature." Normally, telegrams and letters of that type would have been filed without reply, but correspondence on this subject seemed to require acknowledgment. The White House developed three form letters for use in responding to "VIP Calley mail," but those disposed of only a small fraction of the correspondence. By 13 May it appeared that acknowledging the rest could take until August and also be prohibitively expensive (costing an estimated $72,300 plus labor). Reluctant to offend Calley's loyal legions, White House staffers thrashed about, searching for a suitable substitute for individual replies.

Capitol Hill also found itself awash in pro-Calley correspondence. Two days after the conviction, Senator Edward Gurney (R. Fla.) wrote the president that his office had "been deluged with telegrams, phone calls and mail, all protesting the severity of the verdict." On 1 April Representative Jim Wright (D. Tex.) informed Nixon that among his constituents "there has been a considerable outcry of strong disapproval, which seems to be quite generally felt." Wright had received spontaneous expressions from an unusually large number of people from across the political spectrum. To Congressman Louis Stokes (D. Ohio) the most striking thing about the messages flowing into his office was "the overwhelming agony and desperate search for understanding they reflect." Representative Elwood H. Hillis (R. Ind.), who had received thousands of letters, chose to pass along 15 from high school students so the president could "have the sentiment of our youth in this regard." A White House aide who checked with the offices of fifteen other congressmen found that the volume of mail and telephone calls received by most representatives from the Northeast and Midwest was moderate, but that directed at legislators from Arizona and California was heavier, and southerners had been deluged. Jim Broyhill (R. N.C.) had received 3,000 letters, and Bill Brock (R. Tenn.), 3,500. A member of Broyhill's staff reported "Greater spontaneity and more volume of mail on this than even [the May 1970 invasion of] Cambodia." This was, according to an aide to Joe McDade (R. Pa.), the "loudest outburst since [the] school prayer issue six years ago." From 98 to 100 percent of the communications received by these legislators opposed the court-martial's action. So did 97 percent of the 2,944 messages sent to Senator William Spong (D. Va.) "I have received hundreds of letters . . . and not one . . . has been in favor of the sentence," Representative Edward A. Garmatz (D. Md.) informed the White House.

Senators and congressmen echoed the sentiments of their constituents. Representative Don Fuqua (D. Fla.) introduced a concurrent resolution offering Calley the opportunity "to present his case to the American people on the floor of the Congress convened in joint session." Other House members submitted a resolution urging the president to grant Calley executive clemency. Although the Pentagon strenuously opposed House Joint Resolution 573, Senator Abraham Ribicoff (D. Conn.) issued a statement in which he, too, urged Nixon to take such action. Ribicoff was a dove, but his hawkish colleague Strom Thurmond (R. S.C.) was equally negative about the court-martial, characterizing it as a serious setback to the army and a threat to national security. Senators Taft and Jacob Javits (R. N.Y.) defended the verdict, but as Javits acknowledged, most of their colleagues disagreed with them.

Numerous members of Congress communicated their support for Calley to the White House. "I feel it is my responsibility to report to you that without exception every one of the many constituents from the Sixth District of Louisiana contacting me are [*sic*] outraged at the conviction of Lieutenant Calley," wrote Representative John R. Rarick (D. La.). He implored the president to grant Calley an immediate pardon. So did Congressmen Walter Flowers (D. Ala.), Walter S. Baring (D. Nev.), and William H. Harsha (R. Ohio). Representatives Ed Jones (D. Tenn.), Richard Fulton (D. Tenn.), James Quillen (R. Tenn.), Richard Ichord (D. Mo.), and Romano L. Mazzoli (D. Ky.) all advocated executive clemency. Mazzoli wanted Nixon to grant it only if the conviction was not reversed by the military appellate courts, but Congressman Joel T. Broyhill (R. Va.) implored the president, in a letter of 31 March, to act immediately "to end the public crucifixion of our defense establishment." Broyhill "urgently recommend[ed]" that, as commander in chief, Nixon "set aside the provisions of the Manual for Court [*sic*] Martial for military review of the Calley case" and direct the solicitor general to refer it and all others arising out of the My Lai incident to the civilian courts.

The president did not take the legally impossible tack Broyhill advocated, but he did act quickly. According to Haldeman, on 31 March the Calley case was the focus of concern at the Western White House in San Clemente, California. The question, he wrote in his diary, was what the president "should or should not do in reaction to this, as public opinion continues to mount." Although there was disagreement within his staff, Nixon was determined to do something immediately. During an early afternoon meeting with his domestic affairs adviser, John Ehrlichman, he advocated acting before "a lot of review" made this more difficult. A couple of hours later, Ehrlichman noted, although Kissinger favored letting "it build up," Nixon's "strong feeling [was] to move on it now." Considering Calley his responsibility, the president was unwilling to delegate the matter to Secretary of Defense Laird. Late in the afternoon he asked Ehrlichman to get recommendations from all five lawyers in his cabinet, and that evening Nixon met personally with one of them, Secretary of the Treasury John Connally, who advocated immediate action to free the lieutenant.

Again on 1 April, "Calley dominated the day," Haldeman noted in his diary. At 0900 he and Ehrlichman met with the president, who insisted that they must act "on the basis of what does us the most good." According to Haldeman, Nixon felt "that maybe there's a position to be taken that an act of compassion on the part of the P[resident] wouldn't be a bad thing to do at this point." Nixon added, "We've got to move now." That was because, as Ehrlichman noted during a noon meeting, he believed they "[h]ad to hold war effort support to end it our way." Ehrlichman thought nothing would be done about Calley that day, but at 1230 Nixon picked up the telephone and called the chairman of the Joint Chiefs of Staff, Admiral Thomas Moorer, in Washington. He ordered that, while appealing his conviction, Calley should be confined in his BOQ apartment rather than the Fort Benning stockade.

In taking this action the president apparently went against the wishes of Secretary Laird, who had urged him to refuse even to comment on the case on the grounds that it would be inappropriate for him to do so when motions could still be filed in the trial court and none of the reviewing authorities, including the president, yet had access to the records of the court-martial. Nixon also seems to have ignored the advice of White House Counsel John Dean. In a memorandum written on 1 April, Dean argued that while the president might use his pardoning power to grant executive clemency at any time, he could not exercise piecemeal the powers of a court-martial convening authority. One such power, although he did not mention it specifically, was changing the conditions of a defendant's confinement. Dean considered it unwise for the president to take some action as a convening authority be-

{ *The Vietnam War on Trial* }

cause this would make him the convening authority for all future aspects of the case. Should something happen that resulted in his disqualification, "the proceedings would be frustrated," because there would then be no higher convening authority to whom the matter could be referred. Dean recommended against intervening in the case at the present time. After Nixon did so anyhow, Eric J. Fygi, of the Office of Legal Counsel, on whose analysis Dean had apparently relied in drafting his 1 April memorandum, character- ized the president's order to Admiral Moorer as "of very doubtful legality." In his opinion, Fygi stated in a 6 April memorandum, the president's authority "as Commander-in-Chief, by itself [was] in- sufficient to authorize [his] action in directing that Calley be re- leased from the stockade."

Nixon took a legally dubious action that the Pentagon consid- ered unwise because he saw political advantage in doing so. The decisive advice came from Special Counsel Charles Colson, who called from Washington to suggest (according to Larry Higby) that "the President could immediately order Calley released to his home pending appellate review of his case." Colson pointed out that a civilian could remain free on bail while appealing, as heavyweight boxing champion Cassius Clay was doing while seeking to overturn his conviction for draft evasion. He argued that keeping Calley out of the stockade would enable the presi- dent to capture public sentiment, without foreclosing any future options. Politically, the action he recommended was a great suc- cess. It elicited spontaneous applause from the House of Repre- sentatives, Nixon recalled, and Governors Wallace and Carter commended his decision.

It also bought time to consider other options, which Nixon and his advisers discussed for most of Friday, 2 April. "This turned out to be pretty much Calley day all day, as we worked on the whole question of the approach to further action," Haldeman wrote in his diary. At first Nixon was anxious for the White House to get out the details of what he had done. The president may even have proposed putting an end to the whole My Lai (4) matter by dismissing the charges against Calley, Medina, and the others in return for their resignations from the army, for at some point Ehrlichman wrote out by hand a proposed statement saying he was doing that. One of the president's aides was urging caution, however. While public opinion overwhelmingly opposed the verdict, Tom Charles Huston warned, hawks and doves condemned it for very different reasons. It was "too soon to get a good feel for just exactly what the impact will be over the long term." Noting that the president would be under heavy pressure to act immediately, Huston argued that hasty action could be risky and prove damaging in the long run. "My recommendation," he wrote in a memorandum, "is that we all sleep on this matter for a few days, until we get a better feel for the depth of public sentiment." Others agreed with Huston. Dean, of course, had urged the president not to become involved in the case "at this time," pointing out that the life sentence Calley had received was likely to be reduced during appellate review and reminding him that the conviction was for "particularly aggravated conduct" that constituted "a gross violation of the customary law of war." When Ehrlichman discussed the case with the director of the Office of Management and Budget, George Schultz, on 1 April, Schultz also warned the president to be careful.

Nixon ultimately heeded such advice. He avoided meeting with Latimer, who had said during a Wednesday television appearance that he would welcome an invitation to talk with the president. During a midafternoon briefing for reporters, Press Secretary Ron Ziegler seemed reluctant to expand at all on what he had said the previous day about Calley's release. Nixon's inclination, Ehrlichman noted, was to commute the lieutenant's sentence. Nevertheless, according to Haldeman, the president "decided finally, after going through all the range of options, to announce now that he will review the case after the final sentence." In other words, as Ehrlichman summarized the decision in handwritten notes, "The President does nothing." Yet he would give the appearance of doing something.

At a press conference on the morning of 3 April, Ziegler announced that the president had decided, "before any final sentence is carried out in the case of Lt. Calley," to "personally review the case and finally decide it." The press secretary then turned the microphone over to Ehrlichman, who described for reporters how court-martial convictions were reviewed within the military legal system. The president could intervene after this process was completed and the sentence put into execution by granting a pardon, he explained, but Nixon was "saying here that he will not wait until that time, but will come into the case prior to the operation of the sentence itself." The president had decided to inject an "extralegal ingredient" normally added only when passing on pardon applications because the Calley case had "captured the interest of the American people," and it "was important for him to make clear at this stage of the proceedings that the entire review process would include more than simply the technical, legal review which the Code of Military Justice provides." In response to a question, Ehrlichman denied that Nixon was trying to, or that his action would, influence the appellate review of Calley's conviction. He also denied that the officers involved in that process would be influenced by the president's action in releasing Calley from the stockade. Ehrlichman insisted the announcement he was making was not meant to denigrate in any way the military judicial system. It was being made simply because Ziegler had gotten so many questions about the case. Ehrlichman denied that public pressure was influencing the administration of justice.

The White House clearly was sensitive to public opinion, however, and the 3 April announcement was intended to appease the masses. "With this whole thing behind him," Haldeman noted, Nixon could now turn his attention to a scheduled address on Vietnam. In addition, announcing that the president would personally review the case after the appellate process was completed justified future silence concerning what he was doing for Lieutenant Calley. "Since the President has made his position very clear that there will be no official Presidential involvement in [Calley's and related] cases while they are being adjudicated . . . , it would be improper and inappropriate for White House Staff members to make any comments or statements . . . regarding these cases," Dean advised his colleagues in a memorandum on 9 April. When the Judge Advocate General inquired in July whether the confinement of Calley to his quarters was intended to remain in effect until the president reviewed the case, Dean, responding in the affirmative, informed him that the White House did not want to create the impression that the president was making a new decision. He also recommended that there "be no further comment by the White House on the case until the final action is taken by the President," a suggestion Ehrlichman endorsed.

The 3 April announcement also bought the White House time to figure out how to dispose of a political hot potato. At the president's request, Ehrlichman formed a small working group to develop options for dealing with the My Lai (4) cases. Dean was a member and did most of the work, conducting extensive research on them, as well as on other allegations of war crimes in Vietnam. Brigadier General Al Haig assisted him by obtaining information from the Pentagon. None of this benefited Calley. When his lawyers wrote a private letter to the president on 27 January 1972, requesting immediate executive clemency, Dean responded that the issues "must first be narrowed to the greatest extent possible," and consequently that it would be "inappropriate to interrupt th[e] process of judicial review."

Although buying time to consider its options, the White House failed to extricate itself from the fires of the Calley controversy. The reason was a military revolt against presidential intervention in the case. The verdict had elicited an emotional reaction from many GIs. Hersh, who was in Vietnam when it came down, felt so threatened by the anger of the soldiers around him that he went into hiding. Out in the Ashau Valley some artillerymen christened one of their guns "Calley's Avenger." Back at Fort Benning about a hundred protesters, most of them GIs, marched on the stockade, demanding the lieutenant's release. Soon infantrymen were double-timing across the post chanting: "Calley, Calley, he's our man. If he can't do it, Medina can."

Professional officers realized, however, that what had happened at My Lai (4) could never be justified, and almost everyone in the military agreed that Nixon's motives for meddling in the case were political. The Pentagon was not at all enthusiastic about his intervention. On 7 April Haig gave Ehrlichman a "SEN-SITIVE" memorandum furnished to him by Secretary Laird, "which portrays the attitude and thinking of the Department of Defense and the Department of the Army on the substantive issues surrounding the Calley trial." "Based on the evidence produced in the public trial . . . ," it contended, "Calley fully deserves to be punished, morally and legally." Letting him off or drastically reducing his sentence would lend substance to charges that his actions "were the product of the war policy" and that Americans did not consider Asian lives worthy of respect. It would also be inconsistent with Nixon's own earlier statement strongly condemning the My Lai incident and promising to see that those responsible for the massacre were punished. For the president to free Calley would provoke a serious international reaction, invite retaliation against American prisoners of war, and send soldiers the message that "anything goes." It would make punishing other GIs for war crimes impossible and undercut the army's efforts to clean up its own problems. Furthermore, "Intervention in the Calley case repudiates the military justice system."

Those responsible for the operation of that system considered it important that war crimes be punished. Two young JAG officers, Captains Norman Cooper and Jordan Paust, published extensive articles on My Lai in the Judge Advocate General's Corps' own law review. While Cooper (whose piece was originally written as a thesis for the JAG School) adopted a somewhat detached tone, Paust, who also contributed articles on war crimes to several civilian legal journals, was more passionate. "We must establish an effective, uniform and consistent law enforcement program not because we wish to punish but because we know that without enforcement there may be no law in the field," he wrote. Major Harvey Brown would certainly have concurred. Although he received hundreds of letters protesting the verdict, the court-martial juror declared publicly that what Calley had done was morally wrong and merited punishment.

While Brown refused to criticize Nixon's intervention, the military lawyers who had prosecuted Calley were less circumspect. On 3 April Captain Daniel, who was about to get out of the army, dispatched an irate four-page letter to the president. Asserting that Calley had received a fair trial in which his rights were fully protected, and that the jury had followed the law and rendered a decision based on the evidence, Daniel expressed shock at the public's reaction to the verdict and its inability to grasp the moral issue the trial presented. He found it even more appalling that "so many of the political leaders of the nation . . . have failed to see the moral issue or having seen it, [are willing] to compromise it for political motives." In light of the president's previous statements concerning My Lai, Daniel was "particularly shocked and dismayed at your decision to intervene in these proceedings in the midst of the public clamor." His action had damaged the military legal system and subjected the entire American judicial process to criticism that it responded to political influence, Daniel told the president. He should have supported not Calley but the jurors, who were being unfairly attacked merely for doing their duty. While My Lai was a tragedy, Daniel concluded, "The greatest tragedy of all will be if political expediency dictates the compromise of such a fundamental moral principle as the inherent unlawfulness of the murder of innocent persons."

His cocounsel echoed the man *Time* called "The Captain Who Told the President Off." Captain Partin declared in a 4 April letter to the president, "1 April 1971 was the most discouraging night of my life." Pointing out that there were 200 prisoners in the Fort Benning stockade who had not even been charged with, let alone convicted of, a capital offense, he accused the president of carving out "a new set of rules for Lt. Calley alone." To Partin it appeared that the only reason Calley had been "afforded such peculiar treatment was the public outcry." By allowing him to remain under house arrest, the president had degraded the hard work of lawyers and the conscientious efforts of jurors. His promise to review the case constituted unwarranted interference. Partin concluded by lashing out at Nixon for failing to condemn those who had threatened violence against the jurors and Judge Kennedy.

Nixon was quite upset by the criticism from the JAG lawyers. On 7 April Senator Harold Hughes (D. Iowa), who (along with several of his colleagues) had received a copy of Daniel's letter from the prosecutor, wrote the president, asking him to "clarify" his actions in the Calley case. According to Haldeman, Nixon wanted Ehrlichman to rush out to answer Daniel's allegations head-on, but Ehrlichman convinced him this was a bad idea because "it was a one-day story, and that would only accentuate it." Haldeman himself was "not really sure that's the case." At an Oval Office meeting the next day, Nixon and Ehrlichman agreed that the job of responding to Daniel and Partin should be delegated to Secretary Resor.

Dean drafted a letter for Resor's signature. The first version faulted Daniel for having "gravely misconstrued the nature and motives of the action taken by your Commander-in-Chief" and lauded Nixon for not succumbing to "emotional pressures and strong vocal demands" to take the case out of the control of the military immediately. The draft actually sent to Resor had been modified substantially. It praised Daniel for his conduct of the trial and expressed respect for the members of the court and the judicial process. It also claimed Nixon had acted out of a desire to quiet fears stirred up by the verdict and sentence and concern about the connection between Calley's case and the broader problem of trials for all war crimes. The president had been advised that his actions were within his power and consistent with upholding the military judicial process, this draft maintained. It also claimed the commanding general of Fort Benning had independently concluded Calley should be confined to his quarters because the stockade's officer confinement facilities were inadequate.

Resor deleted that lie and returned the letter, recommending that it be signed "by an attorney on the White House staff." "I believe that it would be inappropriate for me to write to [Daniel and Partin] concerning the Calley case," the secretary declared. His stated reason was that he was required to act as the final approving authority should the Court of Military Appeals affirm a sentence that included dismissal from the army. Forced to do its own dirty work, the White House answered Daniel on 21 April with a bland note, which acknowledged receipt of his letter and stated that the president believed it would be inappropriate for him to respond in detail to the points the prosecutor had raised because the case was on appeal and he would be reviewing it later. This reply was signed by Fred Fielding, an assistant to Dean.

Long before Daniel received Fielding's polite brush-off, Nixon had responded to him publicly. Asked during a 16 April press conference about the prosecutor's charge that he had undermined the military system of justice, the president began by expressing respect for Daniel and the members of the court. He went on to insist that the two steps he had taken were "completely consistent with upholding the judicial process of the Armed Forces." Confining Calley to his quarters was proper, Nixon claimed, because civilians convicted of crimes could remain free on bail while appealing. His announcement that he would review the case personally before final sentence was imposed was preferable to passing the buck to someone else. Asked what had motivated him to act, the president acknowledged that the widespread public interest in the case had been a factor, but he insisted that when people were stirred up about an issue, the president had a responsibility to quiet their fears. He had done that. Public fears about the Calley case had subsided because people knew it would receive "a final review by the President."

Although they did not have the calming effect he claimed, Nixon's actions were popular. The *Philadelphia Inquirer* criticized them, and William Raspberry, an African-American columnist for the *Washington Post*, found releasing Calley while he was appealing inconsistent with the president's endorsement of preventive detention for accused street criminals. A *Post* editorial faulted Nixon for seeking publicity and political advantage by intervening "in a process that should have been allowed to run its own course." Senator Birch Bayh (D. Ind.) also accused him of playing politics with the Calley case. Ten liberal Democratic congressmen issued a joint declaration calling his intervention "extremely improvident," and Senator George McGovern (D.S.D.) put out a critical statement. "President Nixon's decision to intervene in the Calley case, first to order the officer's release from the stockade and [then] to announce his intention to review the case and to make a final determination on the sentence, represents an unfortunate interference with the processes of military justice," the *New York Times* editorialized.

These were the voices of the minority. Although the White House worried that the president's intervention in the Calley case would subject the administration to criticism from all sides, 70 percent of the mail it received by 14 April was favorable. Colson found leaders of veterans' organizations solidly behind Nixon's actions. Cooper Holt, the executive director of the VFW, commended the "courage and independence of the President." Even George Meany of the AFL-CIO supported the president's decision to assume responsibility for the final disposition of the case, Colson learned, although he was unlikely to say so publicly. Representative Barber Conable (R. N.Y.) reported to the White House that his constituents' response to Nixon's order confining Calley in his apartment had been excellent, and Congressman Brock said he had received many letters lauding the president.

Polls confirmed what the White House was hearing. A Louis Harris survey discovered 80 percent of Americans agreed with the president's decision to allow Calley to remain in his officer's quarters while appealing. The Opinion Research Corporation found 75 percent of those it interviewed approved of Nixon's announcement that he would make the final decision about what should be done with the lieutenant, while a mere 17 percent disapproved. Twenty-seven percent of those questioned by the Harris organization rated the president's reaction to the Calley court-martial "excellent," and another 31 percent considered it "pretty good." Only 18 percent gave it a "poor" evaluation. The principal complaint regarding Nixon's handling of the case was that he had not gone far enough. The Harris survey found 34 percent of Americans thought he should have immediately given Calley executive clemency. Fifty-five percent, however, supported the president's failure to do that. Asked if Nixon had gone as far as he could to show he did not agree with the decision in the Calley case, 57 percent said yes. Only 30 percent said no.

Public support for the president extended to his confrontation with Captain Daniel. On that issue as well, some publications challenged the chief executive. The *New York Times* praised Daniel, calling his letter a magnificent expression of American idealism, and *Life* agreed with the prosecutor that Nixon should have been more concerned with the orderly processes of military justice. "The timing, tenor and content of Captain Daniel's letter could not be improved on," *The Nation* editorialized. Senator Taft, however, supported the president, and again the liberal media found itself at odds with public opinion. Asked whether President Nixon had interfered with the system of military justice and prejudged the Calley case before he ruled on it as commander in chief, 58 percent of those interviewed by the Harris organization said no; just 26 percent answered yes. Fifty-eight percent also disagreed with the statement that "President Nixon has come close to undermining the system of military justice by showing sympathy with Lt. Calley"; just 28 percent agreed with it. According to the Opinion Research Corporation, 75 percent of Americans supported Nixon's decision to intervene in the case; only 14 percent shared Daniel's view that it was wrong.

There are a number of reasons why Americans rallied behind a president who intervened in a legal proceeding for political purposes and made a hero out of a soldier whose fellow officers, after hearing all the evidence, convicted him of mass murder. One was a certain skepticism about the whole concept of war crimes. "War is murder and weapons are made for only one purpose," Oscar Schau of Smithfield, Texas, wrote to the U.S. Court of Military Appeals. Another likely contributing factor was popular distrust of military justice. Most of the millions of Americans who served in the armed forces during World War II acquired a very negative impression of a system that, to men fresh from civilian life, seemed harsh, unfair, and dominated by command influence. Congressional enactment of the UCMJ in 1950 reduced the differences between civilian and military criminal procedure, but there remained a widespread impression that military justice was an oxymoron. Also fueling the public's repudiation of the Calley verdict and its support for Nixon was a certain amount of, if not racism, at least xenophobic nationalism. In their study of the reaction to the trial, Herbert C. Kelman and Lee H.

Lawrence found that, where war crimes were concerned, Americans applied different standards to foreigners than to their own. Considerably more of them endorsed the convictions of Japan's General Yamashita, whom the United States had executed for atrocities committed by his troops in the Philippines during World War II, and the German war criminals tried at Nuremberg than favored punishing their own country's soldiers for similar conduct.

While many factors contributed to the popular lionization of Lieutenant Calley, two were primarily responsible. One was the growing disaffection with the war in Vietnam. Polling data camouflage the connection between the two phenomena. Kelman and Lawrence found that those who disapproved of the court-martial were very evenly divided on the war. Twenty-eight percent identified themselves as hawks, 28 percent as doves, and 29 percent as middle-of-the-road. Forty-two percent of respondents to a Louis Harris survey agreed with the proposition that the My Lai incident proved U.S. involvement in Vietnam had been morally wrong all along, while 44 percent disagreed with it. Although these numbers suggest support for Lieutenant Calley was unrelated to feelings about the war, as Tom Huston recognized, "You have two conflicting points of view united in a single conclusion."

Hawks opposed the conviction of Lieutenant Calley because they thought he was being punished simply for waging a war they supported. Colson found leaders of veterans' organizations unanimous in the belief that if this was the way America treated its military personnel, it should abandon the struggle in Vietnam immediately. "It is unspeakable that we should be fighting a war and have G.I.'s court-martialed for killing," Mrs. John Schwei of Grand Prairie, Texas, wrote to the Court of Military Appeals. She and other hawks thought Calley was being sent to prison merely for doing his duty. He had not dodged the draft like Clay but instead had volunteered to fight for his country, and now it was punishing him. "This young educated man did not burn his draft card or run away to Canada, but instead became a leader of men in . . . the . . . army," Bill Worthy of Dallas complained to the president. The outpouring of emotion from people like Worthy, as the conservative journal *National Review* recognized, had little to do with Calley himself. What angered hawks was that a soldier was being sanctioned for trying to win the war.

What upset doves, on the other hand, was that Calley was being punished for what they considered the inevitable consequences of a mistaken national policy. "The events of My Lai, for which Lieutenant Calley has been found guilty, are reflective of the tragedy of the entire Vietnam war," wrote Senator Abe Ribicoff (D. Conn.) to the president. The *New Yorker* echoed his sentiments, and Telford Taylor concluded an article entitled "Judging Calley Is Not Enough" by declaring, "It is high time that the people of the United States squarely face the human consequences of their Vietnam venture." All who had supported this policy must share Calley's guilt, Senator Mark Hatfield (R. Ore.) maintained. The way to make the nation accountable for his crimes, Yale Law School professor Burke Marshall argued, was to end the war immediately.

Because hawks and doves were attacking the outcome of the court-martial from totally different directions, Huston, although convinced the Calley case would have a considerable impact on the public's attitude toward the war, was reluctant to predict what its effect would be. Nixon was sure the case would unite Americans behind his policies, and he was determined to exploit it, for opposition to those policies was mounting. His initial honeymoon with the country on Vietnam ended in May 1970 when, to buy time for Vietnamization to work, he ordered American troops to attack Communist staging areas in theoretically neutral Cambodia. College campuses exploded in protest, and several students were killed by National Guard troops at Kent State University in Ohio. A Nixon-approved ARVN incursion into Laos in February 1971 also fanned the fires of opposition. "At this moment that uneasily dormant beast of public protest—our nightmare, our challenge . . . burst forth again," Kissinger recalls. The Vietnam Veterans Against the War (VVAW) staged their "Winter Soldier" hearings in Detroit to establish that the atrocities committed at My Lai (4) were far from isolated occurrences, then mapped plans for mid-April demonstrations in Washington.

{ *The Vietnam War on Trial* }

In the aftermath of the Laotian incursion, the House Democratic caucus adopted a resolution urging that the war be ended by the close of 1972, and early April found Dean worrying that Minnesota would soon join Massachusetts in seeking a judicial ruling forbidding the government to send its drafted citizens to fight in an undeclared war. Even within the military, disaffection was widespread. In 1971, 17 percent of all soldiers went AWOL and 7 percent deserted. A poll done for the White House on 6–7 March found only 41 percent of Americans approved of the president's handling of Vietnam, while 47 percent disapproved. Nixon hoped to turn the public around with a televised address on the war, which he delivered on 7 April, and he was temporarily successful in doing so. A poll done on 12–13 April showed approval for his handling of Vietnam had risen to 48 percent, while disapproval had dropped to 40 percent. For the president, however, the crucial problem was how to hold enough support for a year and a half to maintain his conduct of the war. He believed that exploiting the Calley case could help him do this. Indeed, Nixon viewed moving on it as essential to keeping support for the administration's policies from evaporating and its backers from becoming discouraged.

Although he believed anger over the Calley verdict would rally America behind his program, what it actually did was expand the legions advocating that the war be ended as soon as possible. A Harris poll found that only a bare plurality of Americans (36 percent to 35 percent) considered the lieutenant not guilty and that 53 percent thought his shooting of Vietnamese civilians at My Lai (4) was unjustified (versus 35 percent who viewed it as justified). People believed he should not be held accountable for deeds they regarded as wrong because they considered his actions no different from those of many other American soldiers in Vietnam. The VVAW supported Calley because, as one member of that organization explained, "What he did is what was done on an everyday basis all over Vietnam by every unit. We knew from our own experiences that this was just normal operating procedure." A Gallup poll found only 24 percent of Americans believed My Lai (4) was an isolated episode; 52 percent thought such incidents were common. Eighty-one percent of respondents to a Harris survey were sure similar occurrences had been hidden; only 6 percent disagreed.

The perception that Calley was being punished for conduct that was common in Vietnam drove hawks and doves, for quite different reasons, to the same conclusion. For supporters of the war the outcome of the court-martial was proof that U.S. forces were being kept from doing what they had to do to win; as the *National Review* pointed out, their angry reaction to the verdict was a way of releasing the frustration they felt over being denied victory. A resolution by officials of Artesia, New Mexico, condemning the Calley court-martial, argued that either the use of drafted troops in Vietnam should be halted or "our elected representatives [should] consider taking all necessary steps for the United States to win." In a memorandum to Pat Buchanan on 2 April, Ehrlichman noted that there was "a strong underlying desire (evidenced by the reaction to the Calley verdict) to get our men and particularly our draftees out of the combat environment." That is, of course, what opponents of the war wanted, too. "I . . . think this trial is additional evidence that our country's involvement in the Indochina conflict must be ended as soon as possible," wrote Senator B. Everett Jordan (D. N.C.) to a constituent. Ironically, Michael Novak noted in *Commonweal*, the outcome of the Calley court-martial seemed "to be crystalizing both hawks and doves in revulsion against the war." As pollster Tom Benham explained to the White House, "the Calley thing" had forced Americans to focus on the negative side of Vietnam and to ask themselves, "What the hell we are doing there?" Two weeks after the verdict, the Harris organization found for the first time that a majority of Americans—56 percent—wanted the war ended and U.S. forces brought home.

While the mounting disaffection with the Vietnam War helped rally the public behind Lieutenant Calley, an increase in popular distrust of government was also a factor. Virtually everyone thought Calley had been made a scapegoat. In a letter to the Court of Military Appeals, Nancy Cooper, a Fort Worth social studies teacher, called him a "sacrificial lamb." "We realized . . .

that Calley was a scapegoat," recalled Joe Urgo of the VVAW, explaining why antiwar veterans supported a convicted murderer. The army denied the little lieutenant was being singled out to bear the entire burden of a difficult war (insisting he was guilty of uniquely infamous atrocities), but the public was not convinced. The military's condemnation of Calley seemed hypocritical and self-serving. Sixty-nine percent of Americans thought he had been singled out unfairly as a scapegoat, a Gallup Poll reported; only 16 percent disagreed. When the Harris organization asked the same question, 77 percent of those it interviewed responded in the affirmative, and just 15 percent answered no. Kelman and Lawrence obtained results nearly identical to Gallup's when they asked whether it was unfair to single out Calley for trial.

Of those Gallup questioned, only 15 percent disapproved of the verdict because they thought no crime had been committed at My Lai (4). Fifty-six percent did so because they believed many others besides Calley shared responsibility for what had happened there. "No one wants to see a single individual saddled with blame that obviously extends to many others," Senator Hughes wrote to President Nixon. Oscar Schau of Smithfield, Texas, spoke for many Americans when he declared: "Lt. Calley is not guilty, the system is guilty." Forty-nine percent of those the Harris organization questioned thought the army should be blamed for the crimes committed at My Lai (4), whereas only 38 percent thought it should not. If Calley were guilty, then so were "many of his superior officers, some of the higher commanders, and so are our political leaders who helped make the decisions which led to this tragedy," declared several residents of Louisville, Kentucky, in a telegram to the president. A theme running through many of the wires the White House received was that Calley was only a fall guy for others higher up in the chain of command. Asked whether he was being "made the scapegoat for the actions of others above him," 70 percent of those responding to a Gallup survey answered yes; only 12 percent said no. Seventy-seven percent of those questioned by the Harris organization thought the soldiers at My Lai (4) were "only following orders from their higher-ups." Seventy-four percent believed Nixon should either stop all trials such as Calley's or see to it that those higher-ups were tried, too.

These respondents seemed to share the attitude encapsulated in the GI maxim "Shit rolls downhill," a saying that reflected the belief of many soldiers that their leaders could not be trusted and always sought to protect themselves by pushing responsibility for whatever went wrong as far down the chain of command as possible. *The Nation* thought that was what had happened in Calley's case: the army had tried to make a scapegoat out of a lieutenant in order to whitewash its own highest echelons.

Antiwar activists had their own slogan: "I love my country but fear my government." So did hippies, many of whose Volkswagen microbuses sported bumper stickers that read, "Question Authority." After 13 June, when the *New York Times* began publishing an illicitly obtained and highly classified Defense Department history of how the United States had become involved in Vietnam, Americans had plenty of reason to question authority. The "Pentagon Papers" proved their leaders had repeatedly deceived them about the war. These revelations did not cause the distrust of "higher-ups" that fueled the firestorm over the Calley court-martial, however, for it had erupted two months earlier. According to Robert D. Putnam, the distrust of government leaders that it reveals did not exist as late as April 1966, when almost two-thirds of all Americans still rejected the proposition that "the people running the country don't really care what happens to you." By April 1971, the poll results concerning Calley suggest, people had changed their minds. The corrosive effect of the Vietnam War had eaten away the confidence they had once had in their leaders and left most of them convinced that those who ran things could not be trusted. The country's civilian and military leaders would sacrifice a "little guy" like Lieutenant Calley to protect themselves or advance their own interests.

Those who bombarded Congress and the White House with telephone calls and mail and who answered pollsters questions identified with Calley. He was Everyman. To them Calley was not a mass murderer but a victim of all that they disliked and distrusted: the war, the "system," and what alienated youth referred to pejoratively as "the Establishment." President Nixon recognized how angry the public was, but his efforts to exploit the powerful emotions unleashed by the court-martial of Lieutenant Calley failed because he did not understand the disaffection with the Vietnam War and the resentment of authority that fueled them. Those forces transformed a convicted mass murderer into one of the most improbable heroes in all of American history.

CHAPTER 11

"Others That Participated . . . or Condoned the Bloody Act"

Among those who wrote to the U.S. Court of Military Appeals, urging it to free Lieutenant Calley, was Robert Landess of Garland, Texas. He acknowledged that the evidence brought forth at the trial had persuaded him Calley was probably guilty. "To pin the entire crime on him is another matter, though." As far as Landess was concerned, "others that participated in the actual crime or condoned the bloody act, should [also] be brought forth and tried." Many Americans agreed with him. One reason the public reacted so strongly to the outcome of the court-martial was that no one else had shared Calley's fate.

People suspected what Seymour Hersh would allege many years later: that the army wanted Calley convicted so it could justify closing an embarrassing case as quickly as possible. Professor William Eckhardt, who as a JAG lawyer oversaw all prosecutions of participants in the massacre, disputes Hersh, maintaining prosecutors never considered reducing the charge to manslaughter if Calley would plead guilty. Even if the army did not really try to entice him into becoming a scapegoat for all those who were culpable in the My Lai affair, it certainly managed to create the appearance of attempting to do so. Although the CID investigated forty-seven officers and enlisted men for crimes allegedly committed during the 16 March operation, and the Peers Commission accused thirty of involvement in a cover-up, only Calley was ever convicted of anything. The army sanctioned just two other soldiers for their roles in the My Lai (4) affair, and whereas the lieutenant received a life sentence, Major General Koster got a one-grade reduction in rank and Brigadier General Young an official censure.

It certainly looked as if Calley had been unfairly singled out. The CID's investigation yielded evidence sufficient to justify prosecuting three other officers for murders allegedly committed during the 16 March operation: Captain Medina; Second Lieutenant Steven Brooks (commander of Charlie Company's Second Platoon); and then–First Lieutenant Thomas Willingham (a platoon leader in Bravo Company). The army also accused Captain Eugene Kotouc, Task Force Barker's intelligence officer, of assaulting and maiming a prisoner he interrogated at a bivouac the evening after the attack on My Lai (4). It filed murder charges against seven enlisted men (Sergeant Charles Hutto, Sergeant Esequiel Torres, then-Corporal Kenneth Schiel, SP-4 William F. Doherty, SP-4 Robert W. T'Souvas, Private Max D. Hutson, and Private Gerald Smith), all of whom had participated in the massacre. In addition, the army prosecuted Staff Sergeant David Mitchell, Staff Sergeant Kenneth L. Hodges, and Hutto for assault with intent to commit murder, and charged Hodges and Hutto with rape and Smith (who had allegedly fondled the breasts of a Vietnamese woman) with "indecent assault." Thus, Calley was only one among fourteen officers and enlisted men alleged to have committed serious offenses in and around My Lai (4) on 16 March.

He was only one among thirty soldiers the Peers Commission accused of helping to hide the crimes committed that day. Although the army did not prosecute him for his rather small contribution to the cover-up, it did file charges against thirteen other officers implicated in it. At the head of the list was Major General Koster, former commander of the Americal Division and now the commandant of the United States Military Academy at West Point. The army accused Koster of failure to obey lawful regulations and dereliction of duty. It filed charges of dereliction of duty and failure to obey a lawful order against his former deputy, Brigadier General Young, as well as against Colonel Nels A. Parson (chief of staff of the Americal Division); Colonel Henderson (commander of the 11th Brigade); now-Colonel Robert B. Luper (commander of an artillery battalion); Lieutenant Colonel David G. Gavin (senior American adviser in the Son Tinh District of

Quang Ngai Province); Lieutenant Colonel William D. Guinn Jr. (deputy U.S. adviser in Quang Ngai Province); Major Charles C. Calhoun (operations officer of Task Force Barker); Major Frederic W. Watke (commander of Company B, 123rd Aviation Battalion); Captain Kenneth W. Boatman (an artillery forward observer); and now-Captain Dennis H. Johnson (from the 52nd Military Intelligence Detachment). In addition, it accused Henderson, as well as Captain Willingham and Major Robert W. McKnight (the operations officer of the 11th Brigade), of making false statements and swearing falsely under oath.

Although many were accused, only Calley was convicted. The reason was not political intervention in the other cases. Although the president rescued Calley from the stockade, the White House displayed no interest in helping the other soldiers accused of My Lai–related offenses. On 31 March 1971, in the middle of the furor over the Fort Benning verdict, F. Lee Bailey, the flamboyant, high-profile Boston attorney who was representing Captain Medina, sent a certified letter to the president. "The public reaction to the very harsh conviction of Lieutenant Calley has demonstrated that very great numbers of people—many of whom are from that citizen bloc which most strongly supports your administration—are quite angry with the verdict," Bailey reminded Nixon. There was, he added, "little basis to surmise that this reaction will be ameliorated by the further conviction of Captain Medina."

Bailey insisted his client was not guilty, but that the government was keeping him from proving it by blocking use of polygraph examination results that would establish the captain's innocence. He did "not mean to suggest that Captain Medina is unwilling to stand trial," the defense attorney claimed, but both the investigating officer and the commander who formally charged him were biased, and so too (because of command influence) was the jury. Bailey hinted darkly that defending his client in a proceeding such as this court-martial might require him to do things that could embarrass the president and his administration. While not asking Nixon directly to drop the case against Medina, Bailey did profess to believe this "prosecution

. . . in its present posture is ill-advised" and expressed "hope that the steps which I am forced to take imminently can somehow be avoided."

His attempt to pressure the White House into rescuing his client from military justice accomplished nothing. Disregarding a recommendation that the Defense Department respond to Bailey's letter, Dean assumed responsibility for doing so. In a memorandum of 13 April forwarding a draft reply to Ehrlichman, he wrote: "As you can see . . . , I am pursuing a course of non-involvement in the Medina case based on the general position the president has taken in the Calley case." In his letter to Bailey, Dean reminded the attorney that Nixon had announced there would be no presidential intervention in the Calley matter while the conviction was being appealed pursuant to the UCMJ. "Therefore, it would be inappropriate to respond to the matters you have raised regarding your client's case, which is presently pending trial under the provisions of the Uniform Code of Military Justice."

When Bailey wrote to the president again on 20 April, apparently trying to get him to assign a different prosecutor to the Medina case, Dean replied, "This is not a matter in which the White House should become involved." The Boston attorney contacted the White House again in August, this time through the Justice Department, seeking help in securing the presence of two South Vietnamese interpreters, whose depositions he considered crucial evidence against Medina. Although threatening to "scream bloody murder" in court if he did not get what he wanted, Bailey was informed that further contact with the White House about this matter would be inappropriate.

His failure to obtain presidential intervention in Medina's case was due to White House resolve to avoid further involvement in any actual or potential My Lai (4) prosecutions. As a memorandum of 15 April from Ehrlichman to Kissinger makes clear, senior members of Nixon's staff realized that "all of these My Lai cases are . . . interrelated." Those of Calley and Medina were "inextricably combined insofar as the president's ultimate decision is concerned." Since Nixon had postponed doing anything meaningful for the lieutenant by announcing that he would finally decide his case only after all appeals were exhausted, it would be unwise to take any action on behalf of Calley's captain. Dean advised the White House staff to make no comments or statements about these "related cases . . . while they are being adjudicated under the procedures of the Uniform Code of Military Justice."

In the meantime, he prepared for Ehrlichman's working group a discussion draft of a memorandum for the president "regarding the war crimes cases in general and the Calley case in particular." This "TOP SECRET" document, which Dean did not complete until 14 May, was intended only "to give us a starting point for our working sessions." It recommended that further public comments by the president about Calley "be very guarded lest it appear the president is attempting to influence the outcome of the case." As for the other soldiers accused of involvement in the massacre and cover-up, by 14 May a number of their cases had already been resolved. Concerning the rest, Dean offered no recommendations or even "presidential options." These should be worked out by the task force, he suggested. Although a memorandum he received from the Defense Department on 10 June indicates Dean was continuing to monitor "My Lai related cases," the White House still had no real policy for dealing with them.

Long before it could develop one, all had ended in a manner favorable to the accused. Some alleged wrongdoers were never even formally charged. One of these was Lieutenant Colonel Barker, who, according to the Peers Commission, had "planned, ordered, and actively directed the execution of an unlawful operation against inhabited hamlets" and intentionally or negligently provided his company commanders with false intelligence that contributed to the killing of numerous noncombatants. Both of these actions would have merited prosecution. In addition, Barker had "probably conspired with MAJ Calhoun and others to suppress information concerning the war crimes committed during the Son My operation." Only the June 1968 helicopter crash that took his life saved him from prosecution.

Lieutenant Brooks also avoided trial by dying. The Peers Commission accused him of ordering the Second Platoon to execute an unlawful operation against an inhabited village, directing and supervising the systematic killing of noncombatants, and possibly killing at least one female civilian himself. Brooks almost certainly would have been prosecuted had he not been killed in action following the My Lai (4) operation.

While Brooks and Barker could not be tried because they were dead, far more offenders avoided trial because they were no longer in the army. Draftees had to serve for only two years, and because of the length of time it took to train them for combat in Vietnam, by the time they completed their one-year tour of duty there, most were within a few months of being discharged. Consequently, as Eckhardt explained to an audience at Tulane University, the two-year cover-up of the massacre meant that by the time it was fully investigated, "90 percent of the people that were involved in this incident were out of the service."

The Supreme Court had held that it was unconstitutional to subject ex-servicemen to trial by courts-martial, and Congress had never given any civilian federal court the authority to try them for crimes committed abroad. The only viable option appeared to be trial before a group of officers sitting as a military commission. There were doubts about the legality of that approach, however. During and just after the Civil War, the Union government had used such commissions to try some Northerners accused of treason, as well as the alleged participants in the plot to assassinate President Lincoln. In *Ex parte Milligan* (1866), however, the Supreme Court had ruled it was unconstitutional to try a civilian before such a body where the civil courts were open and functioning. By the 1960s judicial decisions on the subject strongly suggested that a military commission might be employed only when the defendant was accused of committing acts of hostile belligerency against the United States.

Article 21 of the UCMJ appeared to confer broader authority, saying such bodies had jurisdiction to try offenses against the common law of war. Since many of the things American soldiers were alleged to have done at My Lai (4) constituted violations of the international law of war, Eckhardt thought, "We perhaps could have tried them by military commission." He believed doing this would be constitutional, but other authorities on military law had serious doubts. As one of them, army captain Norman Cooper, recognized, "Trial of civilians in a military tribunal of any kind would probably meet with public disfavor and legal censure." Concerned that any effort to employ this procedure would trigger protracted litigation over its legality, the attorney general rejected the idea. On 8 April 1971 the Defense and Justice Departments announced that efforts to prosecute discharged servicemen were being dropped, due to constitutional limits on military jurisdiction and the fact that no civilian federal court could try them. Because of that decision, according to Eckhardt, "the government . . . could only proceed after the 10 percent who were left in the military."

That limitation severely constrained Eckhardt, who was then a major in the Judge Advocate General's Corps, in prosecuting the crimes committed during the assault on My Lai (4). Major Eckhardt, age forty, had earned a bachelor's degree and an ROTC commission at the University of Mississippi in 1963 and had graduated with honors from the University of Virginia School of Law three years later. Within six weeks after receiving his law degree, he was on his way to Vietnam. There Eckhardt served as both a prosecutor and a defense attorney. He and five other lawyers handled all the army's trial work for the entire country. After returning to the United States, he attended the JAG officers career course at Fort Lee, Virginia.

Eckhardt was a student there when the My Lai (4) story broke. "It was awful," he thought. The army ordered him to the headquarters of the Third Army at Fort McPherson in Atlanta, Georgia, "to be the prosecutor of the ground action." That made him lead government lawyer in most of the cases involving crimes committed against Vietnamese civilians during the 16 March 1968 operation, for the army had transferred almost all of the soldiers charged with such offenses to Fort McPherson. Only Calley and Sergeant Mitchell, now stationed at Fort Hood, Texas, stood trial elsewhere, and Eckhardt consulted with and nominally supervised the lawyers who prosecuted them.

Eckhardt's assignment was not a pleasant one. "The first day I got there," he remembers, "I looked at [the My Lai] case files and thought that I was going to throw up. I threw the files against the wall and went and ran five or six miles." The facts were far worse than the public realized. Over 500 Vietnamese had been killed; Eckhardt knew that in part because "the enemy gave us a list of the names of those who were in the ditch." Besides the murders, the files documented "the sexual abuse, the rapes, the sodomy, the looting." To Eckhardt this was "the most horrible thing" he had "ever seen." "We're clearly going to court," he told his superiors.

Although Major Eckhardt was determined to punish those responsible for the orgy of wrongdoing at My Lai (4), he and his fellow prosecutors could not convict them. Only when the defendants sought extraordinary pretrial relief from judges did the government prevail. Private Hutson's military lawyer, Captain William Lanham, failed to persuade the U.S. Court of Military Appeals to issue a writ of mandamus directing the summary court-martial convening authority to provide him with at least two qualified military investigators or FBI agents or to give him money to hire private detectives so the defense could conduct an independent investigation of the My Lai (4) incident. Such assistance was available to indigent defendants in civilian federal criminal cases, and the court was "not without sympathy for defense counsel," but the judges believed they lacked the legal authority to grant Lanham's request.

They also denied a petition for a writ of mandamus filed by SP-4 Doherty's civilian counsel, Frank J. McGee Jr. McGee contended that because of the publicity surrounding the Calley case, there was a "fair risk" that his client would be denied his right to an impartial Article 32 investigation. The defense attorney wanted an order delaying Calley's court-martial until the charges against Doherty were either dismissed or referred to trial. Observing that there was no indication the investigating officer had been influenced by the Fort Benning proceeding, the Court of Military Appeals took the position that McGee had failed to provide a foundation for the relief he was seeking.

Although unsuccessful in the Court of Military Appeals, defense attorneys consistently prevailed before juries. The first of their clients to win acquittal was Sergeant Mitchell. The not-guilty verdict in his trial was a direct result of the Hébert sub-committee's meddling in the My Lai matter. The Mitchell court-martial, which began on 6 October 1970, had barely gotten under way when the military judge, Colonel George R. Robin-son, announced that, because of the Hébert panel's refusal to make available transcripts of its hearings, he would not permit any soldiers who had appeared before it to testify. Eckhardt thought this ruling (based on the Jencks Act) was just what Rep-resentatives Hébert and Rivers wanted; he later accused Congress of "calculatingly setting out to destroy the prosecu-tion" of the My Lai (4) defendants. Certainly, Hébert had been warned by Secretary of the Army Resor and fellow congressman Abner J. Mikva (D. Ill.), later a federal judge, that failure to turn over the transcripts of his subcommittee's hearings could prevent successful prosecution of those accused of committing crimes at My Lai (4). Clearly, by classifying its hearings, the House Armed Services Committee wrecked the government's case against Mitchell. Hamstrung by Judge Robinson's ruling, the prosecutor, Captain Michael Swann, called only three of the dozens of wit-nesses he had been expected to proffer. Dennis Conti placed Mitchell at the irrigation ditch, and Greg Olsen said he had seen Mitchell take aim at the villagers in the ditch and open fire. Charles Sledge testified that Mitchell had joined Calley in killing civilians at that location.

Defense attorney Ossie Brown, a civilian volunteer, countered with the testimony of over twenty former soldiers. Some swore that the government's witnesses were known liars. Others dis-puted the prosecution's contention that Mitchell had been at the irrigation ditch. Most who admitted seeing any killing at all at-tributed it to Lieutenant Calley. A tearful Mitchell testified in his own defense. He claimed not to be sure what had happened on 16 March or even who was in his squad that day. "But I'm posi-tive I did not shoot anyone," he declared. In his closing argu-ment, Brown contended that Mitchell and the other men who had participated in the assault on My Lai (4) were just soldiers doing their duty. "Some elements," he claimed, were trying to undermine and destroy the military and the country. Insisting, "We need soldiers such as Sergeant Mitchell," he urged the jury "not to betray him."

It did not. In Eckhardt's opinion, most military men believed that a conviction in a My Lai case would be "a slap in the face of the army" and would undermine the war effort. Certainly this seems to have been the sentiment of the Mitchell jury, which was out for less than seven hours and, according to several jurors, actually reached a verdict in far less time than that. The jurors delayed returning only because longer deliberations would look better. Their verdict was not guilty.

Prosecutors at Fort McPherson fared no better than had Captain Swann. The first My Lai defendant to be tried there was Sergeant Hutto, whose court-martial began in early January 1971, while Calley was still on trial at nearby Fort Benning. Unlike Colonel Robinson, the military judge in the Hutto proceeding did not prevent anyone from testifying because of the House Armed Services Committee's refusal to supply transcripts of its hearings, and this seemed like an easy case. Although none of the three witnesses called by the prosecutor, Captain Franklin Wurtzel, could recall seeing the defendant fire a single shot, he had admitted to the CID killing a group of unarmed civilians with an M-60 machine gun. Hutto's signed statement containing this damning admission was read to the jury, and he did not take the stand to refute it.

Instead, his civilian attorney, Edward Magill of Miami, based his defense on the testimony of a clinical psychologist, Dr. Norman Reichberg. According to Hutto's statement, during the assault on My Lai (4) "orders came down to kill all the people." Reichberg testified that the defendant, who had grown up in a poor, rural part of Louisiana, lacked the capacity to make a judgment concerning whether such a directive was legal or illegal. Hutto's personality was marked by a total lack of creativity and a willingness to believe others and to submit to orders from authority figures. In his closing argument Magill hammered on the theme that his client had never thought to question the instructions he was given. Indeed, he did not even know there was such a thing as an illegal order. "The only thing the Army ever said to Charlie Hutto is that he was to obey orders without question." The six officers on the jury apparently accepted this argument. It took them less than two hours to acquit Hutto.

The Hutto verdict upset Eckhardt, for he knew that the prosecution had produced sufficient evidence of all the elements of murder. "You're darn right we did," he told the audience at a Tulane University conference on My Lai. "I know that because the law of evidence at that time required that you have a prima facie case before you put [a defendant's] confession in, and the confession went in." Eckhardt did not believe the verdict could be attributed to any failure to establish what the prosecution was required to prove.

While reluctant to "knock the jury," he related an experience that suggested he doubted that it had weighed the evidence fairly. On "the first day of prosecution," Eckhardt said, he went alone to the Fort McPherson officers club. There he overheard a conversation at two adjacent tables, apparently about the Calley trial. The thrust of it was "how in the world could such a fine, upstanding officer be charged with such a horrible incident." Unfortunately for Eckhardt and his prosecutors, "that was your jury."

As he saw it, "the problem for the government was who sat on courts-martial." During another trial Eckhardt asked a potential juror, a colonel who had served with one of the army's finest units, the 101st Airborne Division, about the law of war. The colonel responded, "There's no such thing." The judge dismissed him for cause, but when Eckhardt showed the transcript of this exchange to his boss, that JAG lawyer exclaimed, "God help us all."

The acquittals of Hutto and Mitchell suggested that, despite the dictates of international law and the army's own regulations, officers sitting as jurors in such cases were likely to accept obedience to orders as a complete defense. Prosecutors carefully reassessed the evidence they had on the other enlisted defendants and concluded their cases against them were not viable. On the lawyers' recommendation and "in the interests of justice," Lieutenant General Albert O. Connor, the commander of the Third

Army and the convening authority in their cases, dismissed the murder charges against Torres, Hutson, T'Souvas, and Smith. A few weeks later the prosecutions of Schiel and Doherty for murder and of Hodges for rape and assault with intent to commit murder were quietly terminated. Aware that history might judge him and his staff harshly for halting these prosecutions, Eckhardt prepared a lengthy written explanation of their reasons for doing so. Although the army had elected not to try the other enlisted men, it utilized an administrative review process to discharge them from the service and to bar all, including those who had planned to make the military a career, from reenlisting.

Captain Willingham also quietly left the service after prosecutors decided not to proceed against him because their evidence was sketchy and inconclusive. They did bring Captain Kotouc to trial just after Calley's court-martial ended, but the result was another failure. Kotouc had tried to intimidate a VC suspect into supplying information by placing his hand on a board and repeatedly thrusting the blade of a seven-inch knife between his fingers. One blow cut off the end of a digit. Kotouc claimed this amputation was an accident. Apparently believing prosecutors had failed to produce sufficient evidence to prove his purpose had been to disfigure the prisoner, the military judge directed a verdict of acquittal on a charge of deliberate maiming.

Someone could also violate Article 124 of the UCMJ simply by engaging in conduct that he was aware might inflict a disabling or disfiguring injury, but the judge rendered a conviction on the basis of such recklessness unlikely. He instructed the jury that directives and army regulations in effect on 16 March 1968 could have led Kotouc to believe that it was lawful for him to threaten violence in order to pry information from a prisoner; if this was what he had been trying to do, his actions were justified. If he had merely been negligent, he had not violated Article 124. "Unless you are satisfied beyond a reasonable doubt that the cutting of the alleged victim was not the result of an accident, you must acquit Capt. Kotouc," the judge told the jury. Having heard his instructions, it took less than an hour to find the defendant not guilty.

Kotouc's acquittal left only Captain Medina still facing prosecution for crimes allegedly committed during the assault on My Lai (4), and Bailey predicted frequently that his client would never come to trial. He and Medina's two military lawyers, Captains Mark J. Kadish and John Truman (a nephew of the former president), filed suit against Secretary Resor, the Judge Advocate General, General Connor, Major Eckhardt, Captain Daniel, and the staff judge advocates of the Third Army and the Infantry Center, claiming they were violating Medina's constitutional rights by conspiring to deny him a fair and impartial trial. The alleged conspiracy had purportedly manifested itself in the government's refusal to let Captain Medina (who had not yet testified at the Calley court-martial) take the stand there to refute testimony blaming him for the massacre and in Eckhardt's unwillingness to utilize him as a witness in the Hutto case. The defense attorneys asked the Court of Military Appeals to order the conspirators not to interfere with the administration of justice by preventing Medina from testifying at Fort Benning and temporarily to prohibit Connor, Eckhardt, and others from referring the charges against the captain to trial. On 7 March 1971, noting that what happened in the Calley proceeding could have no legal effect on Medina, and observing that there did not appear to be any reason why, if the charges against him were actually referred to a court-martial, he could not thereafter obtain relief through the normal processes of trial and appeal, the court dismissed their petition. Bailey also failed to get the charges against his client dropped because of undue command influence.

Ironically, he himself was trying to invoke command influence from the very highest level. While the White House was being bombarded with complaints about the Calley conviction, it received not only Bailey's vaguely threatening letter of 31 March but also a telegram from Medina's fellow Latino, Congressman Henry B. Gonzalez (D. Tex.), which urged "an indefinite postponement of [his] court-martial trial." Asserting that the passions and emotions developing in the country over the Calley case made a fair trial for Medina impossible, Gonzalez argued that "a second national blood-letting would only give aid and comfort to the enemy." Both his appeal and Bailey's threats were unsuccessful.

So was what seems to have been an attempt by the defense attorney to get Eckhardt removed from the case. Claiming to be concerned about how the press would react if Medina avoided punishment because his lawyers were more skilled and experienced than the prosecutors, in a letter that he sent to Nixon on 20 April, Bailey asked for the assignment of a senior trial counsel who "has not been involved in any of the other My Lai cases." The White House brushed him off. Medina came to trial in late August, and his lawyer found himself confronting Eckhardt.

The Medina trial posed a far more difficult legal issue than had the earlier My Lai courts-martial. The former company commander was charged with two counts of aggravated assault and with personally murdering an adult female and a small boy. His defenses to these allegations were that he thought the woman was armed; that the killing of the child had occurred because he countermanded too late what might have been understood as an order to shoot him; and that he had not assaulted a prisoner over whose head he admitted firing a rifle twice.

Medina was also tried for the premeditated murder of not fewer than 100 Vietnamese civilians killed by his men. If he had directed them to commit those killings, he would have been guilty under ordinary principles of criminal law, applicable in civilian as well as military courts. Eckhardt came to realize, however, that the only former members of Charlie Company who claimed Medina had issued an explicit order to shoot civilians were ones who had themselves killed villagers. At Bailey's request, the captain took a series of lie detector tests. These revealed that he was telling the truth when he answered no to the question, "Did you intentionally infer to your men that they were to kill unarmed, unresisting noncombatants?" On the other hand, Medina was not being truthful when he denied knowing that his troops were killing such persons between 0730 and 0930 on the morning of 16 March. To Eckhardt, these results suggested that probably Charlie Company "got out of control and he refused to stop it." As far as the prosecutor was concerned,

"Knowing this was going on and calculatingly doing nothing about it was murder."

Yet he realized that normally the law punishes only acts; in the few instances where it imposes criminal liability for inaction, the reason is that the defendant was under a legal duty to do what he failed to do. Prosecutors could find no direct support for the proposition that a commander had a duty to control his troops that included finding out if they were misbehaving. The prosecution was, Eckhardt reports, "forced to weave and to modify isolated portions of dated military field manuals and to rely on tangential dicta by the military courts." The best his lawyers could come up with was paragraph 501 of *The Law of Land Warfare*, a Department of the Army field manual. It declared that a commander was responsible for the acts of his subordinates if he knew or should have known that those troops were about to commit or had committed a war crime and failed "to take necessary and reasonable steps to insure compliance with the law of war or to punish violators thereof." Eckhardt needed to win acceptance of the broad definition of command responsibility set out in paragraph 501, at least if the court believed Medina, for the defendant testified that he had been unaware of what his men were doing because he had remained on the periphery of My Lai (4) during most of the intense firing.

Bailey argued that his client was not responsible for the murders committed by his men because he had not wanted anyone but the enemy killed and had ordered a cease-fire as soon as he learned that they were shooting civilians (a claim Eckhardt believed). The nub of his defense was that responsibility for the My Lai murders reached no higher than Lieutenant Calley. Bailey seemed to know the law better than the military judge, Colonel Kenneth A. Howard, and to exploit that advantage whenever possible.

As if that did not make the prosecution's situation difficult enough, its cause was repeatedly undermined by its own witnesses. Eckhardt called fifty of them during the first two weeks of the trial alone, but quantity could not compensate for a lack of quality. Only one of these witnesses put Medina at the scene of a killing, and he admitted the captain had his head down and was talking on the radio when a member of his command group shot a small boy. Under cross-examination, Gene Oliver testified that he, rather than the defendant, had shot the child Medina was accused of killing. When Bailey asked Michael Bernhardt whether he would lie if he thought doing so would serve the ends of justice, Bernhardt acknowledged that he would. Gerald Hemin recalled overhearing Medina and Henderson discuss the killings, but he thought Colonel Henderson was a major and admitted drinking four quarts of wine in one night and using LSD. Frederick J. Widmer, who, according to another witness, had shot a small boy shortly after Medina walked by, refused to say anything at all, invoking the Fifth Amendment and persisting in remaining silent even after the prosecution offered him immunity. The military judge cited Widmer for contempt (although a civilian federal court later reversed his action). Calley, too, appeared only long enough for his lawyer to invoke his privilege against compulsory self-incrimination. According to Mary McCarthy, a young reporter whispered, "I get the feeling somebody is betraying Eckhardt."

Its case damaged by its own witnesses, the prosecution (apparently because Eckhardt believed Medina's claims concerning his location on the morning of 16 March) failed to call other former soldiers, such as Paul Meadlo and Jay Roberts, whose testimony in earlier proceedings had placed the captain within the hamlet when the killing was going on. The prosecutor was able to have the polygraph examiner relate the defendant's answers to the questions he had asked him, but unfortunately the results of the lie detector tests themselves were inadmissible. Nor could Eckhardt get Haeberle's photographs into evidence.

The prosecution also had to overcome the detailed, confident, and impressive testimony of Medina himself. The defendant firmly denied knowing that his men had killed civilians. If the jury believed him, it could not convict Medina of those homicides, for Judge Howard instructed the members of the court that a commander was responsible for war crimes committed by his troops only if he *knew* they were committing or were about to commit them and wrongfully failed to act. He emphasized that *actual knowledge* was required. "Thus," he told them, "mere presence at the scene without knowledge will not suffice." Nor could they infer the required knowledge from the fact that the killers were Medina's subordinates. Ruling there was insufficient evidence to support a conviction for premeditated murder, Howard let the jury consider only whether to convict the captain of involuntary manslaughter in the deaths of the civilians his men had killed. He dismissed entirely the murder charge involving the boy Oliver had admitted shooting.

After deliberating for only about an hour on 22 September, jurors acquitted Medina of the remaining charges. They had been waiting to be persuaded he was not innocent, one of them, Colonel Robert Nelson, told reporters. "It was rather apparent we were not convinced." That evening Bailey threw a victory party at the Atlanta Airport Hilton. Some observers attributed his triumph to the fact that Howard and four of the five jurors were southerners, but McCarthy, who had sat through the trial, disagreed. She thought the prosecution lost because it presented a weak case, which proved only that Medina had been guilty of dereliction of duty.

It had originally accused him of suppressing information, which seemed more consistent with the evidence, but Eckhardt elected to press instead the more serious charge of murder. Unlike Medina, Colonel Henderson was tried for dereliction of duty. His case was referred to a court-martial by Lieutenant General Jonathan O. Seaman, commander of the First Army, headquartered at Fort Meade, Maryland, who had been given responsibility for deciding which officers should be prosecuted for the cover-up. Henderson's military lawyers hoped to use portions of the Peers Report to persuade Seaman not to try him, but on 25 November 1970 the Court of Military Appeals rejected their request for access to this material, which had not yet been made public. A civilian lawyer, Henry Rothblatt, then sought during pretrial hearings to keep testimony Henderson had given to the Peers Commission and during the inspector general's investigation from being used against him. He, too, was unsuccessful.

{ *The Vietnam War on Trial* }

Henderson fared better when his case got to trial. In a sixty-two-day proceeding, which began late in the summer of 1971, 106 witnesses gave 6,000 pages of testimony. The most important came from helicopter pilots, who said they had reported indiscriminate killing at My Lai (4). Largely on the basis of their testimony, the prosecutor, Major Carroll Tichenor, maintained that "beyond question" Henderson knew within two days after the 16 March operation that a massacre had taken place; he covered it up to preserve his military career and ensure his promotion to general. Henderson acknowledged not giving Hugh Thompson's allegations as much credence as they deserved, but he adamantly denied knowing there had been "excessive killings" at My Lai (4). Medina supported him, testifying that after his men told him they had killed at least 106 Vietnamese civilians, he reported to Henderson that the number did not exceed 28. The jury, composed of two generals and five colonels, found Henderson (an officer with a long and distinguished military career) and his witnesses more persuasive than the prosecution's case. In late December, after less than four hours of deliberation, it acquitted him of all charges. "With that verdict," *Time* reported, "the Army closed its judicial books on My Lai."

It had never even tried the other participants in the cover-up. General Seaman dismissed charges of dereliction of duty and failure to obey lawful regulations against all of them. In the cases of Brigadier General Young, Colonel Parson, Colonel Luper, and Major McKnight, he did so fairly early in the prosecutorial process, after staff judge advocates advised him that there was simply not enough evidence to justify proceeding against those officers. The other cover-up defendants all underwent formal Article 32 investigations, but none had his case referred to trial. The officer who investigated General Koster, Brigadier General B. L. Evans, found that the former commander of the Americal Division had been remiss in not reporting the deaths of twenty civilians and in not ordering a proper investigation. Pointing to Koster's fine character and long career of outstanding service, however, Evans concluded that the charges against him should be dismissed. Seaman did so "in the interests of justice."

General Koster did not escape entirely unscathed. Having decided not to expose him to a public trial, Seaman dressed him down in private. In a blistering letter of censure he declared, "I feel compelled, not only by time-honored command principles, but also by the peculiar facts of this case, to hold you personally responsible for the failure of the Americal Division to make the required report or to pass on in some other fashion information vital to and required by your superior commanders." Seaman's letter of reprimand effectively ended the once-promising career of a general some had predicted would one day become Chief of Staff. The man who held that job, General Westmoreland, added to Koster's humiliation by recommending that he be demoted one grade to brigadier general and stripped of his Distinguished Service Medal. Koster soon retired from the army. General Young also lost his Distinguished Service Medal, and in addition received a formal letter of censure from the secretary of the army.

To Young and Koster the destruction of their military careers no doubt seemed like substantial punishment. To many others it did not. The *New York Times*, Representative Samuel Stratton (D. N.Y.), and Robert McCrate, the Peers Commission's civilian legal adviser, all blasted General Seaman's disposition of the Koster case. For the army, what appeared to be a move designed to prevent a full public airing of the malfeasance of high-ranking officers proved to be a public relations disaster. That was almost inevitable, for compared with the life sentence Lieutenant Calley had received, the sanctions imposed on Koster and Young were trivial.

Furthermore, they were the only punishment any other participant in the My Lai (4) affair received. The fact that everyone else accused of wrongdoing during and after the massacre managed to avoid being punished seemed to confirm that Calley was being made a scapegoat. Why should he alone suffer for what had happened at My Lai (4)? To Robert Landess the answer to that question was obvious: he should not. If it was impossible to try the others responsible for the killings and the cover-up, he wrote in his letter to the Court of Military Appeals, "then I suggest that you either free Calley or drastically reduce his punishment."

CHAPTER 12

"Hasn't He Suffered Enough?"

On 16 September 1974, just over a month after assuming the presidency, Gerald Ford received a telegram from a woman in Lieutenant Calley's home state. Virginia Trotter of Fort Lauderdale, Florida, complained that Calley had been rotting in prison for the past six years. "Hasn't he suffered enough[?]" she asked. Actually, Calley had spent only a few months in prison, and by early November he would be a free man. The widely held belief that he was being punished while the rest of those who had committed crimes during and after the My Lai massacre avoided punishment was at best a wild exaggeration. As a result of reductions in his sentence by a general and the secretary of the army, the intervention of a federal district court, and the operation of the military parole system, Lieutenant Calley avoided spending the rest of his life in prison. In fact, he spent less time in a cell than many people convicted of minor misdemeanors. His deliverance went largely unnoticed because, during the more than four years that his case was on appeal, it faded from public consciousness. Interest in Lieutenant Calley's fate waned along with the military conflict that had precipitated his court-martial.

By late 1975 both the Calley case and the Vietnam War were over. For the United States the war had ended officially on 27 January 1973 when Secretary of State William Rogers and North Vietnam's Le Duc Tho signed a peace agreement in Paris. The end did not come easily. Anxious to achieve a settlement before the 1972 presidential election, the chief American negotiator, Henry Kissinger, had worked out a deal with Tho by October of that year. Under it the United States would have left Vietnam, while the North Vietnamese kept troops in the South but could not increase their numbers. The government of U.S. ally Nguyen Van Thieu would remain in power but acknowledge the legitimacy of the Communist National Liberation Front and explore the prospect of a coalition government. Thieu objected to this deal, and after Kissinger presented his demands to the North Vietnamese, the talks collapsed on 13 December.

Five days later Nixon launched a massive bombing campaign against North Vietnam. Wave after wave of B-52s pounded bridges, power plants, railroad lines, and industrial installations, and more than a thousand North Vietnamese civilians died. Although this Christmas bombing offensive ignited outraged reaction at home and abroad, and Nixon's approval rating plummeted, it did get North Vietnam back to the bargaining table. The agreement that Kissinger and Tho reached on 9 January differed only cosmetically from the one Thieu had scuttled earlier, however, and the South Vietnamese leader had to be pressured into accepting it. He went along only after being promised billions of dollars in military and economic aid and receiving assurances that the United States would "respond with full force" if North Vietnam violated the agreement.

The cease-fire for which the Paris peace accords provided proved to be at best temporary. Fighting between North and South Vietnam raged on, and the South Vietnamese actually suffered more battle deaths in 1973 than in any previous year except 1968. Meanwhile, the United States was disengaging from the hostilities. By the end of March all its prisoners of war (POWs) had been repatriated, and all its troops, except for 159 marines, left behind to guard the U.S. embassy in Saigon, had withdrawn from Vietnam.

Few Americans wanted a return to Vietnam. Angry that Nixon was bombing Cambodia to support anti-Communist forces there and the cease-fire in Vietnam, Congress voted in June to require an immediate cessation of all military operations in and over Indochina. Nixon's veto of this legislation was sustained, but he had to accept a compromise that imposed a 15 August deadline. When the president requested $1 billion in aid for South Vietnam, Congress slashed the amount to $700 million.

On 8 August 1974 the Watergate scandal forced Nixon to re-sign from office, and Ford, who replaced him in the White House, was too busy trying to establish his own legitimacy and authority to do much for South Vietnam. North Vietnamese commanders ordered their forces to liberate people and hold territory in the South, and in intense fighting during the first three months of 1975, the South Vietnamese armed forces collapsed. Although it was obvious they were being routed, Congress was unwilling to authorize military assistance for South Vietnam. On 23 April President Ford received wild applause when he proclaimed at Tulane University that "the war in Vietnam is over as far as America is concerned." Six days later it was over for South Vietnam, too. Communist forces captured Saigon, as the United States beat an inglorious retreat from its embassy in what soon became known as Ho Chi Minh City.

While the war in which Rusty Calley had fought staggered to an ignominious end, he was appealing his case through the military and civilian judicial systems. His conviction was reviewed first by the Third Army convening authority, General Albert O. Connor. On 18 August 1971 Connor approved the court-martial's findings of guilt and its decision to sentence Calley to dismissal from the army and forfeiture of all pay and allowances. Connor reduced the term of imprisonment the court had imposed from life to twenty years, however. An ordinary defendant would have been immediately incarcerated in the United States Disciplinary Barracks at Fort Leavenworth, Kansas, but after the Judge Advocate General's office checked with the White House to verify that Nixon intended Calley's confinement to quarters to continue until he had appealed his case all the way up to the president, Connor directed that he remain under house arrest.

Being confined to his Fort Benning apartment was tougher than it seemed. Calley was not permitted to leave his quarters, or even to talk with the other officers who lived in the six-unit BOQ complex. He had to exercise in a small, fenced backyard, where his workouts consisted mainly of badminton games with one of his guards. Calley could not use the base gymnasium, cinema, or canteen or even buy food at a local supermarket. Anne Moore had to do his grocery shopping for him. In eighteen months he was allowed out of his quarters only to see a dentist and to visit his terminally ill father, whose funeral he chose not to attend because of concern that his presence would turn it into a media circus. Calley resented being accompanied by military police whenever he did get out of his apartment and being under constant guard even at home.

To fight boredom, he took correspondence courses in accounting, history, and oceanography and built large gasoline-powered model airplanes. For company he acquired a beagle, a mynah bird, and two aquariums full of fish. Isolation began to wear on him, though, and the lieutenant told visitors that the president had not done him a favor by placing him under house arrest; at least at Fort Leavenworth, he could have socialized and had access to educational facilities.

In late 1972 army psychiatrists examined Calley and concluded that further confinement to his quarters at Fort Benning would be extremely detrimental to his mental health. The imposed isolation was reinforcing negative features of his personality. Finding him unstable and prone to moods of deep depression, the psychiatrists expressed concern about his suicidal tendencies. At their urging, the secretary of the army requested that Calley be transferred to Fort Leavenworth, where he could develop normal social relationships. The country was focused on welcoming home the first of its repatriated POWs, however, and with the Watergate scandal beginning to undermine his presidency, the last thing Nixon wanted to do was divert attention from an event that promised beneficial publicity by resuscitating the My Lai controversy. He told Ehrlichman that it would be a mistake to move on Calley now. The president did nothing, and the lieutenant remained confined to his BOQ apartment.

While he battled boredom and depression there, the Army Court of Military Review considered his appeal. This tribunal had far more authority than a civilian appellate court, being empowered not only to decide legal issues but also to weigh evidence, assess the credibility of witnesses, and resolve disputed questions of fact. On 1 May 1972 Latimer and two JAG lawyers,

Captains J. Houston Gordon and Richard M. Evans, asked it to consider thirty-two alleged errors in the Calley case, involving the jurisdiction of the court-martial, unfair pretrial publicity, unlawful command influence, erroneous rulings and instructions by Judge Kennedy, denial of the right to a fair trial, violation of various constitutional rights, and inadequate posttrial review. The government took until 17 August to file a reply brief, and the court did not hand down a decision until 16 February 1973.

Although empowered to reduce Calley's sentence, set aside all or any part of the findings of guilt, order a new hearing, or dismiss the charges entirely, the Court of Military Review did none of these things. Its sixty-three-page opinion rejected the contention that the court-martial had been without jurisdiction over Calley because he had been improperly retained on active duty. Although conceding his case had become a cause célèbre, the court denied that the massive and sensational pretrial publicity had deprived him of a fair trial. It also disputed the contention that unlawful command influence (allegedly exercised by numerous high-ranking military and civilian officials, including General Westmoreland and President Nixon) had fatally infected all proceedings involving Calley, including its own. Such individuals had made a multitude of public statements about the My Lai (4) incident, the Court of Military Review acknowledged, but these had been "neither coercive in nature nor specifically directed to potential court members who might serve on [Calley's] court-martial." The court considered the evidence sufficient to prove that the defendant had personally participated in, and also ordered subordinates to commit, the mass summary execution of unresisting men, women, and children and detected "no impediment to the findings that [he] acted with murderous *mens rea*, including premeditation." The refusal of the Hébert Subcommittee to turn over records of its hearings had not resulted in any violation of Calley's rights, the court ruled, for the testimony of the "key government witnesses" (Sledge, Meadlo, Conti, Dursi, and Turner) had been unaffected by this action and the defense had been provided with volumes of pretrial statements made during various army investigations by men who subsequently testified for the prosecution. The court also held that the Judge Advocate General had acted properly in denying a defense petition for a new trial, for although Calley's counsel had found a previously unavailable witness, former PFC Charles Gruver, who could testify about Medina's briefing and the massacre, they had failed to establish that his testimony would change the outcome. The Court of Military Review did find that Judge Kennedy had erred in granting more than one peremptory challenge to each side, but it considered this error harmless. In any event, by failing to object at the time, defense counsel had waived the right to raise this issue on appeal. Finally, the sentence Calley had received was appropriate.

His lawyers appealed the decision of the Court of Military Review to the United States Court of Military Appeals. This tribunal, which sat in Washington, consisted of three civilian judges and was the court of last resort for all branches of the armed forces. On 2 April 1973 Latimer, Gordon, and Evans presented it with a massive 422-page petition for review, raising thirty issues that, they claimed, required reversal of Calley's conviction. Most were substantially similar to ones already considered by the Army Court of Military Review.

After studying this petition and the trial record, Ralph DeLaVergne, a commissioner for the Court of Military Appeals, concluded that all the issues raised by defense counsel were either without merit or unworthy of further consideration. He recommended that the court decline to hear the case. The chief commissioner agreed "with his coverage of the issues and with his assessment of their merits," but he recognized that the judges might think the seriousness of Calley's crimes warranted something more than a simple denial of review. They did. On 23 May, going against DeLaVergne's recommendation, the court agreed to consider three issues.

In early October it heard oral argument on the adequacy of Judge Kennedy's instructions, the sufficiency of the evidence showing Calley had possessed the state of mind required to make his killings murder rather than manslaughter, and whether adverse publicity had kept him from receiving a fair trial. Appearing before a court on which he had served for a decade, Latimer turned in another disappointing performance. Frequently getting lost in his notes and repeating himself, he seemed out of his depth.

To no one's surprise, the Court of Military Appeals affirmed the Army Court of Military Review. Its 21 December decision was not unanimous, however. In an opinion by Judge Robert E. Quinn, the court rejected the contention that pretrial publicity had denied Calley his constitutional right to a fair trial. Quinn pointed out that most stories and editorials about My Lai had not attributed responsibility for the massacre to anyone in particular, that those items which mentioned Calley generally supported him, and that Judge Kennedy had given the defense ample opportunity to challenge for cause any jurors who might have been prejudiced by the media coverage. The court also held that there was sufficient evidence for reasonable jurors to find the defendant guilty of the crimes with which he was charged. Responding to the contention that it was inadequate to support convictions for murder rather than manslaughter, Quinn declared that the record contained evidence tending to prove Calley had directed and personally participated in the intentional killing of unarmed Vietnamese men, women, and children; that he knew these prisoners were supposed to be treated with respect and held for interrogation; and that he had executed them without regard to their age, condition, "or possibility of suspicion." It was the jury's job to decide between his claim that Medina had ordered him to kill everyone in the village and the captain's denial that he had done so.

Finally, Quinn held, Judge Kennedy had properly instructed the jury concerning what it must find in order to convict Calley of murder rather than manslaughter and had not harmed him by what he told jurors concerning when an illegal order would excuse a soldier's actions. Kennedy had stated that to provide an accused with a defense, an order must be one that the defendant did not actually know was illegal and, under the circumstances "a man of ordinary sense and understanding" would not have recognized as unlawful. Calley's counsel wanted the Court of Military Appeals to rule that superior orders excused a subordinate's conduct unless they were so palpably or manifestly illegal that a person of "the commonest understanding" would recognize their illegality. Quinn believed that in this case it really did not matter which formulation was used. He declared, "An order to kill infants and unarmed civilians who were so demonstrably incapable of resistance to the armed might of a military force as were those killed by Lieutenant Calley is, in my opinion, so palpably illegal that whatever conceptional difference there may be . . . the difference could not have had any . . . impact on a court of lay members."

Quinn's colleagues disagreed with his handling of this issue. In a concurring opinion Judge Robert Duncan agreed with him that Kennedy had applied the proper standard, which he had taken directly from the *Manual for Courts-Martial*, but Duncan faulted him for presuming that Calley knew he could not kill the people of My Lai (4). Chief Judge William Darden disagreed with Quinn about the standard. He considered the one set forth in the *Manual* "too strict in a combat environment" and criticized it for permitting "serious punishment of persons whose training and attitude incline them either to be enthusiastic about compliance with orders or not to challenge the authority of their superiors." Darden wanted that standard replaced with the "palpable illegality to the commonest understanding" test advocated by Calley's lawyers. That one would properly balance the interests involved and also promote "fairness by permitting the military jury to consider the particular accused's intelligence, grade, training and other elements directly related to the issue of whether he should have known an order was illegal." Since the defense of superior orders had been submitted to the jury under what he considered an improper standard, Darden wanted Calley to be given a rehearing.

Perhaps inspired by Darden's opinion, on 7 January 1974, the lieutenant's lawyers filed a petition for reconsideration, which alleged that the standard the court had adopted was unfair and unjust. It also contended that the Court of Military Appeals had denied Calley the presumption of innocence at trial and had erred in holding that he had not been prejudiced by the pretrial publicity. These arguments were to no avail. On 4 February the court denied their petition.

The White House was no more receptive to the entreaties of Calley's lawyers than were the military appellate courts. Nixon's aides monitored the case and kept the president informed about its progress. Sometime before General O'Connor reduced the lieutenant's sentence, Ehrlichman prepared a handwritten outline of the entire appellate process. Dean wrote a memorandum on Calley's confinement, and in November he had his assistant, David Wilson, draft one for the president on the litigation, explaining that the matter was then being considered by the Court of Military Review. He was, Dean told Nixon, just trying to provide "a brief report to bring you up to date on the status of the case."

While keeping abreast of how it was progressing, the White House continued to adhere to the hands-off policy it had adopted following the president's April announcements. That is clearly the course the Pentagon favored. Ehrlichman received a memorandum from the Department of Defense, written on 2 April 1971, which warned, "The precedent of intervention in the review process will subject the president, the Secretary of Defense and the Secretaries of the Military Departments to pleas for summary intervention in other cases." To demonstrate the magnitude of the problem this could pose, the memo pointed out that in fiscal 1969 there had been a total of 109,345 courts-martial.

Letting normal appellate review run its course posed a potential political problem, however. Dean foresaw the possibility that this process might reach its conclusion just before the 1972 presidential election. Consequently, he asked Eric Fygi to give him his "views as to various actions that might be taken to preclude politicizing what we agree should be a judicious and impartial presidential review." In a 23 June 1971 memorandum Fygi warned against trying to slow down the military appellate process. Doing that, he believed, would "be most undesirable and of questionable legality." For one thing, there was at least one military case holding that the accused had a right to speedy appellate review. In addition, presidential action to influence the pace of the appeals process would be susceptible "to legal attack and general criticism as unlawful command influence." Fygi pointed out that should the case reach the president at a politically inconvenient time, he could delay acting on it by claiming there needed to be a thorough review of the matter by his staff before he could make a decision. Fygi recommended resort to this stall tactic.

He and Dean obviously believed that further White House intervention in the Calley case posed large political risks that ought to be avoided. Thus, the lieutenant's lawyers faced a formidable challenge when, even before asking the Army Court of Military Review to hear his case, they tried to persuade the president to grant him clemency. Latimer believed that Nixon could pardon Calley at any time, and he had expressed his opinion publicly on television. On 27 January 1972 he and Captain Gordon wrote privately to the president, requesting that Nixon consider their client's case immediately and grant him clemency in any form deemed appropriate. Dean recommended against doing what they asked. After reading their letter, Nixon concurred. The next day the counsel to the president wrote to Latimer and Gordon, saying that in order for the "final review" the president had promised to be fair and just, the issues in the case must "first be narrowed to the greatest extent possible." For this reason, "It would be inappropriate to interrupt [the] process of judicial review."

The White House brushed off pleas for early intervention not only from Calley's attorneys but also from Dr. Albert LaVerne, the psychiatrist whose attempt to testify at the court-martial had ended so disastrously. As a result of examining the lieutenant for the defense, LaVerne had developed a strong conviction that Calley suffered from a severe mental disorder that rendered him incapable of premeditating or formulating the intent to kill. After the court-martial, the psychiatrist "pursued the cause of freeing Calley with missionary zeal, presenting his conclusions to everybody connected with the case," Dean told Ehrlichman. "This effort has included the unethical public release of the confidential medical examination he conducted." LaVerne also wrote several letters to the White House, including one on 31 May, in which he implored the president to appoint an impartial panel of prominent civilian psychiatrists and psychologists to examine Calley and "settle once and for all the question of [his] sanity." He argued that it would be unwise to delay further final disposition of this explosive case. Obviously, Dean did not agree. The White House had responded to previous letters from LaVerne with "the briefest of acknowledgments," but on 8 June Dean recommended that this time it tell him to present his psychological evidence to Latimer, who could then use it in making a plea to the president on Calley's behalf. Ehrlichman adopted Dean's suggestion.

While the White House seemed determined to avoid taking any action on Calley's behalf, Secretary of the Army Howard "Bo" Callaway did not share its reluctance to come to his aid. After the Court of Military Appeals handed down its decision, the Judge Advocate General, Major General George Prugh, advised Callaway in an 8 February 1974 memorandum to approve the lieutenant's sentence and order it into execution "unless the President otherwise directs." Callaway spent two months reviewing the record and other documents in the case and sought guidance from the Army and Air Force Clemency and Parole Board. Then, on 15 April, as he informed the president, he "ordered into execution the sentence as affirmed by the United States Court of Military Review and the United States Court of Military Appeals." This directive meant that approximately ten days later Calley would cease to be an officer.

Callaway added, however, that pursuant to his authority as secretary of the army, he had taken a separate action, remitting "the unexecuted portion of the sentence to confinement in excess of ten years." This meant that he had slashed Calley's term of imprisonment in half. It also meant that the convicted mass murderer would become eligible for parole in just seven months, on 19 November 1974. Callaway concluded his memorandum to the president by offering to have "the appropriate officials" brief him on the matter. The secretary had reportedly reduced Calley's sentence because he considered the possibility that the lieutenant might have sincerely believed he was acting in accordance with superior orders a mitigating factor.

Some newspapers nevertheless found what the *Washington Star-News* characterized as his "extraordinary act of compassion" disturbing. After all, opponents of the war were being punished far more severely than this convicted killer merely for deserting from the military or evading the draft. Noting that President Nixon was now obliged to carry out his promise to review the sentence, the *Star-News* commented, "We think the breaks have mostly been with Calley, and the President would do well to leave things as they are."

Perhaps he read its editorial, for that is precisely what Nixon did. Acting on instructions from the president, White House aide J. Fred Buzhardt informed Calley's lawyers that because the record compiled during the trial and appeals was so voluminous, he could base his review of the case entirely on it and would not need to meet with them. Then Buzhardt prepared a memorandum for Nixon, laying out the three alternatives open to him: (1) approve Secretary Callaway's action and do nothing more; (2) reduce Calley's sentence still further; or (3) grant him a full pardon. Buzhardt recommended the first option. The president concurred and later that day sent Callaway a one-sentence memorandum, which stated simply: "I have reviewed the record of the case of United States vs. Calley and have decided that no further action by me in this matter is necessary or appropriate." That is how Nixon fulfilled the promise he had made three years earlier to an outraged and applauding public to personally and finally decide the Calley case.

Nixon's impersonal decision was not final either. The army terminated Calley's officer status at 1600 hours on the afternoon of 4 May, but it could go no further with implementation of the sentence the president had approved. The reason was that on 27 February Judge J. Robert Elliott of the United States District Court for the Middle District of Georgia, Columbus Division, had enjoined the secretary and the commanding general of Fort Benning from changing Calley's place of custody or increasing the conditions of his confinement.

Elliott, a sixty-four-year-old jurist formerly best known for his service as Georgia's Democratic national committeeman during the 1950s and for enjoining civil rights protests at Albany, Georgia, in 1962, had also ordered the convicted killer released on $1,000 personal bond. He had taken these actions because he thought an application for a writ of habeas corpus, which Calley's lawyers had filed on 11 February, raised substantial legal questions. Explaining his decision to release the convicted murderer on bail before ruling on that petition, Elliott observed that the lieutenant had been a model prisoner during almost three years of confinement, that his past conduct showed he was unlikely to flee, and that he presented no danger to himself or others. Liberated from house arrest by Elliott's ruling, Calley began taking flight instruction at the Fort Benning Flying Club and weighing numerous job offers. According to the *Philadelphia Inquirer*, he was seen driving around Columbus in a small but expensive Mercedes sports car.

The United States Court of Appeals for the Fifth Circuit ended his cruising in what the *Inquirer* called a "spiffy little auto" by reversing Elliott's orders. Calley's lawyers managed to get two members of the three-judge panel that was originally supposed to hear the government's appeal, Thomas Gee and Elbert Tuttle, to disqualify themselves just two hours before the hearing because of their extensive military backgrounds. This was a hollow victory. On 13 June Chief Judge John R. Brown and Judges John Minor Wisdom and J. P. Coleman ruled that in releasing Calley, Elliot had failed to follow the law as laid down by the Supreme Court. It provided that a military prisoner was entitled to release on bail pending review of a postconviction habeas corpus petition only if he both raised substantial constitutional claims on which he was likely to prevail and could point to exceptional circumstances that made special treatment of his case necessary to ensure the effectiveness of the habeas corpus remedy. The panel returned Calley to military custody until Elliott ruled on the merits of his case, emphasizing that the army now had the authority to prescribe both "the place . . . and the conditions of his custody."

His attorneys requested a rehearing before the entire Fifth Circuit, sitting en banc. Although a majority of the judges voted to reject their petition, Coleman did ask to have the record show that he had voted for it, and Judges Griffin Bell and Lewis R. Morgan filed a brief but blistering dissent. Complaining that the panel had denied rehearing before a vote could be taken on the en banc motion, thereby allowing Calley to be sent immediately to the Fort Benning stockade, they protested, "This court is not an adjunct of the army nor an institution serving at its beck and call." Noting that Calley was the only person involved in the My Lai (4) incident who had been convicted of anything, Bell and Morgan accused the military of seeking to redeem itself by denying him due process.

By the time they filed their futile protest on 19 July, the former lieutenant was already in the Disciplinary Barracks at Fort Leavenworth. The army had ordered him transferred there on 26 June. In late July Kenneth Henson, a Columbus attorney now representing Calley, announced plans to travel there to seek his early release. Henson's efforts to persuade the Army and Air Force Clemency and Parole Board to free his client achieved no immediate results, but the habeas corpus petition that he, Latimer, and Gordon (now out of the army and practicing law in Covington, Tennessee) had filed with Judge Elliott did. On 25 September Elliott ordered Calley "released forthwith from his present confinement in the United States Disciplinary Barracks at Fort Leavenworth, Kansas, and . . . discharged from custody or restraint of any nature."

The judge justified his action in a sixty-three-page opinion, which held that the former lieutenant's constitutional rights had been violated in several ways. First, he had been denied a fair and impartial trial by the intense and highly detrimental media coverage that preceded his court-martial. "Never in the history of the military justice system, and perhaps in the history of American courts, has any accused ever encountered such intense and continuous prejudicial publicity," Elliott declared. He endorsed the *Montgomery Advertiser*'s contention that Lieutenant Calley had been tried and found guilty in news accounts. Elliott acknowledged that Judge Kennedy had tried to protect the defendant's rights by instructing prospective witnesses not to discuss their testimony with or disclose evidence to anyone other than the attorneys, but he pointed out that Kennedy's orders had been violated repeatedly and that his efforts to control the media had proved futile. Elliott filled his opinion with lists of television broadcasts and summaries of and quotations from scores of articles. He even included a photograph of a *Time* magazine cover that depicted the defendant, accompanied by the headline "The Massacre: Where Does the Guilt Lie?". The widespread exploitation of the case by those on both sides of the debate over the Vietnam War, Elliott concluded, had effectively destroyed Calley's defense. He determined that "in the circumstances here presented it was not humanly possible for the jurors not to be improperly influenced." The First Amendment guaranteed the press the right to publish the news, but the Fifth Amendment's due process clause guaranteed individuals the right to a fair trial. Because Calley had been denied that right, his conviction must be set aside.

Elliott found three other reasons for voiding it. One was the refusal of Judge Kennedy to issue subpoenas to certain witnesses the defense wanted to call. Most were high-ranking civilian and military officials, up to and including President Nixon, who had allegedly exercised improper command influence in the case, but one was a former soldier whose testimony it wanted to use to impeach Dennis Conti. Kennedy's refusal to subpoena these witnesses had violated Calley's rights under the Fifth and Sixth Amendments, Judge Elliott believed. His rights had also been violated by the refusal of the Hébert subcommittee to turn over the testimony of witnesses who appeared before it and then at his court-martial. Elliott was inclined to think the Jencks Act required production of this material, but even if it did not, "there nevertheless was a clear violation of Petitioner's constitutional right to confrontation and compulsory process resulting from the refusal of the Congress to honor the subpoenas issued by the military judge." Its action had also deprived Calley of due process, as had the failure of the prosecution to identify the precise individuals he was accused of slaying, an omission that subjected him to the possibility of being convicted more than once for the same killing. In a final section of his opinion, accurately entitled "Obiter," Elliot quoted General William T. Sherman's famous pronouncement that "war is hell" and expressed his personal opinion that Calley had been abused for doing what he had been trained and ordered to do. He viewed the former lieutenant's conviction as "a cathartic to cleanse the national conscience and the impellent to improve the army's image."

Although Elliott concluded his lengthy opinion by ordering Calley's immediate discharge from custody, he failed to liberate the former lieutenant from Fort Leavenworth. Unwilling to acquiesce in the district judge's ruling, the army returned to the Fifth Circuit the day after he issued it. With the permission of Solicitor General Robert Bork, it asked Chief Judge Brown to delay Calley's release for fifteen days while it considered how to respond to Elliott's decision. Brown granted a temporary stay. Calley's lawyers asked Justice Lewis Powell of the U.S. Supreme Court to vacate it, but Powell referred their request to the full Court. By the time it was ready to act on 18 November, the Fifth Circuit, meeting en banc, had decided that the former lieutenant should be released, pending a ruling on appeals by both sides from Judge Elliott's decision. Brown and his colleagues also determined to take the unusual step of hearing the Calley case en banc.

By the time they decided it, on 10 September 1975, Calley had been out of prison for ten months. Back in June 1972 Latimer had begun trying to get his case heard by the Army and Air Force Clemency and Parole Board. Prisoners confined in the Disciplinary Barracks automatically received such a hearing not less than six nor more than eight months after being sentenced, but because Calley was not at Leavenworth, no one appeared to have jurisdiction to convene one for him. Latimer wrote to the secretary of the army, requesting that he authorize someone to do this. Three months later, Calley filed a formal request for clemency. It repeated the now familiar theme that of all the soldiers charged in the My Lai (4) incident, "amazingly" only he had been convicted. Justice demanded clemency in Calley's case, the petition argued, for he had suffered enough, any deterrent effect that punishing him might have had already been achieved, and the self-restraint and courage he had exhibited during his trial and detention showed he did not need rehabilitation. Calley requested that "the sentence to confinement be remitted or any further confinement be suspended." In order that he might appear personally before the Clemency and Parole Board, he asked it to establish a subsidiary board at Fort Benning. On 16 September Robert F. Froehlke, then secretary of the army, granted this request, and on 14 November the Department of the Army ordered a three-member panel to conduct a hearing there and make recommendations concerning possible amelioration of Calley's sentence or the advancement or waiver of his parole eligibility date. On 14 May 1973 Froehlke turned down Calley's request for clemency.

On 8 November 1974 his successor, Bo Callaway, announced that the army was paroling the former lieutenant. It was the Fifth Circuit's decision that day to order him released on bail that precipitated this announcement. Army procedures permitted parole of a prisoner after he had completed one-third of his sentence, and, because all of the time Calley had spent confined in his apartment counted toward this minimum, he would become eligible on 19 November. Finding that his behavior and psychological condition qualified him for release from the Disciplinary Barracks, the Clemency and Parole Board recommended paroling him then. Although Callaway had considered proposing a pardon, he accepted the board's recommendation. The secretary signed the parole order on 30 October and planned to make it public on 15 November, the Friday before the Tuesday on which Calley would be released from prison. The Fifth Circuit's action inspired him to make his announcement a week earlier, partly to avoid looking silly, but also because he had received legal advice that there were serious doubts about whether, once Calley was released on bail, the army would any longer have the authority to parole him.

He would then be legally in the custody of Elliott's federal district court and no longer under military jurisdiction. In hopes of keeping Calley at least technically in its custody and making his release subject to some conditions, the army offered during a 9 November hearing in Elliott's courtroom to make his parole effective immediately. Gordon spurned that proposal, as did the judge. Elliott remarked sarcastically that the offer seemed rather inconsistent with the army's earlier insistence that releasing Calley would have disastrous consequences. He again freed the convicted mass murderer on $1,000 personal bond. "There are no other conditions," the judge declared.

Although Calley walked out of Elliott's courtroom a free man, Arnold Vickery, an attorney for the army, told reporters he was not on parole. Nor would he be on 19 November. Callaway had already made it clear, however, that Calley would not be returning to prison, no matter who won in the Fifth Circuit. The army was appealing only, as it explained in a letter to Senator Hugh Scott (R. Pa.), because Elliott's opinion had "far-ranging legal implications" for a military justice system whose integrity Callaway considered himself duty bound to protect.

The secretary won this fight over principle. By an eight-to-five margin (with Chief Judge Brown and Judge Gee not participating), the Fifth Circuit reversed Elliot's decision. "This Court is convinced," wrote Judge Robert A. Ainsworth, "that Lieutenant Calley received a fair trial from the military court-martial which convicted him." A "careful and painstaking review" of the case had satisfied the majority that "no violation of [his] constitutional or fundamental rights has occurred, and that the findings of guilty were returned by impartial members based on evidence presented at a fairly conducted trial." Ainsworth attacked Elliott's conclusion that Calley had been denied a fair trial by prejudicial pretrial publicity with a scatter-gun, pointing out that some of the coverage of the case had been favorable to the defendant, that the military judge had taken steps to exclude from the jury anyone who had formed an opinion regarding the defendant's guilt or innocence, that the record did not show bias on the part of any juror, and that Kennedy had done as much as the Constitution allowed to control the news media.

Addressing the issue of the trial judge's failure to issue the subpoenas Calley's counsel had requested, he observed that what the witness they wanted to use to impeach Conti might have said would have "been merely cumulative of other testimony to the same effect." Under prior Fifth Circuit decisions, refusing to compel the testimony of the high-ranking officials the defense wanted to question about command influence was proper if the prosecution had demonstrated the untruth of the allegations on which its requests for subpoenas were based, and after extensive hearings Kennedy had found there was no support for its claims. In holding he should have subpoenaed the individuals in question, Elliott had gone beyond what a civilian judge was authorized to do when reviewing the conduct of a court-martial in a habeas corpus action.

As for his holding that the bill of particulars had been insufficiently specific concerning whom Calley had killed, "It is difficult to understand how a defendant is deprived of fair notice of the charges against him when he confirms that the alleged incidents happened and that he participated in them." Ainsworth also rejected Elliott's holding that the failure of the Hébert subcommittee to turn over the testimony of witnesses who appeared before it required Calley's release. There had been no violation of his due process rights because the prosecution was not responsible for the subcommittee's actions. Even if these did violate the Jencks Act, that could not entitle Calley to release because it was just a statute, and only a constitutional violation could justify habeas corpus relief.

Five members of the court disagreed with Ainsworth on that issue. Dissenting for himself and Judges Morgan, Homer Thornberry, Walter P. Gewin, and Charles Clark, Griffin Bell analogized this case to *United States v. Nixon* (1974), in which the Supreme Court had recently held that the president must turn over privileged material required for the fair administration of justice in a criminal case. "We would hold that the government, through Congress, caused the army . . . to deny Lt. Calley due process of law in withholding the testimony of the witnesses who testified against [him]," Bell wrote. He and the other dissenters thought Elliott should be directed to examine the statements that witnesses had made to the Hébert subcommittee and insisted that, if he found these to be material, he should issue the writ of habeas corpus "conditioned on the retrial of Lt. Calley within a reasonable time."

There was not going to be a retrial of Lieutenant Calley, however. The day after the Court of Appeals ruled, the army announced that, although he still had ten days to serve before becoming eligible for parole, it would not seek to return him to prison. Not content with this concession, the former lieutenant's legal team pressed on with what had by now become an essentially theoretical struggle. It asked the Supreme Court to review the Fifth Circuit's decision, but on 5 April 1976, the Court denied Calley's petition for a writ of certiorari. That defeat did not cost him much. The army promptly announced that it was transferring Calley to parole status. This action left him subject to certain conditions on which it did not bother to elaborate, but with the exception of those, he was a free man.

Of course, for all practical purposes Rusty Calley had been a free man for seventeen months. By the time the Supreme Court rejected his last appeal, he had already settled into civilian life in Columbus. Calley had given some lectures on college campuses and earned some money as a consultant for an ABC television special about his trial and for appearing on *AM America* to promote that program. Apparently grateful for the support he had received from George Wallace four years earlier, in November 1975 Calley volunteered to work in Wallace's presidential campaign. In the summer of 1976 he married Penny Vick, the daughter of a prominent Columbus jeweler, V. V. Vick. The candlelight ceremony at Saint Paul's Methodist Church was reportedly one of the major social events in the small west Georgia city. Calley became the manager of his father-in-law's jewelry store, and the following year he and his wife moved into a three-bedroom brick bungalow on Hilton Avenue.

In 1981 the Army Clemency Board turned down his request for clemency, but that did not seem to matter much to his neighbors in intensely pro-military Columbus. So tightly did they close ranks around Calley that by 1993 it was nearly impossible to find anyone in town who considered him anything other than a scapegoat. A retired first sergeant, who had fought in both Vietnam and Korea and now ran a clock shop a few doors down from V. V. Vick Jeweler in the Cross Country Plaza mall, told a United Press International reporter that Calley was "a hell of a fine fellow" who "got a bum rap." A barber in the same shopping center considered him "a good man, a fine man."

Like many Vietnam veterans, by the 1990s Calley was substantially heavier than he had been in his army days; while adding weight, he had also lost much of the reddish hair that earned him the nickname "Rusty." Most of the 105 members of Charlie Company who had accompanied him into My Lai (4) remained alive, and they, too, were settling into middle age. Not all had done as well as Calley at putting the massacre behind them. One had locked himself up behind barred windows in his tiny Mississippi house, there to struggle with drugs, pain, and tormenting memories that would never go away.

In a sense America was like that distraught veteran. For the nation, Vietnam was a tormenting memory that would never go away. For a time nobody seemed to want to talk, or even think, much about it. As the children of the men who had fought there came of age and grew curious about a conflict in which their fathers had participated, but which they often seemed reluctant to discuss, interest in Vietnam revived. Movies, novels, and college courses about the war were not all there was to this revival, though. It also spawned arguments among members of the Vietnam generation, now old enough to contend for national political leadership, over who had fought and who had not, and anguished revelations from veterans, such as former Nebraska Senator Bob Kerrey, about dark deeds they had committed in vicious little engagements long ago, now forgotten by everyone but their Vietnamese victims and themselves.

"I think most Americans understood that the My Lai massacre was not representative of our people, of the war we were fighting, of our men who were fighting it," Richard Nixon wrote in his memoirs. Yet many Americans thought it embodied the very essence of the Vietnam War. They viewed My Lai (4) as the ultimate evidence of why the United States should never have become involved in that conflict in the first place. Certainly William L. Calley Jr. did not belong in Vietnam, at least not as a platoon commander. But his country sent him. He did horrible things there, and then he came home to stand trial for his crimes. In a very real sense, Calley represented all those who had fought in Vietnam. If he was a criminal, he was also a victim, a victim of policies and leaders that had sent him to fight the wrong war, in the wrong place, at the wrong time.

His court-martial was about much more than whether Lieutenant Calley had committed murder. He had, and professional soldiers, horrified by the unprofessional way he had conducted himself at My Lai (4), did their duty as jurors and convicted him. Americans could not accept their verdict, however, because it seemed to them like a condemnation of all the young men they had sent to fight in Vietnam and ultimately of themselves for sending them there. Much more than just a little lieutenant had been on trial at Fort Benning. The Calley court-martial was a trial of the army that fought the Vietnam War and ultimately of that war itself. The evidence presented in a Fort Benning courtroom condemned them both. Neither found vindication in the ambiguous outcome of the court-martial of Lieutenant Calley.

8 June 1943	William L. "Rusty" Calley Jr. is born.
1945	Ho Chi Minh launches a nationalist revolution in Vietnam to prevent France from reasserting colonial control over an area the Japanese had dominated during World War II.
1946	France launches a war against Ho Chi Minh's movement in Vietnam.
May 1954	France is defeated by Ho Chi Minh at the battle of Dienbienphu.
21 July 1954	Geneva Accords divide Vietnam along seventeenth parallel.
1954–1961	Eisenhower administration becomes increasingly involved in Vietnam in the vacuum created by the French defeat.
January 1961– November 1963	U.S. commitment to preserving non-Communist South Vietnam deepens as Kennedy administration increases the number of American military advisers and combat support troops stationed there from about 700 to about 16,000.
Spring 1964	United States expands covert operations against North Vietnam.
2–4 August 1964	North Vietnamese patrol boats attack U.S. destroyer *Maddox* in the Gulf of Tonkin and allegedly attack U.S. destroyer *C. Turner Joy*.
7 August 1964	Congress passes Gulf of Tonkin Resolution, authorizing President Lyndon B. Johnson "to take all necessary measures to repel any armed attack against the forces of the United

States and to prevent further aggression."

13 February 1965	Johnson initiates bombing campaign against North Vietnam, code-named Operation Rolling Thunder.
May 1965	United States initiates offensive ground operations in South Vietnam.
19 December 1966	Captain Ernest Medina takes command of C Company, 1st Battalion, 20th Infantry ("Charlie Company").
15 September 1967	Calley becomes a second lieutenant, completing Officer Candidate School at Fort Benning in bottom 23 percent of his class.
16–22 October 1967	Nationwide "Stop the Draft Week" protests are held.
1 December 1967	Calley and rest of Charlie Company arrive in South Vietnam.
1 January 1968	Task Force Barker activated.
3 January 1968	Operating out of LZ Carrington, near Duc Pho in the southernmost part of Quang Ngai Province, Charlie Company conducts its first combat assault.
26 January 1968	Charlie Company is assigned to Task Force Barker.
30–31 January 1968	North Vietnamese and Vietcong launch Tet Offensive, in which they are defeated militarily but inflict a political defeat on the Johnson administration, destroying much of the support for its war in Vietnam.
25 February 1968	Charlie Company loses three dead and twelve wounded in minefield.

14 March 1968	Sergeant George Cox killed when booby-trapped shell explodes.
15 March 1968	Following memorial service for Cox, Medina briefs Calley and the rest of Charlie Company on next day's operation at My Lai (4).
16 March 1968	Charlie Company murders approximately 500 Vietnamese civilians at My Lai (4).
17 March 1968	Brigadier General George H. Young learns of the massacre at My Lai but fails to order a thorough investigation. This failure is the result of Young's own apathy and deception by those below him, such as Colonel Oran Henderson, commander of the 11th Brigade.
20 April 1968	General William Westmoreland, commander of all American forces in Vietnam, visits the Americal Division and is briefed on a number of recent operations, including the one at My Lai (4), but no one mentions civilian casualties to him.
24 April 1968	Colonel Henderson prepares a watered-down written report on the incident for his superiors, which vastly understates the number of civilian casualties at My Lai (4). Major General Samuel Koster, commander of the Americal Division, receives this report but fails to order a follow-up investigation.
April 1968	Ron Ridenhour hears from Charles Gruver about the horrific events at My Lai and makes it his personal mission to find out what happened there.

September 1968	Calley becomes a civil affairs officer, in which capacity he does what his commanding officer considers a remarkable job of assisting, and hence winning the hearts and minds of, the Vietnamese people.
29 March 1969	Ridenhour sends five-page letter regarding what he has learned about My Lai to Congressman Morris "Mo" Udall and other officials in Washington.
4 April 1969	Secretary of Defense Melvin Laird receives a copy of Ridenhour's letter from Congressman Udall.
9 April 1969	A copy of Ridenhour's letter is forwarded to the army. U.S. forces in Vietnam reach peak strength of 535,000.
12 April 1969	Colonel John G. Hill of the office of the Chief of Staff writes Ridenhour, informing him that an investigation of the My Lai incident (conducted by Colonel William Wilson of the Inspector General's Office) is under way.
9–13 June 1969	After being hustled out of Vietnam, Calley is questioned in the offices of the Inspector General in Washington, where helicopter pilot Hugh Thompson picks him out of a lineup.
16 July 1969	Colonel Wilson interviews Paul Meadlo, who confesses to joining Calley in murdering civilians on 16 March 1968.
17 July 1969	Colonel Wilson submits a written report of his findings, along with the

	transcripts of interviews with thirty-six witnesses.
4 August 1969	Chief Warrant Officer Andre C. R. Feher commences CID investigation of the My Lai incident. His team will gather the evidence used to prosecute Calley and others accused of crimes committed on 16 March.
5 September 1969	Brigadier General Oscar E. Davis, interim commander of Fort Benning, charges Calley with the multiple murders of "Oriental human beings" one day before he is due to be discharged from the army.
15 October 1969	Antiwar movement stages first national Moratorium Day.
22 October 1969	Freelance journalist Seymour Hersh receives a tip regarding the army's prosecution of Calley.
13 November 1969	After a diligent three-week investigation, Hersh reports the story of what happened at My Lai to the general public, triggering a media frenzy and a public and political furor.
13–15 November 1969	Antiwar activists stage "March Against Death" in Washington.
20 November 1969	*Cleveland Plain Dealer* publishes graphic color photographs of the My Lai massacre, taken by a former army photographer, Ronald Haeberle.
24 November 1969	Paul Meadlo interviewed by Mike Wallace on CBS television. Lieutenant General William Peers appointed to head army inquiry into the original investigation of the My Lai incident.

	Representative L. Mendel Rivers announces that Investigative Subcommittee of House Armed Services Committee will look into the My Lai incident.
25 November 1969	The military judge, Colonel Reid Kennedy, holds first Article 39(a) hearing in Calley case.
5 December 1969	*Life* magazine runs a ten-page story regarding the My Lai massacre, including Haeberle's graphic photographs of some of the dead.
8 December 1969	President Richard Nixon tells reporters that the My Lai massacre was "an isolated incident," emphasizing that 1.2 million Americans had served in Vietnam, 40,000 had died there, and "virtually all of them have helped the people of Vietnam in one way or another."
16 December 1969	Trying to prevent pretrial disclosure from tainting Calley's trial, Colonel Kennedy directs the prosecutor to request that the attorney general prosecute potential witnesses who violate his nondisclosure order and take legal action against members of the media who publish their statements.
14 March 1970	The Peers Commission completes its investigation. The report contains a brutal summary of atrocities, cover-up, and dereliction of duty.
17 March 1970	The results of the Peers Commission's investigation are announced to the press. Its report leads to the filing of charges against fourteen officers for

	offenses allegedly committed in connection with the cover-up of the My Lai massacre.
15 July 1970	House Armed Services subcommittee, chaired by Representative H. Edward Hébert, releases a fifty-three-page report, which accuses the military and the State Department of suppressing evidence.
16 July 1970	At a press conference, Hébert remarks that the soldiers accused of committing atrocities at My Lai should have been allowed to plead not guilty by reason of insanity.
17 November 1970	Calley's court-martial commences at Fort Benning, Georgia. After a twenty-two-minute opening statement, Captain Aubrey Daniel begins presentation of prosecution's case.
20 November 1970	Sergeant David Mitchell is acquitted of all charges in court-martial at Fort Hood, Texas.
10 December 1970	Calley's attorney, George Latimer, begins his case in chief for Calley's defense.
14 January 1971	Sergeant Charles Hutto is acquitted in court-martial at Fort McPherson, Georgia.
18 January 1971	Out of the presence of the jury, Judge Kennedy hears the testimony of Dr. Albert A. LaVerne, which in his opinion raises the issue of Calley's sanity, necessitating that he adjourn the trial for three weeks while the defendant is examined by a sanity board at Walter Reed Army Hospital.

29 January 1971	Charges against General Koster are dismissed.
22 February 1971	Calley takes the stand in his own defense.
29 March 1971	The jury announces its verdict, finding Calley guilty of the premeditated murders of at least twenty-two individuals.
31 March 1971	Calley is sentenced to life in prison at hard labor. His trial ends after forty-five days, making it one of the longest courts-martial in American history.
1 April 1971	Public outcry against the verdict leads President Nixon to order that Calley be confined to his BOQ apartment, rather than the Fort Benning stockade, while appealing his conviction.
3 April 1971	The president promises the public he will personally review Calley's case after his appeals within the military legal system are exhausted. Captain Daniel dispatches an irate four-page letter to Nixon, criticizing the president for intervening in the case.
4 April 1971	Daniel's co-counsel, Captain John Partin, also sends an irate letter to the president.
8 April 1971	The Defense and Justice Departments announce that efforts to prosecute discharged servicemen are being dropped, due to constitutional limits on military jurisdiction and the fact that no civilian federal court can try them.
16 April 1971	Nixon responds to Daniel's criticism at a press conference.

21 April 1971	The White House answers Captain Daniel's letter, stating that it would be inappropriate for the president to respond in detail to the points it raises because the case is on appeal and the president will be reviewing it later.
29 April 1971	Captain Eugene Kotouc is acquitted of maiming a Vietcong suspect with a knife.
13 May 1971	The White House accumulates 260,000 letters and cards and approximately 75,000 telegrams, 99 percent of which oppose the verdict.
17 August 1971	Court-martial of Captain Medina begins.
18 August 1971	After reviewing Calley's case, the Third Army convening authority, General Albert O'Connor, approves court-martial's finding of guilt and its decision to sentence Calley to dismissal from the army and forfeiture of all pay and allowances, but he reduces his life sentence to twenty years.
23 August 1971	Court-martial of Colonel Henderson for his role in the cover-up begins.
22 September 1971	Captain Medina's court-martial ends with his acquittal on all charges.
17 December 1971	Colonel Henderson is found not guilty of all charges against him.
27 January 1972	Calley's lawyers write to President Nixon, requesting that he immediately grant their client executive clemency.
1 May 1972	Latimer and JAG lawyers Captain J. Houston Gordon and Richard M. Evans ask the Army Court of Military

Review to consider thirty-two alleged errors in the Calley case, involving the jurisdiction of the court-martial, unfair pretrial publicity, unlawful command influence, erroneous rulings and instructions by Judge Kennedy, denial of the right to a fair trial, violations of various constitutional rights, and inadequate post-trial review.

27 January 1973	The Vietnam War officially ends for the United States when Secretary of State William Rogers and North Vietnam's Le Duc Tho sign a peace agreement in Paris.
16 February 1973	In a sixty-three-page opinion, the Court of Military Review rejects Calley's appeal.
29 March 1973	Last of American ground troops leave Vietnam. Only marines guarding the American embassy remain.
2 April 1973	Calley's lawyers appeal decision of the Court of Military Review to the U.S. Court of Military Appeals.
14 May 1973	Secretary of the Army Robert F. Froehlke turns down Calley's request for clemency.
21 December 1973	Court of Military Appeals affirms the decision of the Court of Military Review.
7 January 1974	Calley's lawyers file a petition for reconsideration with the Court of Military Appeals.
4 February 1974	Court of Military Appeals denies Calley's petition for reconsideration.
11 February 1974	Calley's lawyers file petition for a writ

	of habeas corpus with the U.S. District Court for the Middle District of Georgia, Columbus Division.
27 February 1974	District Judge J. Robert Elliott enjoins the secretary of the army and the commanding general of Fort Benning from changing Calley's place of custody or increasing the conditions of his confinement. Elliott also orders Calley released on $1,000 personal bond.
15 April 1974	Secretary of the Army Howard "Bo" Callaway orders into execution the sentence affirmed by the Court of Military Review and the Court of Military Appeals, but he remits the unexecuted portion of the sentence to confinement in excess of ten years, effectively slashing Calley's term of imprisonment in half and making him eligible for parole on 19 November 1974.
3 May 1974	President Nixon states he will take no further action in the Calley case.
13 June 1974	The U.S. Court of Appeals for the Fifth Circuit rules that Judge Elliott failed to follow the law as laid down by the Supreme Court and orders Calley returned to military custody.
26 June 1974	Army orders Calley transferred from Fort Benning to the Disciplinary Barracks at Fort Leavenworth, Kansas.
8 August 1974	Watergate scandal forces President Nixon to resign from office.
25 September 1974	Judge Elliott orders Calley released from Fort Leavenworth.

26 September 1974	Army seeks to delay Calley's release for fifteen days while it considers how to respond to Judge Elliott's order; Chief Judge John Brown of the Fifth Circuit grants it a stay.
8 November 1974	Fifth Circuit en banc orders Calley released on bail pending its ruling on appeals by both sides from Judge Elliott's ruling. Secretary Callaway announces the army is paroling Calley.
13 November 1974	Peers Report is released to the public in part.
30 April 1975	North Vietnamese overrun Saigon. Vietnam war ends.
10 September 1975	Fifth Circuit Court of Appeals, sitting en banc, reverses Judge Elliott, 8 to 5.
11 September 1975	Army announces it will not seek to return Calley to prison.
5 April 1976	U.S. Supreme Court denies Calley's petition for writ of certiorari.
Summer 1976	Calley weds Penny Vick, daughter of prominent Columbus, Georgia, jeweler.
1981	Army Clemency Board rejects Calley's request for clemency.
Present	Calley lives in Columbus, where he manages a jewelry store.

BIBLIOGRAPHICAL ESSAY

Note from the Series Editors: The following bibliographical essay contains the major primary and secondary sources the author consulted for this volume. We have asked all authors in the series to omit formal citations in order to make our volumes more readable, inexpensive, and appealing for students and general readers. In adopting this format, Landmark Law Cases and American Society follows the precedent of a number of highly regarded and widely consulted series.

The only book-length account of the Calley court-martial is Richard Hammer, *The Court-Martial of Lieutenant Calley* (New York: Coward, McCann and Geohegan, 1971), written by a journalist who covered the trial for the *New York Times*. The Record of the Calley General Court Martial, in Records of the Judge Advocate General (Army), Record Group 153.2.3, National Archives Annex, College Park, Maryland, includes a complete transcript of the proceedings. It is an excellent source of information on not only the trial but also the My Lai massacre and the units and individual soldiers involved in that affair.

Among the subjects on which the transcript is particularly enlightening is Lieutenant Calley himself. The testimony of Dr. Wilbur Hamman, a psychiatrist who appeared as a defense witness, is especially informative concerning Calley's early life, for the defendant seems to have been more forthcoming and candid in his interviews with Dr. Hamman than he was on the witness stand. His own testimony does reveal a great deal about his background, actions, and thoughts, however. Since it was delivered under oath, and he was speaking directly, rather than through an intermediary, it is almost certainly more reliable than John Sack's *Lieutenant Calley: His Own Story* (New York: Viking, 1971). Yet this disjointed "as told to" autobiographical account is sometimes surprisingly candid, as where Calley, discussing an engagement in which his RTO was killed because he allowed his men to walk single file across the top of a four-foot dike, states: "I admit it. I was stupid that day" (p. 54). Hammer's *The Court-Martial of Lieutenant*

Calley contains some details about the lieutenant's background not available elsewhere, which he apparently obtained from official records. These facts include the defendant's standing in his high school class and in OCS and the fact that, while working for the Florida East Coast Railroad, he was "late to work often, failed to complete paperwork correctly, and even once got fifteen demerits for permitting several cars on his train to break free from his idling engine" (p. 57).

There is a vast literature on the war in which Lieutenant Calley fought and in which he committed mass murder. The best overviews of the Vietnam conflict are Robert D. Schulzinger, *A Time for War: The United States and Vietnam, 1941–1975* (New York: Oxford University Press, 1997), and George Herring, *America's Longest War: The United States and Vietnam, 1950–1975*, 3d ed. (New York: Knopf, 1996). James S. Olson and Randy Roberts, *Where the Domino Fell: America and Vietnam*, 2d ed. (New York: St. Martin's, 1996), provides an even more concise summary. Stanley Karnow's *Vietnam: A History*, 2d rev. ed. (New York: Penguin, 1997), which was written by a journalist who was also developing a television series on the war for the Public Broadcasting Service, is longer and more detailed. Phillip B. Davidson, *The Vietnam War: The History 1946–1975* (New York: Oxford University Press, 1991), recounts the struggle over South Vietnam from a North Vietnamese perspective.

David Levy, *The Debate over Vietnam* (Baltimore: Johns Hopkins University Press, 1991), although short and without footnotes, provides an excellent summary of the controversy within the United States over the war. Also helpful in understanding domestic protest against American involvement in Vietnam is Terry H. Anderson's well-researched and entertainingly written *The Movement and the Sixties: Protest in America from Greensboro to Wounded Knee* (New York: Oxford University Press, 1995).

The most thorough study of the Selective Service System, which was used to mobilize American manpower for the war, is George Q. Flynn, *The Draft, 1940–1973* (Lawrence: University Press of Kansas, 1993). Lawrence M. Baskir and William A. Strauss, *Chance and Circumstance: The Draft, the War, and the Viet-*

nam Generation (New York: Knopf, 1978), which was written by two men who held executive positions with President Gerald Ford's Clemency Board, is less scholarly, is not as richly documented, and contains fewer statistics, but it takes a broader view of the social consequences of Selective Service. Besides being informative concerning how the government obtained the soldiers who fought in Vietnam, Ronald H. Spector's *After Tet: The Bloodiest Year in Vietnam* (New York: Vintage, 1993) also provides useful information on the composition of American forces there and on the training of officers and noncommissioned officers (NCOs). Spector provides further information on these topics in "The Vietnam War and the Army's Self-Image," in *The Second Indochina War: Proceedings of a Symposium Held in Airlie, Virginia, 7–9 November 1984,* ed. John Schlight (Washington, D.C.: United States Army Center for Military History, 1986), 169–85.

Spector's *After Tet* provides a thorough discussion of infantry warfare in Vietnam and an understanding of the experiences of those who served as "grunts." Even better at conveying what it felt like to live and fight as an infantryman is Philip Caputo, *A Rumor of War* (New York: Bantam, 1977), written by an especially perceptive Marine Corps officer who saw combat in the same general area as Calley. Like Caputo's book, Gregory L. Vistica's "What Happened in Than Phong," *New York Times Magazine,* 29 April 2001, 50–57, 66–68, 133, provides insights into what caused Americans to commit war crimes in Vietnam. The best source of information about the flaws in the organization and training of Charlie Company, which made it especially susceptible to the pressures that drove U.S. troops to engage in such behavior, is the trial testimony of the company's commanding officer, Captain Ernest Medina.

The many books on the My Lai massacre also offer insights into how the composition of Charlie Company and its experiences prior to 16 March 1968 contributed to what happened that day in My Lai (4). The best-researched and most comprehensive of these is Michael Bilton and Kevin Sim, *Four Hours in My Lai: A War Crime and Its Aftermath* (New York: Viking, 1992). Among other things, Bilton and Sim report that Charlie Company eventually stopped taking prisoners: "There was one guy Medina had to shoot the prisoners. . . . [T]hey would walk them down toward the beach, or behind some sand dunes, and shoot them" (p. 77). They add that Medina beat suspects himself during interrogation (p. 79). Their account of the events of 16 March contains allegations of rape, including a report that Sergeant Kenneth Hodges took a young Vietnamese girl into a hooch, from which she emerged fifteen minutes later wearing no pants and with her blouse unbuttoned (p. 131). Bilton and Sim quote a member of Charlie Company's Second Platoon, Vernardo Simpson, as saying, when describing what he did to the inhabitants of My Lai (4): "I cut their throats, cut off their hands, cut out their tongue [*sic*], their hair, scalped them. I did it. A lot of people were doing it, and I just followed" (p. 130). Even after the massacre, according to Bilton and Sim, Calley continued to exhibit brutality toward Vietnamese civilians; Sergeant Thomas Kinch reported that he vented his anger toward one woman by slapping her and at another by kicking her in the stomach (pp. 197–98).

Also extremely enlightening concerning what transpired on 16 March and why it happened is Seymour M. Hersh's *My Lai 4: A Report on the Massacre and Its Aftermath* (New York: Random House, 1970). Hersh, the journalist whose brilliant investigative reporting brought to light what had happened in Son My on 16 March 1968, relies heavily on interviews with members of Charlie Company. In *My Lai 4* he reports that before the massacre another member of the company questioned a suspect and concluded he was not a Vietcong, but Herbert Carter nevertheless knocked the man into a well, and Calley shot him (pp. 32–33). Hersh quotes Charles Gruver as telling him about a small boy he observed on 16 March who was standing by a trail with a wounded arm. "Then the captain's RTO put a burst of 16 [M-16 rifle fire] into him" (p. 71). James Bergthold reported to Hersh that he had seen an old man who had been shot in both legs; figuring the man was going to die anyhow, he decided, "I might as well kill him." According to Hersh, Bergthold told him he put the barrel of a .45 pistol against the man's forehead and blew off the top of his head (p. 73). Several GIs told Hersh they saw Lieutenant Calley run after a bloody but unhurt two-year-old boy, throw him into a ditch, and shoot him (pp. 63–64). Hersh also details a long-running conflict between Calley and his platoon sergeant, Isaiah Cowan, which boiled over following the massacre when the lieutenant called in artillery fire on a location dangerously close to his own platoon's position and spurned Cowan's pleas to cancel this order. According to Hersh, Captain Medina transferred the lieutenant to another platoon in response to an "It's either Calley or me" ultimatum from his own platoon sergeant (pp. 88–89). Much of what Hersh reports in his book can also be found in his article "My Lai 4," *Harper's*, August 12, 1970, 53–84.

Also valuable on the massacre is James S. Olson and Randy Roberts, *My Lai: A Brief History with Documents* (Boston: Bedford Books, 1998). It provides numerous eyewitness accounts of the massacre and other primary sources, along with a concise narrative. Also informative is Richard Hammer, *One Morning in the War: The Tragedy of Son My* (New York: Coward-McCann, 1970). David L. Anderson, ed., *Facing My Lai: Moving Beyond the Massacre* (Lawrence: University Press of Kansas, 1998), is a collection of presentations made during a conference at Tulane University. It includes a revealing account by helicopter pilot Hugh Thompson of what he observed on 16 March. For more information on his role in that day's events, see Trent Angers, *The Forgotten Hero of My Lai: The Hugh Thompson Story* (Lafayette, La.: Acadian House, 1999). Thompson's testimony at Calley's court-martial is also quite illuminating concerning the events of 16 March, as is the evidence given by Captain Medina, Sergeant Cowan, Charles Sledge, James Joseph Dursi, Thomas Turner, Dennis Conti, Michael Bernhardt, and Robert Earl Maples. Telford Taylor provides a contemporary comparison between My Lai and Nazi war crimes in *Nuremberg and Vietnam: An American Tragedy* (Chicago: Quadrangle Books, 1970).

There is a good deal of information about what happened on 16 March, and even more about subsequent efforts to cover up the massacre, in the numerous books that discuss the investigation conducted by the Peers Commission and lay out its findings. The most important of these is *Report of the Department of the Army Review of the Preliminary Investigation into the My Lai Inci-*

dent (Washington, D.C.: Government Printing Office, 1970). W. R. Peers, *The My Lai Inquiry* (New York: Norton, 1979), provides invaluable insights into the conduct of the panel's inquiry. Also informative is Joseph Goldstein, Burke Marshall, and Jack Schwartz, eds., *The My Lai Massacre and Its Cover-Up* (Boston: Free Press, 1976). Seymour Hersh's *Cover-Up: The Army's Secret Investigation of the Massacre at My Lai 4* (New York: Random House, 1972) makes greater use of unofficial sources of information than do the other books on this subject. There is also a great deal of information about the cover-up in Bilton and Sim, *Four Hours at My Lai*, which reports, among other things, that two days after the massacre the assistant commander of the Americal Division, Brigadier General George H. Young, told a group officers with whom he met at LZ Dottie, "Only five of us know about this"; he implied that they should keep quiet about the allegations made by Hugh Thompson and other helicopter pilots, at least until those allegations could be investigated (p. 177).

Bilton and Sim also provide the best account of how Ronald Ridenhour came to write the letter that exposed the massacre and triggered the Peers Commission's inquiry. Olson and Roberts reprint the letter itself in *My Lai: A Brief History with Documents*. Colonel William Wilson, "I Had Prayed to God That This Thing Was Fiction . . . ," *American Heritage*, February 1990, 44–53, is a detailed account of the resulting Inspector General's investigation, written by the officer who conducted it. Bilton and Sim also offer substantial information about the IG investigation; it is they who report that Sergeant Lawrence La Croix lied to Wilson (pp. 224–25). Hammer's *The Court-Martial of Lieutenant Calley* provides a discussion, apparently based on interviews, of how charges came to be filed against Lieutenant Calley. For the official version of that occurrence, see the Records and the opinion of the Court of Military Review in *United States v. William L. Calley, Jr.*, 46 C.M.R. 1121, 1152–53 (1973). The complete records of the Article 32 investigation are available in the Records of the Calley General Court Martial.

The best source of information on Seymour Hersh's exposure of the massacre and the dealings of Ronald Haeberle, Paul

Meadlo, and other witnesses with the press is Bilton and Sim, *Four Hours at My Lai*. Anderson, *Facing My Lai*, which includes remarks by Hersh on how he obtained the story of the massacre and came to publish it (as well as a discussion of the hostility directed at him by soldiers in Vietnam after the verdict in the Calley court-martial was announced), is also helpful. The most complete analysis of the press's coverage of and reaction to the My Lai massacre is William M. Hammond, *Public Affairs: The Military and the Media, 1968–1973* (Washington, D.C.: Center for Military History, 1973).

The Gallup Poll: Public Opinion 1935–1971 (New York: Random House, 1972), vol. 3, and Public Opinion Online (Roper Center at the University of Connecticut, 1989) both contain valuable data on public attitudes toward the Vietnam War. William L. Lunch and Peter W. Sperlich, "American Public Opinion and the War in Vietnam," *Western Political Quarterly* 32 (March 1979): 21–44, offers analysis as well as numbers. This article and the Gallup and Roper Polls deal with the war in general, but the *Wall Street Journal* conducted a survey dealing specifically with My Lai, the results of which appeared on 1 December 1969, at pp. 1, 18. On 22 December 1969, at p. A-9, the *Washington Post* ran a story reporting the results of a poll on the massacre, done by the *Minneapolis Tribune*.

Most of the books that discuss how the Nixon White House reacted to the public's growing disaffection with the Vietnam War also contain opinion poll data. These include Levy, *The Debate over Vietnam*, and Schulzinger, *A Time for War*. Particularly valuable is Jeffrey Kimball's massive and quite detailed *Nixon's Vietnam War* (Lawrence: University Press of Kansas, 1997). Another source of useful insights is Henry Kissinger's autobiographical *The White House Years* (Boston: Little, Brown, 1979).

The White House reaction to the revelation of the My Lai massacre must be pieced together from a variety of primary sources. The most valuable published ones are Richard Nixon's *RN: The Memoirs of Richard Nixon* (New York: Grosset and Dunlap, 1978) and H. R. Haldeman's *The Haldeman Diaries: Inside the Nixon White House* (New York: Putnam's, 1994). There is informative manuscript material in the President's Office Files, the Files of Ron Ziegler, the Files of John Dean, the Files of John Ehrlichman, and File CF NE 18-4 of the White House Central Files, all of which are housed in the Nixon Presidential Materials Project at the National Archives Annex in College Park, Maryland.

Mark D. Carson, "F. Edward Hébert and the Congressional Investigation of the My Lai Massacre," *Louisiana History* 37 (winter 1996): 61–79, is good on the probe conducted by the House Armed Services Committee. Also helpful on that subject are U.S. Congress, House, Investigating Subcommittee of the House Committee on the Armed Services, *Investigation of the My Lai Incident: Hearings . . . Under Authority of H. Res. 105*, 91st Cong., 2nd sess., 1970 (Washington, D.C.: Government Printing Office, 1976), and the same committee's *Investigation of the My Lai Incident: Report of the Armed Forces Investigating Subcommittee of the Committee on the Armed Forces*, 91st Cong., 2nd sess., 1970.

By far the best source of information on the court-martial of Lieutenant Calley is the official Records, which provide a complete transcript of the proceedings. Hammer's *The Court-Martial of Lieutenant Calley* furnishes comments by an eyewitness observer, as well as information about events occurring both inside and outside the courtroom that were not part of the official proceedings. For example, it is Hammer who reports that defense attorney Richard Kay leaked confidential information to reporters he was trying to impress (pp. 63–64). Sack's *Lieutenant Calley: His Own Story* provides the defendant's perspective on the trial, along with his reactions to what was happening. It includes interviews first published as "The Concluding Confessions of Lieutenant Calley: The Lieutenant's Account of the Day at Mylai Four, the Aftermath of the Trial," *Esquire*, September 1971, 85–89, 224–28. Joseph DiMona includes a chapter on the Calley case in *Great Court-Martial Cases* (New York: Grosset and Dunlap, 1972), 246–86. In addition, the trial received extensive coverage in the *New York Times* and other major newspapers, as well as in *Newsweek*, *Time*, and *U.S. News & World Report*.

Wayne Greenhaw, *The Making of a Hero: A Behind the Scenes View of the Lt. William Calley Affair* (Louisville, Ky.: Touchstone,

1971), is a journalistic account that deals with the aftermath of the trial, as well as the massacre and the court-martial. By far the best source of information on public reaction to the verdict is Public Opinion Online, which includes the results of surveys on the subject done by the Gallup Poll, Louis Harris and Associates, and the Opinion Research Corporation (which did polling for the Nixon White House). Also quite helpful is Herbert C. Kelman and Lee H. Lawrence, "American Response to the Trial of Lt. William L. Calley," *Psychology Today*, June 1972, 41–55, 78–81, which is republished in *The Military in America: From the Colonial Era to the Present*, ed. Peter Karsten (New York: Free Press, 1980), 431–46. One can also glean a good deal about reaction to the conviction of Lieutenant Calley, at least in Texas, from letters received by the United States Court of Military Appeals and now held by its successor institution, the United States Court of Appeals for the Armed Forces. There are huge numbers of letters and telegrams about the case from all over the country in the holdings of the Nixon Materials Project, especially under the Ex ND8/Calley and GEN ND8/Calley classifications in the White House Central Files.

The largest amount of material on the White House response to the Calley verdict is in the Files of John Dean. The Files of John D. Ehrlichman contain useful handwritten notes on meetings with the president, as well as important memorandums and transcripts of press conferences dealing with the president's intervention in the case. There are also a number of important memorandums and other items in the Files of H. R. Haldeman. Other sources of information on public reaction to Calley's conviction and the White House response to it are the Files of Patrick Buchanan, Charles Colson, Ron Ziegler, and J. Fred Buzhardt. A transcript of Nixon's 16 April 1971 press conference, at which he discussed the case, is found in the President's Personal Files, also held by the Nixon Materials Project.

Nixon comments briefly on his intervention in the Calley case in his memoir *RN*. There is far more information on that subject in the published *Haldeman Diaries*. Jeffery Kimball provides a brief but well-researched account in *Nixon's Vietnam War*, and Bilton and Sim include a discussion of Nixon's efforts on behalf of

Calley in *Four Hours at My Lai*. William M. Hammond's *Public Affairs* discusses the Calley court-martial and its aftermath, but his account, especially those parts dealing with the White House response to the case, is unreliable because it contains a large number of factual errors and distortions.

Of far greater value are a number of articles that appeared in popular periodicals, which contain information on reaction to the trial, the verdict, and/or Captain Daniel's confrontation with President Nixon. These include "The Hero Calley," *Time*, 15 February 1971, p. 14; "Judgement at Fort Benning," *Time*, 12 April 1971, pp. 27–32; "The Wound Reopened," *Time*, 12 April 1971, pp. 13–16; "Unlikely Villain," *Time*, 12 April 1971, p. 17; "The Calley Affair (Cont.)," *Time*, 19 April 1971, pp. 13–14; "Second Thoughts About Calley," *Newsweek*, 19 April 1971, pp. 29–30; "The Captain Who Told the President Off," *Newsweek*, 19 April 1971, p. 30; and "The Case That Will Not Go Quietly Away," *Life*, 23 April 1971, pp. 22–27.

A number of popular periodicals and newspapers ran articles and/or editorials that expressed opinions on the outcome of the Calley court-martial and/or the public's reaction to it. The most significant articles include Telford Taylor, "Judging Calley Is Not Enough," *Life*, 9 April 1971, pp. 20–23; Peter Steinfels, "Calley and the Public Conscience," *Commonweal*, 16 April 1971, p. 128; "Calley for President," *National Review*, 20 April 1971, pp. 408–10; David Lawrence, "War Is Hell," *U.S. News & World Report*, 26 April 1971, p. 96; Michael Novak, "The Battle Hymn of Lt. Calley . . . and the Republic," *Commonweal*, 30 April 1971, pp. 183–86; and Joseph Goldstein, "The Meaning of Calley," *New Republic*, 8 May 1971, pp. 13–14. For editorials, see *Washington Evening Star*, 1 April 1971; *Chicago Tribune*, 2 April 1971; "Calley and Company," *New Republic*, 3 April 1971, pp. 10–11; "The President and Mylai," *New York Times*, 4 April 1971; "The Calley Case and the President," *Washington Post*, 4 April 1971; "Lieutenant Calley and the President," *Life*, 15 April 1971, p. 40; "The Talk of the Town," *New Yorker*, 17 April 1971, pp. 31–33; and "The Captain and the President," *The Nation*, 19 April

1971), pp. 482–83. For an African-American perspective on Nixon's handling of the case, see William Raspberry, "Calley Release Bit Inconsistent," *Washington Post*, 4 April 1971.

For insights into the growing distrust of authority and government that fueled the reaction against the Calley verdict, see Robert D. Putnam, *Bowling Alone: The Collapse and Rebirth of American Community* (New York: Simon and Schuster, 1995), and Terry H. Anderson, *The Movement and the Sixties*. Anderson also discusses the growing disaffection with the war, both among civilians and within the armed forces. For the views of former fighting men who became opponents of American involvement in Vietnam, see Richard Stacewicz, *Winter Soldiers: An Oral History of the Vietnam Veterans Against the War* (New York: Twayne, 1997).

Hammer provides sketchy but useful discussions of the other cases that arose out of the My Lai massacre and cover-up in *The Court-Martial of Lieutenant Calley*, and Bilton and Sim summarize them in *Four Hours at My Lai*. William Eckhardt greatly enhanced my knowledge and understanding of the ground action cases in a telephone interview on 19 December 2001. The best analysis of the legal issues raised by the courts-martial of defendants other than Calley is Norman G. Cooper, "My Lai and Military Justice: What Next?" *Military Law Review* 59 (1973): 93–127. Charles W. Corddry III, "Jurisdiction to Try Discharged Servicemen for Violations of the Laws of War," *JAG Journal* 26 (fall 1971): 63–76, and Jordan J. Paust, "After My Lai: The Case for War Crime Jurisdiction over Civilians in Federal District Courts," *Texas Law Review* 50 (1971): 6–34, examine jurisdictional issues posed by the fact that many of those who committed offenses at My Lai were out of the army by the time their crimes came to light. Both Cooper's article and Paust's "My Lai and Vietnam: Norms, Myths, and Leader Responsibility," *Military Law Review* 59 (1973): 93–127, provide insights into how young Judge Advocate General's Corps officers reacted to the massacre. Jeffrey F. Addicott and William A. Hudson Jr., "The Twenty-Fifth Anniversary of My Lai: A Time to Inculcate the Lessons," *Military Law Review* 139 (1993): 153–85, is a useful retrospective.

A number of law review articles discuss the command responsibility issue raised by the trial of Captain Medina. These include Roger S. Clark, "Medina: An Essay on the Principles of Criminal Liability for Homicide," *Rutgers-Camden Law Journal* 5 (1973): 59–78; Kenneth A. Howard, "Command Responsibility for War Crimes," *Journal of Public Law* 21 (1972): 7–22; Michael L. Smidt, "Yamashita, Medina, and Beyond: Command Responsibility in Contemporary Military Operations," *Military Law Review* 164 (2000): 155–254; and William G. Eckhardt, "Command Criminal Responsibility: A Plea for a Workable Standard," *Military Law Review* 97 (1982): 1–34. Mary McCarthy, *Medina* (New York: Harcourt, Brace, Jovanovich, 1972), originally published in a slightly different form in the *New Yorker*, provides the perspective of a journalist who attended the captain's court-martial. For a news magazine account, see "The Case Against Medina," *Time*, 30 August 1971, p. 24. The ruling of the United States Court of Military Appeals on his pretrial motion alleging a conspiracy against him is reported as *Medina v. Resor*, 20 U.S.C.M.A. 403 (1971). The Files of John Dean and the Ex ND8/M category in the White House Central Files at the Nixon Materials Project contain the correspondence and other material documenting the efforts of F. Lee Bailey and Representative Henry B. Gonzalez to persuade the White House to intervene in Medina's case.

Dean's papers also include information on the White House's handling of the other My Lai cases, as do the Files of John Ehrlichman. William G. Eckhardt, who as a major in the Judge Advocate General's Corps was in charge of all prosecutions arising out of the ground operations at My Lai 4, provides a useful overview of those cases in "My Lai: An American Tragedy," *UMKC Law Review* 68 (summer 2000): 671–703. Even more enlightening are Eckhardt's remarks at the Tulane conference, published in David L. Anderson, ed., *Facing My Lai*. For rulings of the Court of Military Appeals in cases arising out of these other prosecutions, see *Doherty v. United States*, 20 U.S.C.M.A. 163 (1970); *Henderson v. Resor*, 20 U.S.C.M.A. 165 (1970); and *Hutson v. United States*, 19 U.S.C.M.A. 437 (1970).

Newsmagazines published a number of articles dealing with

the cases of My Lai suspects other than Calley and Medina. These include "The Army: Henderson in the Dock," *Newsweek*, 6 September 1971, p. 17; "Trials: More About My Lai," *Time*, 27 September 1971, p. 32; "My Lai Killings—12 out of 13 Accused Are Free," *U.S. News & World Report*, 4 October 1971, p. 101; "Courts-Martial: End of the Affair," *Newsweek*, 4 October 1971, p. 2; "My Lai: The End of the Affair," *Newsweek*, 27 December 1971, pp. 18–19; and "The War: Court Adjourns on My Lai," *Time*, 27 December 1971, p. 8.

The best sources of information on Calley's military appeals and his efforts to get his conviction overturned by the civilian federal courts are the published judicial opinions in those cases. The ruling of the Court of Military Review is reported as *United States v. Calley*, 46 C.M.R. 1131 (1973), and the decision of the United States Court of Military Appeals as *United States v. Calley*, 22 U.S.C.M.A. 534 (1973). Jonathan Lurie provides an insightful discussion of the latter ruing in *Pursuing Military Justice: The History of the United States Court of Appeals for the Armed Forces, 1951–1980* (Princeton, N.J.: Princeton University Press, 1988), abridged as *Military Justice in America: The U.S. Court of Appeals for the Armed Forces* (Lawrence: University Press of Kansas, 2001). For Judge Elliott's opinion granting Calley a writ of habeas corpus, see *Calley v. Callaway*, 382 F.Supp. 650 (M.D. Ga. 1974); for the decision of the Fifth Circuit Court of Appeals reversing Elliott, see *Calley v. Callaway*, 519 F.2d 184 (5th. Cir. 1975), *cert. denied* 425 U.S. 911 (1976). Information on the battle between Elliott and the army over whether Calley should be free on bail or confined in the Disciplinary Barracks at Fort Leavenworth pending resolution of the habeas corpus litigation appears in *Calley v. Callaway*, 496 F.2d 701 (5th Cir. 1974), *Calley v. Callaway*, 497 F.2d 1384 (5th Cir. 1974), and *Calley v. Callaway*, 419 U.S. 1015 (1974).

For further information on the bail dispute, see *New York Times*, 27 September 1974. *Columbus Ledger-Inquirer,* 20 February 2001, contains a lengthy article on Judge Elliott, and the *Memphis Commercial-Appeal*, 10 November 1999, has a short one on his freeing of Calley on bail. The Calley File at the United States Court of Appeals for the Armed Forces contains the Petition for Grant of

Review and Brief in Support of Petition for Grant of Review that George Latimer filed with its predecessor institution, the United States Court of Military Appeals, as well as Commissioner Ralph J. DeLaVergne's lengthy analysis of Calley's appeal and other valuable memorandums, correspondence, and newspaper clippings.

The best sources of information on the White House's response to Latimer's efforts to obtain executive clemency for his client and the limited nature of President Nixon's review of the Calley case are the Files of John Dean and the Files of John Ehrlichman in the Nixon Materials Project. The former collection also contains Dean's assessment of psychiatrist Dr. Albert LaVerne's campaign to secure Calley's freedom. In a memorandum of 8 June 1972, found in box 14, he declared, "This effort has included the unethical public release of the confidential medical examination he conducted." The Ex ND 813 classification in the White House Central Files at the Nixon Materials Project contains the president's short letter of 3 May 1974 refusing to take any action in the case and the advice from J. Fred Buzhardt on which it was based. There is also some useful material in the Files of H. R. Haldeman.

For documents revealing the actions taken by the Department of the Army in Calley's case subsequent to his conviction by the Fort Benning court-martial, see box 1, Records of the Calley General Court Martial. There is correspondence from the public in box 26 of Records of the Calley General Court Martial. For additional information on the army's final disposition of the case, see Facts on File World News Digest, 20 September 1975, and "Reinstated," Newsweek, 22 September 1975, p. 85. The New York Times reported on Calley's parole on 28 November 1972, 27 July 1974, 10 November 1974, and 12 September 1975. For editorial comment, see New York Times, 22 November 1974.

On what became of Calley after he dropped out of the spotlight, see New York Times, 2 April 1975, 24 November 1975, and 6 April 1976. There is also relevant material in the Toronto Star, 24 September 1989, and in a story run by United Press International on 16 March 1993.

INDEX

{ *The Vietnam War on Trial* }

Equipment, military, 44
"Establishment," 215
Eszterhas, Joe, 120
Evans, Brigadier General B. L., 233
Evans, Richard M., 239
Executive clemency, 196–98,
    201–3, 207, 244
Ex parte Milligan, 221

Fagan, Staff Sergeant Martin, 58
Fair trial, right to, 150
Feher, Chief Warrant Officer
    Andre C. R., 110, 111–12, 116
Fielding, Fred, 206
Fifth Amendment, 142, 163, 249
Firepower, 16, 17
First Amendment, 249
First Cavalry Division, 13
First Platoon, 59, 60, 62–64,
    70–73, 75, 77
"Five S's," 42, 49
Fleet Reserve, 194
Florida East Coast Railroad, 29
Flowers, Walter, 197
Flynn, George Q., 31
Fonda, Jane, 21
Ford, Colonel Clifford H., 1, 154,
    188, 190
Ford, Gerald, 235, 237
Foreign Relations Committee,
    Senate, hearings of, 15
Fort Benning, Georgia, 2, 6, 118,
    202
Fort Leavenworth, Kansas, 238,
    248
Fort McPherson, Georgia, 225–26
Forty-eighth Local Force Battalion
    (Vietcong), 51–52, 54, 57, 60,
    61
France, 7
Franklin, Colonel Joseph R. (Ross),
    123
Froehlke, Robert F., 238, 250–52
Fulbright, J. William, 12, 14, 21
Fulton, Richard, 197
Fuqua, Don, 196
Fygi, Eric J., 199, 243–44

Gallup poll, 21, 130, 132, 193, 211,
    213
Garfolo, Gary, 57, 77

Garmatz, Edward A., 196
Gavin, Lieutenant Colonel David
    G., 217
Gee, Thomas, 247–52
General Counsel, Army, 124, 127
Geneva Accords, 7
Geneva Convention on the Laws of
    War, 42
Geneva peace conference, 7
German war criminals, 209
Gewin, Walter P., 253
Gibson, Major Glenn D., 93, 108
GIs
    deaths of, 16, 44, 45
    feelings toward Vietnamese, 47,
        48, 51, 56
    killings, 63–65, 67, 69, 72
    reaction to Calley verdict, 202
    See also "Grunts"
Goldberg, Arthur, 129, 136
Goldwater, Barry, 11
Gonzalez, Henry B., 228
Goodell, Charles, 133
"Gooks," 48
Goralski, Robert, 118
Gordon, Captain J. Houston, 239,
    244, 251, 253
"Ground pounders," 46
Ground war, 18
"Grunts"
    combat in Vietnam, xi, 36, 37,
        43–44
    killings, 59, 65, 74, 131–32
    limited understanding of
        massacre, 79–80
    living conditions, 43
    rules of engagement, 49
    See also GIs
Gruver, Charles "Butch," 69, 101,
    103–4, 105–6, 240
Grzesik, Ronald, 109
Guam, legislature, 192–93
Gubser, Charles, 138, 140
Guerrilla squads and platoons, 45
Guerrilla warfare, 17
Guinn, Lieutenant Colonel
    William D., 218
Gulf of Tonkin incident, 11, 12
Gulf of Tonkin Resolution, 12, 133
Gulf War, 2
Gurney, Edward, 195

Medina, Ernest, *continued*
as draft volunteer, 37
heroism, 55
hostility toward Vietnamese, 56,
272
investigation of, 87–88, 93, 107
killing of women and children,
58, 67–68
My Lai role, 57, 75, 86
OCS, 38
orders, 58, 61–65, 67, 70, 103,
140, 166, 173–74
orders cease-fire in My Lai, 75
promoted to captain, 38
quoted, 40, 41, 58, 77, 104
and radio operators, 67, 69
responsibility for massacre,
168–69, 171
and Silver Star, 55
testimony, 115, 181–83
training, 38, 42
transferred, 273
and troops, 38, 41, 54, 58, 60, 68
Metcalfe, Geoff, 169
Mikel, Mary, 194
Mikva, Abner, 142–43, 224
Military Academy. *See* West Point
Military appellate process, 243
Military Assistance Command,
Vietnam (MACV), 91
Military commission, 222, 223
Military judges, 227, 229, 231, 240
Military justice, x, 201, 203, 205–8
Military service, 23, 121
Military strategists, 16
Military tribunal. *See* Military
commission
Miller, Colonel Hubert, 128
Miller, Colonel Robert W., 122, 128
Millians, Chief Warrant Officer
Dan R., 108, 159
Milwaukee Journal, 119
Mines, 45, 54, 55, 56, 88
Minh, Duong, 170
Minneapolis Tribune, 130, 131
Minnesota, 211
Minorities, racial, 26
Mitchell, Staff Sergeant David
court martial of, 142, 217, 222,
224–27, 225
My Lai role, 71–72, 162

privilege against self
incrimination, 115, 180–81
service in army, 39
Mollenhoff, Clark, 135
Montgomery Advertiser, 248
Moore, Anne, 145, 194, 237
Moorer, Admiral Thomas, 198,
199
Moratorium Day, 133
Morgan, Lewis R., 247–48,
253
Moyers, Bill, 20
Moynihan, Daniel Patrick, 136
M-16 rifle, 44
Muste, A. J., 21
Mutinies (combat refusals),
132
My Khe, 60
My Lai (4)
attacked, 63
devastation, 64, 78, 126, 157
enemy soldiers, 63
free fire zone, 158, 167
inhabitants, 62, 63, 65, 75
landscape, 60, 64
LZ, 63
village, 1, 120
My Lai Incident Subcommittee (of
House Armed Services
Committee). *See* Armed
Services Investigative
Subcommittee
My Lai massacre
atrocities, ix, x, 69, 156, 204
condemned, 129, 203
deaths, 64, 68, 130, 160
destruction, 64, 121–22
killings, 131, 135, 138, 140, 144,
216, 219, 223, 233, 255
questions raised, xi, 129
rampage, 1
responsibility for, 3–4, 202
search and destroy mission, 60,
61, 132, 158
truth about, 96, 97, 134, 199,
211
victims, 70–72, 74–75

Nation, The, 192, 208, 214
National Guard, 25, 26
National Guardsmen, 2